MW01443582

ACROSS THE KENTUCKY COLOR LINE

Cultural Landscapes of Race
from the Lost Cause to Integration

LEE DURHAM STONE

Copyright © 2023

Lee Durham Stone

ALL RIGHTS RESERVED

No part of this book may be reproduced or transmitted in any form or by any means without prior written permission from the author, except for educational and scholarly use, which is permitted and encouraged with proper citation to this work.

ISBN-13: 979-8393499808

*A knowledge of history is, above all, a means of responsibility—
of responsibility to the past
and of responsibility to the future.*

—John F. Kennedy

CONTENTS

Acknowledgments..v

Prologue 8

Chapter 1 Introduction: Place, Memory, and Historiography.............12

Chapter 2 Jim Crow and the Lost Cause..23

Chapter 3 Out of the 'Silent Archives' 36

Chapter 4 Working the 'Steamboat Sublime,' Main Street, and 'Caverns of Night' 54

Chapter 5 Trial and Execution of Harrison Alexander 73

Chapter 6 Endemic Violence 91

Chapter 7 Possum Hunter Reign of Terror 104

Chapter 8 The Strange Case of Dr. R. T. Bailey............................133

Chapter 9 Black Soldiers in the World Wars.................................140

Chapter 10 Complexity, Continuity, and Racialized Spaces 148

Chapter 11 Jim Crow Education 167

Chapter 12 School Integration, 'as Conditions Warrant'..................179

Chapter 13 Resistance and Change..203

Epilogue 221

Notes 226

About the Author 292

Index 293

FIGURES

Map 1: Western Kentucky iii

Map 2: Muhlenberg and Seven Contiguous Counties iv

Table 1: Black Kentucky Miners, 1900-1980 70

Table 2: Muhlenberg Mining Fatalities, 1964-1980 248

Map 1: Western Kentucky

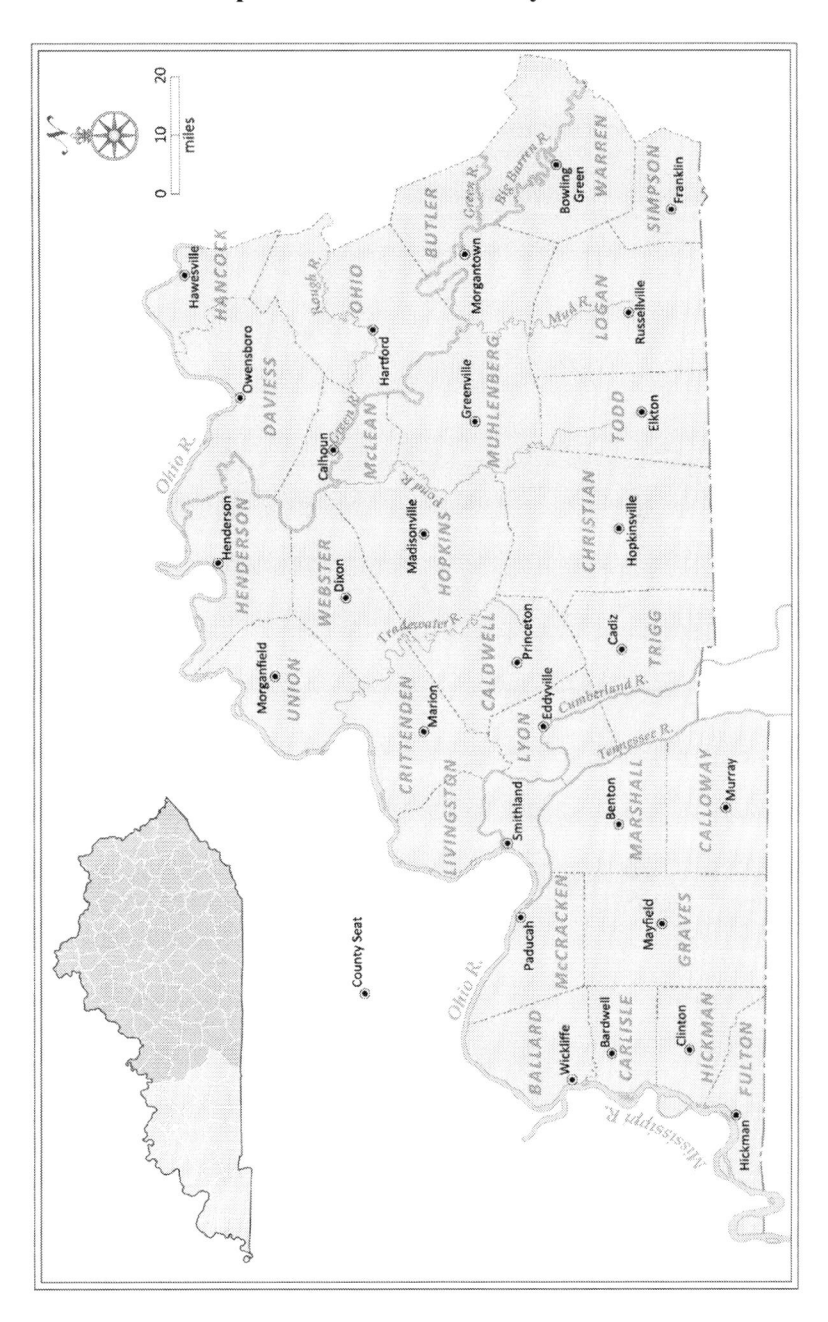

Source: Cartography by Richard A. Gilbreath, as commissioned by the author (2023).

Map 2: Muhlenberg and Seven Contiguous Counties

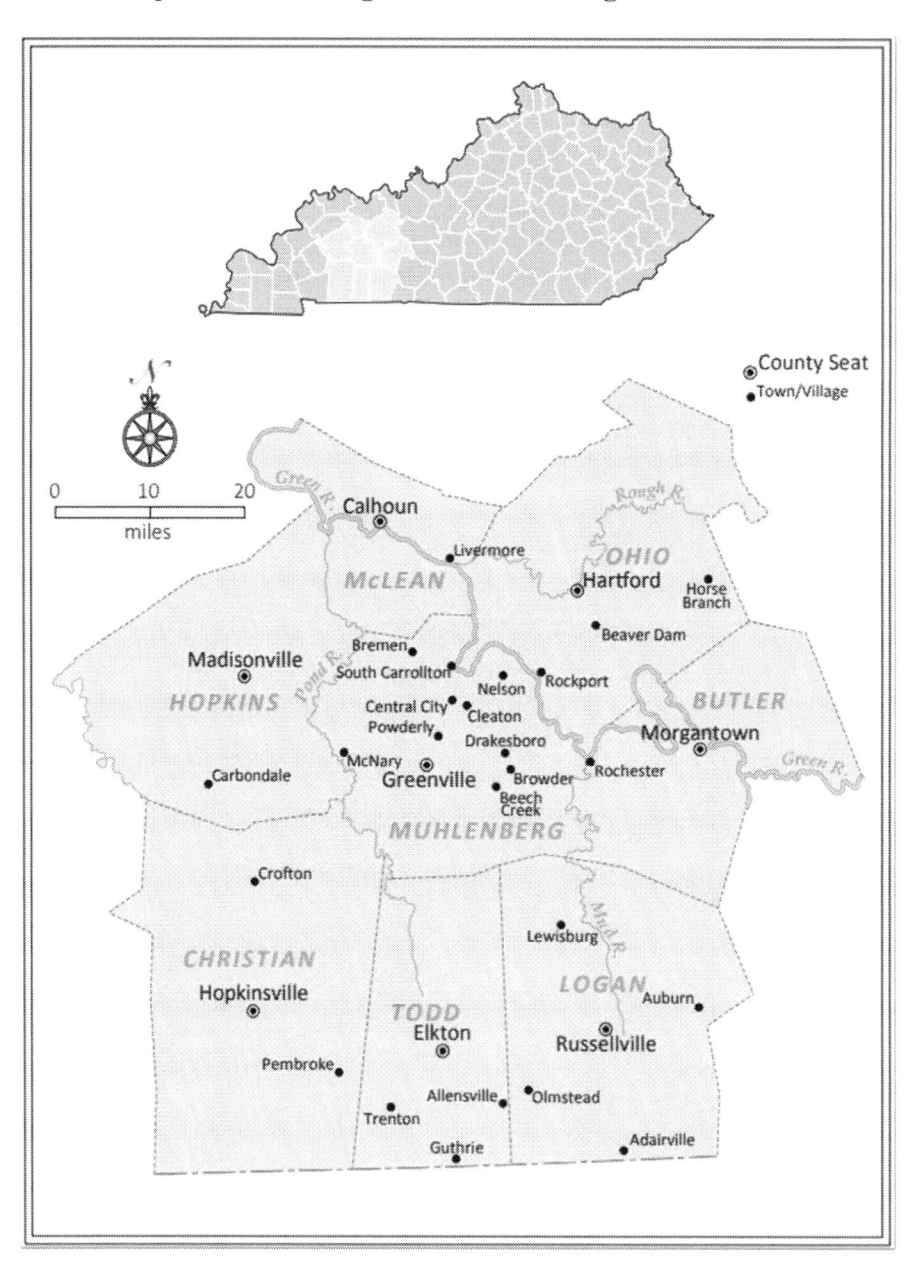

Source: Cartography by Richard A. Gilbreath, as commissioned by the author (2023).

ACKNOWLEDGMENTS

I have many people to thank for their aid and interest in this project. After returning to Kentucky in 2011, my classmate Margaret Williams reminded me of the 4th-grade school trip to the Central City State Theater in 1957 to see *The Ten Commandments* movie and that the Black school kids waited separately in the alley (see the Prologue). This reminder and its segregated tableau piqued my interest in the Bluegrass State's Black history (which turned out to be a white history, too).

At this point, I telephoned Larry Elliott (Louisville, formerly of Greenville) to ask his opinion on my attempt at such a project. His terse response: "It's past due." Because of that, I might never have begun the intense study required to produce this book without his encouragement. Larry and I had several more helpful conversations that set me on the way.

In time, Annie Louise Bard (Central City) sent me a long letter about her life. She also participated in the interview session I conducted with Rev. Otis Cunningham (Central City), Roger Frazier (Drakesboro), and Willie Parker (Drakesboro). George Humphreys (Drakesboro, author of *The Fall of Kentucky's Rock* [2022], published by the University Press of Kentucky) recorded this session, now archived at the Louie B. Nunn Center for Oral History, University of Kentucky Libraries (see the citation in Chapter 12 notes). Over some years, George and I have had many conversations about my ongoing project, much of which centered on his encouragement to continue working on getting it published.

Others to whom I owe thanks include Jay Divine (St. Louis), Roger Givens (Morgantown, and author of *African-American Life in Butler County, Kentucky*), Bill Hicks (Montgomery, AL), Tom Noe (Russellville, who is working on a history manuscript), Mark Stone (managing editor of the *Central City Times-Argus*), Larry Stone, Jr. (Spanish Fort, AL), and Hugh Sweatt (Central City), who provided a valuable anecdote. Dorann O'Neal Lam and J. P. Johnson (librarian in the Lexington Public Library) have been forthcoming in finding information. In addition, Dorothy Martin, a former Muhlenberg teacher, was generous with her time in two telephone interviews in 2018 and 2021. Finally, Jeff Taylor (Central City and Hopkinsville) read a chapter, offered helpful advice, and supplied a meaningful story about his childhood experience in a segregated restaurant in Central City (see Chapter 10).

This book would not have been possible without four previous works used extensively herein. These include the books by Otto A. Rothert (*A History of Muhlenberg County* [1913]), Leslie Shively Smith (*Around Muhlenberg* [1979]), Paul Camplin (*A New History of Muhlenberg* [1984]), and Mike Moore (*The Hanging of Harrison Alexander* [2005]). (See the Notes for the complete citations.)

I also realize that I stand on the shoulders of many Kentucky and Southern historians who have proved indispensable to comprehending the history of the Commonwealth and the South. These include several works by George C. Wright and James C. Klotter. However, I consulted and used many others. (Again, see the Notes.)

Finally, even with a decade of diligent research, I am sure errors have crept in. Any mistakes herein are mine.

PROLOGUE

It may first be necessary to realize that the past does not tell its own story.[1]

A queue of Black schoolchildren lines up in single file before a narrow unmarked door in a grimy side alley.[2] They patiently wait to enter a cavernous vaudeville-era theater. With eyes big and silent, they gaze at a queue of white children as these stare uncomprehendingly back at them. The time is spring 1957. The place is Central City, Muhlenberg County, Kentucky.[3]

Unbeknownst to these children, one year before, in February 1956, Reverend Martin Luther King, Jr., and eighty-eight other Montgomery civil rights leaders had voluntarily turned themselves in for arrest for violating an Alabama business boycott law. Thus, a new activist phase of the civil rights movement had begun. Moreover, none of these children could foresee that they would be sitting in integrated classrooms seven years later with some of the same children at whom they leer that day.

The white children wait on the spacious front sidewalk. They are fidgety while waiting to file through the wide front doors under the flashing lights marquee to watch the Cecil B. DeMille-directed blockbuster movie *The Ten Commandments*. Inside, they watch the film from a privileged position on the main floor. Even though the children from the Works Progress Administration-built Central City Colored School (the name chiseled above its front door) down the train tracks are also public-school students, they head through the narrow side door and upstairs, relegated to the dark second-class balcony.

These children—the ones still living—and I, along with Black political scientist Adolph Reed, Jr. (b. 1947) and white Civil War scholar and former president of Harvard University Drew Gilpin Faust (b. 1947), are the age cohort "for which the Jim Crow regime is a living memory—for good and ill."[4] We are the witnesses—the "living memory"—of that critical era that thankfully transformed into something else. Moreover, their parents, grandparents, and great-grandparents lived through the events and times depicted in this book, like the terror of the Possum Hunter movement (1914-1916) examined in Chapter 7.

The movie theater in Hopkinsville similarly assigned the acclaimed national journalist Ted Poston (1906-1974) to the balcony "peanut gallery," as he described it in good humor. With contrasting emotions, poet Maya Angelou (1928-2014) truculently expressed her experience of this social slight as a child in small-town Arkansas. The town theater required her to enter "a really crummy little door" on the side. Angelou realized painfully that the world would treat her differently, as determined by her socially assigned color grouping. In Muhlenberg, before World War II, Maggie Dulin (1924-2017) recalled the ten-cent admission to the Drakesboro movie theater that relegated Black moviegoers upstairs and white patrons down.[5]

Poston, Angelou, and Dulin's experiences of discrimination are reminiscent of the physical separation and social distance imprinted on the child consciousness of writer and anthropologist Zora Neale Hurston. She recounted, "I remember the very day I became colored."[6] On the other side of the *color line*, Southern writer and sociologist Katherine Du Pre Lumpkin (1897-1988) recalled the personally traumatic event in 1905 in Georgia when she realized her whiteness.[7] This conscious awareness happened when she was an impressionable eight-year-old and witnessed her father, a former enslaver and Confederate soldier, beating their Black family cook for her insolence.[8]

The white Central City schoolchildren at the theater assimilated something similar but reversed from the Black children. After they see the latter and file through the front doors to take the choice seats on the main floor, they subconsciously absorb the cultural facticity of their privileged whiteness, as did Lumpkin.

These segregated children watch a Hollywood spectacle whose story depicts the physical and spiritual conflicts of an oppressed people seeking to enter a promised land. This film flashes cinematically onto their mental screens the struggle to attain this sacred covenant. Their release from bondage and striving to enter the land of Canaan—a poignant subject in Negro spirituals (aka *Sorrow Songs*)—was a central theme used metaphorically in the post-World War II social movement for racial equality and democracy.[9] Rev. King, Jr., called it a "promissory note" held by Black Americans waiting with extraordinary, unending patience to cash at the "bank of justice."[10]

Nevertheless, these Black schoolchildren, their teachers, and the nationwide Black movie-going public vicariously witness an indelible social irony in that living moment. They watch a freed tribe—the Israelites—finally reach their Promised Land. Conversely, however, 1950s Black Americans dwell in a precarious position. Symbolically, they are waiting in Pharaoh's Land on the far shore of the Red Sea. Alternatively, perhaps they are closer, undergoing the trials in the desert—the wandering antecedent stage to reaching their "home over Jordan."

On that movie day, the Black and white children sense some of the strange meanings of the social spacing between privilege and second-classness for the first time in their young lives, as did Zora Neale Hurston and Katherine Du Pre Lumpkin. On opposite sides of the color line, the two segregated groups learn a meaningfully social and spatial lesson—subconsciously in the "hidden curriculum," the spectrum of learning outcomes not found in the formal syllabus.[11] They perceive social hierarchy, privilege, and separation. In other words, this episode teaches them *otherness*. It becomes part of both groups' felt history, as experienced in segregated felt space.

This promise of a better place is merely a potential when viewed from the second-class balcony of the segregated small-town lifeworld. The Promised Land—not yet seen from the mountaintop—would have to bide its time. The arduous climb up the incline would be slow and long.

This book is about that long climb and the boulders littering the way up the steep wilderness slope.

Chapter 1

INTRODUCTION: PLACE, MEMORY, AND HISTORIOGRAPHY

*You can't be universal without being provincial.
It's like trying to embrace the wind.*[1]

Parochial events in the territory one hundred miles up the Green River, a middle-level Kentucky stream flowing into the Ohio River, help us understand the United States. Closely examining bygone happenings at this smaller scale feeds into and supplements the currents and eddies in the more expansive cultural flows. "There is a time for understanding the particular, and there is a time for understanding the whole," historian Gordon Wood pronounces, pointing to this scaling-up effect.[2] In the present case, the particular that helps define the whole is Muhlenberg County, its seven contiguous neighboring counties, and the rest of western Kentucky.[3]

In 1903, W. E. B. Du Bois (1868-1963) famously observed: "The problem of the twentieth century is the problem of the color-line."[4] His sociological diagnosis—and accurate prediction—sets the platform from which this current project examines the historical anti-Black color line and human crossings in the Kentucky cultural landscape.

More precisely, this study investigates the intertwined social history of the Black/white *place-world*—the biracial unfolding in the actively lived-in past.[5] To achieve this, it focuses on the *whereness* and *whenness* of African-descended people in the twentieth century (and some antecedent events), including the Second Reconstruction years after World War II.

The method herein contextualizes western Kentucky in the broader areal associations of the nation, stretching the always dynamic social terrain over timespace. Local historians, Joseph Amato advises, must connect their local places to others further afield.[6] For instance, cultural anthropologist Jack Glazier studied memory and the color line in Hopkinsville and Christian County. "Understanding the dynamics of race in this corner of western Kentucky," Glazier argues, "requires a tacking back and forth between the particularities of place and the broader historical and social processes of which they are a part."[7] Similarly, when feasible, the present study embeds Muhlenberg and the western region in their spatiohistorical settings by merging them with the more extensive geographic-historical terrain. Thus, in exploring these connections, this effort emplaces this region in the micro and macro circuits of timespace.

Social relations are the products of the geometry of the relations of power. This survey diagnoses more than a century of power relations that crisscrossed the color line in a particular delineated spatial setting. Observers can detect these associations in the *cultural landscape* as "the visible human imprint[s] on the land," resulting from the complex cultural interactions between the dwellers and their natural environments. Here, we could think of how coal mining has changed the landscape.

However, this study applies the notion of the cultural landscape as a lens in a more expansive project—as "moments in a networked process of social relations across time and space."[8] Geographer and cultural theorist Don Mitchell addresses these social relations when he writes: "But the question, of course, is always *which* people landscapes invite in and which people can find no place in them."[9] By delving into a particular social form of this regional cultural landscape, this book intends to illuminate its *racialization of space*—in other words, how race plays out in particular places, with material presences and absences in the cultural landscape.[10] These presences and absences occur in, for example, the micro-spaces in which theaters segregate their seating arrangements, to the middle scale where societies site monuments and memorials in public spaces, and to the larger scale where socioeconomic forces place ethnic neighborhoods in towns and cities.

Scholars have often overlooked and erased Black western Kentuckians in written accounts of Green River Country—the present work's theme. These subjects have lived "without history." Alternatively, to use bell hooks' term, the regime of *dominator culture* has viewed them through a lens that has distorted their lived experiences.[11]

However, cultural silences about the past are not synonymous with "collective amnesia." Historical (collective) amnesia is a misleading term since "archival cultures," as is ours, "do not forget the past, even metaphorically."[12] On the contrary, the past is often blocked, occluded, made opaque, or even intentionally "disremembered." For this reason, the historian's task is to gather, expose, and interpret the extant archives. "As a historian," Martha S. Jones announces, "I break silences."[13] The present work, examining the relevant source materials, intends the same.

The absence of written accounts of the Black experience in western Kentucky calls for shining a light into these *archives of silence*.[14] Here, we should understand that memory and history are not oppositional. Accordingly, historian Paul Ricoeur argues that memory is the "womb of history." He means that "memory remains the guardian of the entire problem of the representative relation of the present to the past."[15] This relation is that memories hold and gestate the past in the act of "historying," as post-modernist historian Alan Munslow labels the process.[16] Furthermore, in this sense, "the past" (and any specific past event) does not exist without memory. To this end, the present narrative disturbs these historical silences at punctuated moments—racialized violence, for instance—to proffer current and future voices to these newly disinterred memories arising from the slag heaps of history.

Caveat lector: Not only are past times foreign, but they can be distressingly surreal. "The past should be so strange," one historian contends, "that you wonder how you and the people you know and love could come from such a time."[17] Though we should not be surprised. "History is not a safe place," Kentucky historian Emily Bingham points out, "nor should we expect it to be."[18]

What is more, strangeness can take on a personal dimension. "To honestly confront our bloody past," as one writer frames it, "makes us strange to ourselves." How so? Because on some level of apprehension, we find it difficult to accept that people—our forebears—were capable of such atrocities that this present survey describes. In their writings, William Shakespeare and novelist Joseph Conrad show that we must reckon with a troubling human contradiction: Only humans act inhumanely.[19]

Furthermore, one can hardly stroll easily and familiarly in this former exotic land without feeling estranged and alienated. Thus, the historian's work, according to Carlo Ginzburg, "destroy[s] our false sense of proximity to people of the past because they come from societies very different from our own." Furthermore, "[t]he more we discover about these [past] people's mental universes, the more we should be shocked by the cultural distance that separates us from them."[20] As this book shows, the Kentucky past was, in truth, at times, appalling. Readers may liken this experience to gazing into the open casket cradling Emmett Till's crushed face.

On the other hand, because of the frequent inhumanity of yesteryear, it may be comforting to believe a vast cultural chasm yawns between our present and that painful foreign past. But was the not-so-long-ago past fundamentally different than the present? One of our tasks is to measure the cultural distance separating us from former times' mental and moral universes. Then, assess the manner and magnitude of that foreign, uncharted, often misremembered past affecting the present.

Historian Winthrop Jordan argues that comprehending history also "impresses upon us those tendencies in human beings which have *not* changed."[21] For this reason, readers—performing as historians—must evaluate the tendencies of those former times that may yet linger. After all, "it is to history," writer James Baldwin declares, "that we owe our frames of reference, our identities, and our aspirations."[24]

Next, we should remind ourselves that "history must be *given* meaning; it does not contain it."[22] Distinguished historian E. H. Carr further reduces the problem to the data: "A fact is like a sack—it won't stand up until you've put something in it."[23] He might have added that the sacks of facts must be loaded into railroad cars and sent to a meaningful destination. Consequently, this book takes historical data, surrounds them with relevant context, and applies meanings and interpretations. It locates historical knowledge in a contextual matrix using verifiable events as raw materials. This historiographical work creates a story in which, hopefully, the data sacks stand up, bolstered by meaningful contextuality. Nonetheless, the reader and society must lay the tracks and decide where the train goes.

In this spirit, to undertake an updated version of Muhlenberg and western Kentucky history, this effort focuses on the intertwined Black/white place-world.[25] This retelling, this active historying, takes the admonition seriously that "the one duty we owe to history," as Irish poet and playwright Oscar Wilde famously quipped, "is to rewrite it."[26] Sometimes, this entails rewriting people into the preexisting collective historical narrative.

Nonetheless, we must be clear about historical revision—the "rewrite"— and its place in the work of historians. Eminent American historian James McPherson, writing as the president of the American Historical Association, explains:

> [R]evision is the lifeblood of historical scholarship. History is a continuing dialogue between the present and the past. Interpretations of the past are subject to change in response to new evidence, new questions asked of the evidence, new perspectives gained by the passage of time. There is no single, eternal, and immutable 'truth' about past events and their meaning. The unending quest of historians for understanding the past—that is, 'revisionism'—is what makes history vital and meaningful.[27]

This responsibility to history means individuals must continually reinterpret bygone eras through fresh eyes and renewed rationales. After all, as historians, psychologists, and life counselors know, we are in constant negotiations with our own historical stories. Thus, our relationship with the past, socially and individually, develops and changes as we move forward. Hence, the current historiography must sometimes alter its rewrite into a corrective "re-right" regarding race relations.

A second caveat is critical. Much of the thematic thrust herein is like what acclaimed Black historian Nell Irvin Painter observed when reviewing a work by historian Leon F. Litwack. "It is a 'white-over-black approach'" presenting "black Southerners as victims rather than black Southerners as people." She laments that this approach was "as though blacks had no existence beyond their connection with whites."[28] In other words, Litwack's account downplays Black *agency*—the capacity of individuals to act on the world.

Readers could fault this present treatment for the same. It does include material on Black businesses, employment in coal mines, Black soldiers in World Wars I and II, education, and other matters that point to Black agency. Still, Painter's critique is accurate to much of the past and current historiography of the Black experience—a "Black trauma narrative." Assuredly, this Black lifeworld is not monolithic and not solely defined by travail.

Nevertheless, tragedy and trauma appear as the leitmotif of the Black experience orchestrated in the present work. This orientation manifests because the available sources are replete with tragic historical events. However, as Pulitzer Prize-winning historian David Blight points out, Black writers have narrated the Black folk memory of inhumane treatment, such that "virtually every major African American writer since emancipation has made these subjects central in his or her work in poetry and prose."[29] These authors include James Baldwin, William Wells Brown, Charles Chesnutt, W. E. B. Du Bois, Paul Lawrence Dunbar, bell hooks, Pauline Hopkins, Langston Hughes, James Weldon Johnson, Toni Morrison, Walter White, and Richard Wright. Indeed, Black writers, according to literary critic Trudier Harris, have served in the communal role as "ritual priests," narrativizing for Black audiences the physical and psychic abuse that has shaped their lives.[30]

However, this study does not intend to posit that tragedy forms an unwavering historical narrative for the subjects examined here or for their descendants. Indeed, this book intends no totalizing cultural script. In writing about lynchings, public execution, murder, suicide, and other horrors—I am reminded of historian Jill Lepore's remark: "All historians are coroners."[31] Still, these traumatic events should not form the plotline of a people's story. Instead, crucially, they help us understand the past, interpret the present, and gaze constructively into the future, hopefully to a time that overcomes the human capacity for cruelty and bloodlust that was instantiated so often in the past.

A second and closely related shortcoming is that this present text tumbles into literary critic Claudia Tate's "protocols of race."[32] Due to this racial protocol, University of Kentucky historian Anastasia Curwood explains: "[M]uch writing about African Americans focuses entirely on social struggle and not on the human experience that would move the analysis beyond a two-dimensional representation of African Americans' lives."[33] Tate uses a psychoanalytic methodology to analyze several acclaimed Black novelists via their texts. Unfortunately, no local historical documents are available for the present study to examine its subjects' interior lives. Nonetheless, this work offers some speculation on internal, emotive events in a few spots.

Therefore, the present work—unsparingly bleak in several passages—will have to stand on its own until someone supplants the racial protocol of struggle to write a fuller, more fleshed-out story of the Black Kentucky experience. That narrative will recount not only personal sorrows but also be full of joy, gladdening hearts, and gladsome stories.

Nonetheless, this present sketch serves a larger purpose. To wit, applying to the Bluegrass State what a cultural historian claims about the nation: The historiography of Kentucky, for better or worse, is a chronicle of debates on the *idea of Kentucky*.[34] This present composition adds to this historical discourse to enrich our understanding of how to think about the Commonwealth of Kentucky. We can expand this to a more capacious idea: Black Americans have been "foundational to the idea of American freedom."[35] And American freedom remains a transhistorical foundational goal with which we still have pronounced present concerns. Any story exploring the struggle toward this ideal should be of inherent personal and national interest.

This effort aims to furnish a factual report for that critical conversation about constructing a "usable past." As an illustration, the *Sankofa*, a bird symbol of the Akan people of Ghana and Côte d'Ivoire, points its body and feet forward while its head reaches to retrieve a precious egg from its back. The symbol's accompanying proverb proposes that "it is not taboo to fetch what is at risk of being left behind." This maxim implies that people should not leave the egg of knowledge in the past unattended. Instead, people of the present must use the past to go forward.

This work uncovers, exposes, and makes western Kentucky's racial record more widely known. It examines the palimpsest of the cultural landscape on which readers can glimpse the geohistorical layers beneath. These layers of Muhlenberg-past, if they but look, sometimes appear as barely visible traces in the precincts of the present. To take a symbol from the coal-mining experience, it shines a carbide lamp into the dark corridors of this past.

As the reader excavates through the temporal strata, she can see a wondrous, complexly layered land, bizarre and foreign, sometimes openly and maliciously bloody, right beneath her feet. She may only vaguely recognize the Kentucky past, but it has perdured, sometimes shrouded, through time. The critical question is whether we would grasp the *Sankofa* egg, claim it, and use it as our own. The worst-case scenario would be to pretend it is not there on the back of the historical bird in the corridors of the silent archives.

Finally, a multicultural scholar voiced a unique way of looking at literature. She mused:

> Books are sometimes *windows*, offering views of worlds that may be real or imagined, familiar or strange. These windows are also *sliding glass doors*, and readers have only to walk through in imagination to become part of whatever world has been created and recreated by the author. When lighting conditions are just right, however, a window can also be a *mirror*. Literature transforms human experience and reflects it back to us, and in that reflection we can see our own lives and experiences as part of the larger human experience.[36]

Similarly, this present volume could function as a mirror reflecting the reader to herself, a window framing hidden histories, or a sliding glass door opening to the Bluegrass State's racialized cultural landscape. It could be all three with conscious effort, creating a portal into the past. Then, we can move forward into the future with the *Sankofa* egg of factual memory and useful knowledge.

Chapter 2

JIM CROW AND THE LOST CAUSE

If we wish to understand the geography of earlier memories, we must look backward at previous relations of power and cultural space.[1]

After 1876, events in the post-Reconstruction period returned the American South to white political dominance, with Jim Crow affliction, hierarchy, segregation, and marginalization. This white Redemption period that returned "home rule" to the former Confederate states featured forms of virulent color prejudice, including many instances of hideous vileness. Indicative of the anti-Blackness, the final decades of the nineteenth century and the early years of the twentieth saw the formation of the second Ku Klux Klan, especially in the 1920s, with intense activity, particularly in Indiana and other places. With the Klan's re-formation, intimidation and lynchings surged. Moreover, the systematic voter disfranchisement of Black citizens across the South became a priority.[2]

The fin de siècle national discourse witnessed the rise of the pseudoscience of so-called "scientific racism." Among its tenets, it purported to show that Black people belonged to an inferior breed (using the theory of polygenesis), a kind of "subspecies out of Africa."[3] This ideology held that "different races were less like siblings and more like separate species descended from multiple ancestors."[4] A common biblical interpretation, lingering since Medieval times, pointed to the "Curse of Ham" that supposedly made African-descended people a servant race in perpetuity. Unsurprisingly, then, the socially constructed "races" were ranked hierarchically.

Evocative of this period, the Kentucky General Assembly passed legislation in 1912 granting pensions to the remaining Confederate veterans and surviving widows. From 1913 to 1931, the Commonwealth awarded $5 million to some 4,700 Confederate veterans or widows.[5] Additionally, horrific lynchings soured race relations as atrocities lit up the American landscape. For example, in the 1895 "race riot" at Spring Valley, Illinois, immigrant miners attacked the Black miners' settlement, driving them and their families out of the immediate area. Others there were, for example, the Wilmington (North Carolina) Race Riot in 1898, the Atlanta Riot, and the Brownsville (Texas) Raid, both in 1906, and the Springfield (Illinois) Race Riot in 1908. The larger-scale events also came closer to western Kentucky. Across the Ohio River in Evansville, in July 1903, a dozen people died, with as many as forty wounded. Black businesses were looted and burned in four days of rioting. Labeling these violent events and many similar ones in this period as "anti-Black riots" is more appropriate as a label than "race riots."

In this post-Reconstruction era, the underlying ideology regarding racialized social and political power and its implementation informed the Jim Crow social order. *Jim Crow* describes the formal and informal subordination and segregation of Black people. Jim Crowism amounted to a constellation of laws and customs, creating a caste hierarchy that enforced discrimination and racial polarization throughout the nation, especially in the former slaveholding states. White citizens called stridently for the enforced segregation underlying this order, crescendoing after the Supreme Court declared the 1875 Civil Rights Act unconstitutional in 1883. Although states and localities codified many laws framing this apartheid-like arrangement, much was "enforced by custom, habit, and violence."[6] In effect, the Jim Crow racial dogma, whether by law or custom, fundamentally defined Blackness as second-classness, with essential elements continuing into the 1960s and after.[7]

In the late nineteenth century, many Black Americans understood the continuing inhumaneness raging against them as a failure of "the notion that accommodation [to the mainstream culture] could mitigate racial tensions."[8] At this nadir, the public intellectual W. E. B Du Bois stepped into the maelstrom with the Niagara Movement and the institutional beginnings in 1905 of the National Association for the Advancement of Colored People (NAACP). The events of this period demonstrate that post-Reconstruction featured much racial struggle and progress, led by Black churches and the NAACP, among many other associations.

The United States underwent enormous changes before and after the turn of the twentieth century. These changes strained political institutions and social arrangements, bringing considerable disorder and heartening progress. From 1880 to 1910, more than a half-million

Americans of color (537,000) left the thirteen-state Southern region. Additionally, more than twice as many white people (1,243,000) out-migrated from this region.[9] But even more significant Black migration began during World War I and continued through the 1960s, numbering in the millions. For many, the experience was like that of novelist, poet, essayist, and short-story writer Richard Wright (1908-1960), who wrote: "I had fled one insecurity and had embraced another."[10]

The severe business-financial panics of 1893 and 1907 punctuated this social upheaval. Again, economic aspects took center stage: "A decade into the new century, America had been whipsawed by a series of recent recessions," a journalist related. "The abuses of the Gilded Age still rankled the citizenry who experienced as great a divide between rich and poor as had been seen. Labor unions fought for a place at the table, and some sought to rein in the influence that corporations had on politics."[11] It was not a peaceful era.

The resulting social disorder also included agrarian protest, labor unrest (e.g., the Great Strike of 1877), the Spanish-American War (1898), the rapidly changing roles of women and the family, and the continuing social question of the place of Black citizens in America. The Black middle class responded to Jim Crowism—with its inhumanity and assault on Black civil and political rights—with the "racial uplift agenda" that sought to carve out an acceptable, non-discriminatory role in society. This struggle and uplift would be heavy and challenging for all the working classes, Black and white.

In the aftermath of the Reconstruction period, the modernizing New South, despite its business boosterism—with Henry Watterson (1840-

1921) editor of the *Louisville Courier-Journal* prominently cheerleading—remained enamored with the cultural values and traditions of the Old (slaveholding) South, which waned only gradually while co-existing with more modern aims. It proceeded "somewhat like the relationship of an older brother with the younger one," observed Kentucky historian Clement Eaton, "at times in reverence, at other times in conflict, but ultimately in compromise."[12] Accordingly, the vestiges of the Old South and post-Reconstruction principles and practices exhibited continuity into subsequent eras.

Nonetheless, some things had changed drastically. Due to the Civil War overthrowing the enslavement economy, a labor revolution appeared in the cultural landscape regarding worker procurement and control. With this, a potent dogma came to re-dominate the former slaveholding states. This doctrine materialized "when the white man's pride and will, and particularly the common white man's," according to influential Southern journalist W. J. Cash, "had concentrated on the *maintenance of superiority* to that black man as the paramount thing in life."[13] Indeed, historians could validly rename this era the Age of Jim Crow due to its pervasive dominator culture.

The end-product of these Southern beliefs and ideals was that Reconstruction (1865-1877) ended on terms dictated by the New South's white social, economic, and political elite. In other words, it transpired as a kind of racial restoration led by the white Southern Democratic Party. With religious overtones of salvation, the notion of redemption expresses the "redeeming" of some of the Old South's values and lifeways.[14] The Redemption struggle intended to "save" the white South, or at least reclaim it, from the "Radical rule" and malevolence (as the former Confederates saw it) of the federal government and the national and state-level Republican Party.

The Redeemer Democratic Party ruthlessly opposed Reconstruction's social goals (we now call "affirmative action") by sanitizing or justifying their disposal of duly elected governments. It mounted a "massive onslaught against the Republican [Party] governments they considered illegitimate and alien."[15] As historian Douglas Egerton asserts: "Reconstruction did not fail. It was violently overthrown."[16] On that ground, Redemption's subversive political intent worked to return political power to white Southerners and their governments. "White Southerners thus perceived 'redemption' as the opposite of Reconstruction," a historian explains. This reversal intended to set up regimes of white "home rule." As a result, they would be free of the federal government's interference that had maintained Black political rights.[17] As a political project, Redemption gained its desired race-based political ends.

As a multi-pronged endeavor to restore white social and economic goals, Redemption included the development of sharecropping (a form of tenant farming) to keep agricultural workers on the land by locking them into inescapable cycles of debt. This system also implemented "convict lease" to requisition prisoners for labor in the primary industries of mining, lumbering, naval stores (turpentine, tar, and other pine-based products), and railroad construction. Redemption also involved segregation in public places, discrimination in employment and professions, and the lynching of thousands of Black people. Finally, an integral tactical maneuver was the rollback of the Black vote.[18]

Fundamentally, the notion of redemption in Southern nationalist thought denoted a "saving" victory. A western Kentucky historian describes this Redemptionist sociology:

> It was a time for Confederate veterans to shine. Throughout the Commonwealth, at camp meetings and political picnics, the old men of the Gray were first in the hearts of Kentuckians. They gathered at reunions, wearing tattered old uniforms, and proudly exhibiting stumps for a leg or an arm—speaking tearfully of Shiloh, Vicksburg, and Chickamauga. Politically, their time had come.[19]

Redemption not only enacted the political, sociological, and deeply personal. It also came to pass as fundamentally historiographical; in other words, it held and promoted a particular ideological interpretation of history. Through the white Democratic Party, Kentucky's redeeming by former Confederates successfully reclaimed the historical narrative from its recent Unionist past.[20] The Bluegrass State, by this reckoning, was retrieved and saved by and for white people.

The so-called "Lost Cause" mythology is a revisionist interpretation of the Southern experience, meaning, and memory of the Civil War. Its goals have included transmitting a neo-Confederate identity and ideology through the rhetoric, ritual, imagery, and cultural productions of literature, textbooks, ceremonies, and monuments. The key institutions perpetuating the Lost Cause memory were the Southern Historical Society, the United Confederate Veterans, and the United Daughters of the Confederacy. In addition, however, ritual and ceremonial activities were vitally important.[21] Mississippi historian Charles Reagan Wilson believes the Lost Cause became integral to a Southern civil religion that invested its historical narratives with a "divine legitimacy."[22] If so, this civil religiousness helps explain its longevity.

Furthermore, the neo-Confederate "cause" was active around the Commonwealth and a part of everyday life. The state's press editorialized praise for former Confederate soldiers and generals. Pamphlets eulogized Confederate officers; historians wrote school textbooks sympathetic to the Lost Cause. Women's Confederate memorial associations conducted ceremonial reinterments of Confederate war dead and, claiming the public space, erected monuments around the state to Rebel soldiers. Local chapters of the United Daughters of the Confederacy (UDC) sponsored monuments in Owensboro in 1900, Madisonville and Paducah in 1909, Princeton in 1912, and Murray in 1917, with a General Robert E. Lee statue. In 2016, Brandenburg (Meade County) accepted and moved the 70-foot Confederate monument dedicated in Louisville in May 1895.

On May 28, 1909, after a "monster parade" a mile long, the UDC unveiled a 29.5-foot Confederate monument on the Hopkins County Courthouse lawn in Madisonville "in the presence of 10,000 cheering people." Atop the granite obelisk pedestal stands an Italian marble statue of "that most picturesque and gallant figure in American history, the Confederate soldier," as the local newspaper lauded.[23] At a gala in the town theater the previous night, Captain J. W. Stone (CSA) praised the work of the UDC. He observed that the Madisonville monument to

Rebel soldiers was the forty-ninth in the Bluegrass State. The captain gloated that "there had not been a single one erected in memory of the Federal soldier in the state."[24] With these actions and others, the Commonwealth re-created itself as a "sentimental Confederacy."[25]

Not to be overlooked, Black Civil War veterans were waging their battle against the nation's false memories of the war. They insisted that they had done their part in remaking and improving America. Indeed, they saved democracy. In 1887, a Black veteran declared, in marvelous wording, that African Americans "washed the blood scars of slavery out of the American flag, and painted liberty there." He continued: "They tore out the Dred Scott decision from the statutes and wrote there, 'All men are equal before God.'" In 1895, a Black Medal of Honor winner castigated white America's ignorance of Black history, particularly its "absolute effacement of the remembrance of the gallant deeds done for the country by its brave black defenders."[26] However, most of the deeds of the U.S. Colored Troops were lost somewhere in the silent archives of battle records.

Like the Confederacy, the Lost Cause civil religion rose from a racial base. The 1915 film *The Birth of a Nation* performed as perhaps the most influential purveyor of redemptionist historiography. Kentucky-born D. W. Griffith modeled his racist film on *The Clansman, an Historical Romance of the Ku Klux Klan* (1905), the popular racist novel by Thomas Dixon, Jr. Griffith's culturally impactful movie glorified the Klan as a heroic, chivalric force that "redeems" and rescues Southern white society. Moreover, these two fictional works depicted the Lost Cause as valorous and emancipation and Reconstruction as tragic mistakes. They also promoted the newer concept of the feared male "black menace."

"[T]he United States had not truly become a nation," Griffith and the Southern Redeemers startlingly inferred, "until the overthrow of Reconstruction in the South."[27] Displayed cinematically, thus was America (and white womanhood) "saved" from the "black beast." As "one of the most useful tools in the arsenal of Jim Crow," a historian argues, the "Black menace was, and remains, a powerful social construct, meant to inspire fear and hostility among whites."[28]

The "black menace" functioned as more than a literary trope; it persisted among white men as an enduring psychosexual fear. Even the U.S. president, Woodrow Wilson, reportedly remarked after screening *The Birth of a Nation* at the White House on March 21, 1915: "It is like writing history with lightning, and my only regret is that it is all so terribly true." Contrarily, historian Henry Louis Gates, Jr., wrote that it was a "silent film that silenced the truth."[29] The sociological perspective Wilson and the white viewing public deemed accurate held that Black men were villainous rapists. This public, including the president, considered the Klan heroic redeemers of Old South culture and saviors of white women. "The white men of the South," Wilson argued previously in his American history book, "were aroused by the mere instinct of self-preservation to rid themselves, by fair means or foul, of the intolerable burden of governments sustained by the votes of ignorant negroes and conducted in the interest of adventurers."[30] For the Princeton University professor with a Ph.D. who became president, the superior race reclaimed its rightful top position.

Otto Rothert (1871-1956), the long-time secretary of Louisville's Filson Club and author of a celebrated history of Muhlenberg County, might have intended to depict the docile, loyal, formerly enslaved "Uncle" John Oates as a positive, anodyne counter-image of the "black menace."[31] After all, he published his book when Confederate monuments, violent racial events, and the racial doctrine of *The Clansman* were culturally dominant. (Griffith's film opened two years later.) Instead, Rothert's portrayal proved less objectionable to the white populace and presented a more benign image. Even so, this rendering was still oppressive, if non-threatening. If "Uncle" John Oates and the formerly enslaved others wanted to remain loyal to their white folks until death, as the white public wanted to believe, then the conditions of hereditary bondage could not have been so bad. However, unfortunately, this historical interpretation gazed into the past, wanting "history" to confirm its present white dominance.

Moreover, the post-Reconstruction era continued as a time of widespread chaos, disorder, lawlessness, and senseless barbarity. Most of this rage and cruelty materialized as the reverse of Griffith's cinematic theme. Instead of whites preyed on by "black beasts," Black Kentuckians became the targets of the continuing racial violence and oppression that surfaced previously during Reconstruction. The intentionally directed, even if ad hoc, white campaigns of domestic trauma "surfaced across the state like angry boils," with the intent "to restore as much of the prewar social and racial order as possible."[32] In analyzing this blatant and continuing oppression and inhumanity, Lexington historian Anne Marshall assigns the blame: "This lawlessness, however, could not be laid at the feet of the federal government or of liberated African Americans. Rather, the fault rested with native whites whose loosely organized campaigns of intimidation, shooting, burning, ransacking, and lynching blanketed the Commonwealth in an atmosphere of terror and disorder for decades."[33]

Simultaneous with this directed anti-Black virulence, state governments across the former slaveholding states diligently formulated a legal order that approached what scholars have correctly labeled *apartheid*—a caste structure of legalized segregation. The plethora of onerous Jim Crow laws and customs implemented a racialized regime of segregated polarization. For instance, Madisonville enacted a segregated residential ordinance in 1910 or 1911, as did Louisville in 1914.[34] In effect, this era formed the so-called nadir of the Black American experience in the United States, a curious designation since it had to rank lower than the dark decades of the trials in the desert of bondage.[35]

However, if the post-Reconstruction era constituted the nadir, it featured more than explosive bloodletting and mushrooming legal sanctions against Black liberty. This era also presented deep-seated psychic and existential challenges. The low point proceeded after the all-too-brief quasi-freedom of the Reconstruction period. It is difficult to imagine the penetrating and suffocating disillusionment and resulting profound despair due to the broken promises and dashed hopes. In effect, this era dug the lowest pit for the Constitutional assurances of the free pursuit of life, liberty, and happiness. A racially liberated America would be a long time coming.

However, the Lost Cause was more than a mere political and cultural exercise: It was a dream with a civic religion at its core. Thus, united were two powerful human forces: theology and history.[36] Together, these powers sacralized the Southern identity as a "chosen people" forged in the crucible of a lost but nobly fought war. The inscription on the Confederate monument in Augusta, Georgia (found verbatim on many others), erected in 1878, points to the sacred romanticism of the Confederacy. "No nation rose so white and fair," the monument touts; "None fell so pure of crime." Fortunately for the United States, the Confederate Army did not continue fighting guerilla warfare after Appomattox. On the other hand, the Lost Cause campaign used historical revisionism and intense, coordinated public propaganda to continue fighting an insurrectionist war of ideas that have not disappeared.

Chapter 3

OUT OF THE 'SILENT ARCHIVES'

The horizon does not disappear as you run toward it.[1]

Besides a few sources, Muhlenberg and western Kentucky's extant historical literature offers a meager Black historical narrative. Historical erasure is a characteristic of the Black experience and sits covered with coal dust in the silent archives. Only a fraction of Black western Kentuckians' historical visibility and documentary presence is available to researchers. Furthermore, sources often presented it as sensationalized news, tragic or salacious, painting negative images, often about Black men in trouble with the law. In 2020, the *Kansas City Star* newspaper admitted this when it confessed it had "disenfranchised, ignored and scorned generations of Black Kansas Citians" since the paper's founding in 1880.[2] Due to this absence, the chronicler, especially in western Kentucky, must piece together the Black Kentucky record from these fragmented sources and situate them in a broader frame.

A local historian wrote about a tragic event, one of only a few instances featuring Black Americans in his text. On June 5, 1892, a southbound excursion train from Owensboro collided with a northbound regular-service train from Russellville on the Owensboro & Nashville

Railroad tracks (formerly the O&R), one mile north of South Carrollton.[3] One-hundred-eighty Black passengers were onboard the excursion train, many from Owensboro. The accident killed five, including a white fireman and a Black porter. The wreck seriously injured another twenty-five, with at least two of these dying later from their injuries.[4]

An exception to this syndrome of Black media nonpresence is the announcements, in 1897, of two Black-owned businesses in South Carrollton. The first features this headline: "EMERY WILLIAMS, (COLORED)." This item lauds Williams and his business establishment:

> There is only one colored person conducting a retail store in town [South Carrolton]. But he is doing a thriving business. For several years he has been handling groceries, tinware, and queensware at his store near the western part of town. He has managed his business in such a manner as to command the respect and confidence of all and a good share of the grocery patronage of his people.[5]

This store announcement points to several historical particularities. First, the label "his people" shows that this business was primarily for Black patrons. This detail also suggests a sufficient threshold of Black citizens living in or near South Carrollton who could support a Black-owned store. A thriving Black business also presumes an adequate minimum of expendable income among Black South Carrolltonians. With the town reaching its demographic peak in 1890 with 525 people, South Carrollton was booming economically. It experienced full employment due to the vast lumbering operations in the area and functioning as Muhlenberg's chief river port. By 1894, the town supported two Black churches.[6] It also had at least two more Black businesspeople. W. S. Kimley ran a grocery. Additionally, Ves Lindley worked as a blacksmith and farrier (a specialist in equine hoof care, including horseshoeing). The business announcement in the West Kentucky College *Reunion* presents Lindley as a "first class man as well as a good workman and deserves the large patronage he constantly receives."[7]

In another development that same year, the state's new U.S. marshal, Republican A. D. James, appointed the Commonwealth's first "colored deputy marshals." One was P. H. Kennedy, a Baptist clergyman of Henderson.[8] Nevertheless, this isolated development did little to change the toxic judicial system for Black Kentuckians.

But sometimes, the hidden became publicly visible, and vitriol surfaced. A prominent instance that captured the nation's attention occurred when Republican president Theodore Roosevelt invited Booker T. Washington, the president of the Tuskegee Institute, to dine at the White House on October 16, 1901. The white South erupted in a paroxysm of denunciations. On its front page, the *Owensboro Daily Messenger* declared: "[T]he president aimed a direct slap at all Southern notions when he placed a negro at the same table with his family." One sub-headline reads: "His mother would disapprove."[9] The Owensboro paper quoted a *New Orleans Times-Democrat* editorial (Oct. 18, 1901, 4): "From that view [of racial equality], even though it be expressed by the chief magistrate of the nation, Americans of the Southern states promptly and emphatically dissent. The negro is not the social equal of the white man. Mr. Roosevelt might as well attempt to rub the stars out of the firmament as to erase that conviction from the heart and brain of the American people."

However, Muhlenberg and regional newspapers scarcely mentioned citizens of color except for sensational stories, like a dramatic death or crime, from the late nineteenth century through much of the twentieth. A case in point: The *Greenville Record*, on May 19, 1910, displayed three articles concerning Black countians. First, in a harrowing account, 16-year-old Robert Hall severed both legs and died due to his attempted jump onto a moving train. Next, a touring vaudeville company appeared at the La Meade Opera House in Greenville, billing a white in blackface comedian "with the funny face."

In the third article, a court sentenced Ben Rosson, a Central City white man previously convicted of murdering a "negro woman" (whose name, tellingly, the paper does not provide), to 13 years of incarceration. However, on delivery by Sheriff T. L. Roll to the State Penitentiary at Eddyville, a writ of habeas corpus returned Rosson to Muhlenberg. The authorities retried him "for a test of his sanity," as it had "been contended all along that Rosson was unbalanced." Subsequently, officers delivered Rosson to the Western Lunatic Asylum in Hopkinsville.[10]

It is pertinent to consider whether the criminal justice system would have given a Black person in a similar position a court verdict short of capital punishment. An apropos contrast is to recall that, 40 years previous, townspeople lynched Bob Gray on the accusation of rape and murder.[11] The 1870 Gray lynching and the 1907 Harrison Alexander rape case (see below) demonstrate that a Black man, even an adolescent, was unlikely to receive fair juridical treatment in Muhlenberg or elsewhere.

The three events above—a tragic death, an announcement of blackface entertainment, and the murder of a Black Muhlenberger—demonstrate the manipulation of Black "news" as an opportunity for sensationalist journalism. To this can be added public disparagement. For instance, on August 20, 1909, the *Central City Muhlenberg Argus*, owned by T. Coleman du Pont, described a suspect nabbed by the deputy sheriff as a "burr-head."[12]

In stark contrast, William Joseph Campbell (1863-1912) provides an extraordinary "invisibly present" Black Muhlenberger. His life story offers a positive and influential historical figure who remains erased and invisible in the historical record.

Throughout his life, Campbell played significant roles as a labor organizer and political operative in local, state, and national labor and political activities. On local and national union boards, he championed "interracial unionism." In his natal state of Alabama, he worked as an organizer for the United Mine Workers and went as an elected delegate to the 1892 Republican National Convention.[13]

On moving with his wife Sallie to Central City in 1894, W. J. Campbell resumed his barbering trade (for which he had trained and worked in Alabama) and again found mining work in one of the DuPont mines around Central City. In 1898, he drafted legislation—the Miners' Pay Bill—passed by the Kentucky General Assembly. The law required timely wage disbursements (by the 16th day of each month) and interest paid on late company payments. It also prohibited the requirement (and coercion) that miners buy from the company or other stores.[14]

Soon, Campbell organized the Republican National League (RNL) clubs for Black and white citizens. It is not clear whether these were integrated organizations. However, interracial organizing was the activity for which Campbell became primarily known. In 1900, local miners sent W. J. Campbell to the United Mine Workers of America (UMWA) national convention. Significantly, the UMWA Constitution barred racial, religious, and ethnic discrimination. Campbell may deserve some credit for this union's position for his dedicated interweaving of political and organizational work at the national level. His work presciently reflected W. E. B. Du Bois's 1935 observation about laborers during Reconstruction. "The theory of race was supplemented by a carefully planned and slowly evolved method, which drove a wedge between the white and black workers," Du Bois argued. "There probably are not today in the world two groups of workers with practically identical interests who hate and fear each other so deeply and persistently," Du Bois continued, "and who are kept so far apart that neither sees anything of common interest."[15] W. J. Campbell saw the common interest.

Kentucky Republicans sent Campbell as a delegate to the national RNL Convention and, in 1901, as a state Republican Campaign Committee member. At the same time, in 1901, the local UMWA District 23 selected him as its secretary-treasurer, perhaps the first Black person in the nation to hold this position. Finally, by 1904, he became a member of the national executive committee of the UMWA, serving as a cabinet officer under the president, John Mitchell, during the phenomenal growth of this union.[16]

Sallie L. (Waddleton) Campbell, the wife of W. J. Campbell, worked as an educator, initially teaching at an early school in Greenville (ca. 1895). In 1905, the Campbells obtained a half-acre of land, either purchased by them or deeded by the Muhlenberg Board of Education for use as a school, probably in Bevier. Sallie Campbell also taught in several other Muhlenberg schools: South Carrollton (ca. 1910) and the Central City Colored School (ca. 1921) (the small schoolhouse on the northeast corner of North First and Pendleton Streets).[17] She also taught in the newer building, the Central City Colored School, built in 1937 by the Works Progress Administration (WPA), just off Legion Drive on Mittie K. Render Avenue.

The Campbells last lived in Drakesboro. After a short life of significant accomplishments in political and labor organizing, on November 28, 1912, W. J. Campbell died at age 49, with burial in Smith Burial Ground (aka Smith Cemetery), an African American cemetery in Drakesboro. UMWA District 23 erected and inscribed a large granite monument.[18]

The above instances point to what Du Bois meant when he wrote of Black social and psychic life "behind a veil." He signified that Black people understood that parts of their lives—sometimes their very existence—were invisible to white society. Nevertheless, Du Bois also knew from his personal experience and as a professional sociologist that Americans of color needed a thorough knowledge of white culture for survival. Du Bois explains this bifurcated complexity:

> It is a peculiar sensation, this *double consciousness*, this sense of always looking at one's self through the eyes of others, of measuring one's soul by the tape of a world that looks on in amused contempt and pity. One ever feels his two-ness,—an American, a Negro: two souls, two thoughts, two unreconciled stirrings; two warring ideals in one dark body, whose dogged strength alone keeps it from being torn asunder.[19]

However, another complication is "the Negro's dilemma." A Kentucky-born administrator of Howard University comments that this predicament means "to want identification with the larger society, but at the same time to be driven along lines of race and common suffering."[20] These "warring ideals," this feeling of "internal twoness," argues historian Ibram X. Kendi, is more precisely termed, a "*dueling consciousness*" that battles internally against itself.[21] Furthermore, the problem of a double and dueling identification with the dominant society and a "community of suffering" is a situation that white people typically do not need to consider due to their position of "white privilege." A local exception might have arisen among coal miners who felt fraternal solidarity with fellow workers, regardless of race. Why? Mutual suffering persisted in the underground, dungeon-like environment with shared daily dangers.

It is easier on the conscience of employers who exploit a class of workers to consider them something less than fully human. This consciousness was part of the cultural climate that viewed Black Americans as, at best, second-class citizens and less than fully human. A cultural signpost of this second-classness was the phenomenon of blackface entertainment. It appeared in Muhlenberg as it did everywhere else.

Blackface minstrelsy—the entertainment genre with white performers wearing black facial makeup—evolved as a typical feature of the long-running caricature of Black Americans as objects of ridicule, humor, and entertainment. Besides the later vaudeville variety shows with some performers in burnt-cork blackface, whites performed in minstrel shows entirely in blackface all over the state during this period. These performances featured comedic "coon" characters and "[N-word] talk."[22] Nationally, minstrelsy materialized as the dominant form of mass entertainment from the end of Reconstruction to World War I.[23] Poet Rita Dove (b. 1952) placed these practices—from the contented and loyal slave trope to minstrel *mammyism* (a museum piece of slavery days)—in the playlist of our "shining, blistered republic."[24]

As a cultural institution, minstrel shows were a potent force for white solidarity across all social strata.[25] The subtext of this form of amusement presented a commentary on supposed comparative racial intelligence, conforming to the early twentieth century's prevailing zeitgeist of racial superiority/inferiority. In a complex psychocultural role-playing reversal, masquerading as Blackness enabled white performers and audiences to display their presumed superior whiteness.

In 1910, Greenville hosted at least one traveling vaudeville show that featured performers in blackface. An ad in the *Greenville Record* proclaimed the "funny" faces displayed by St. Clair, the blackfaced vaudevillian at the La Meade Opera House. At the opera house earlier that year, the paper described the act of Mrs. D. H. Kincheloe,

Madisonville, as a "negro impersonator" who "has few equals." Kincheloe entertained with "her delineations of darkey [*sic*] characters." Her "representation of the negro piano player was almost perfect, and highly enjoyable," declared the paper.[26] Racialized hilarities endured through the years as an integral part of this type of programming.

In 1906, four years before the vaudeville and Negro impersonator performances in Greenville, the Kentucky General Assembly passed the Uncle Tom's Cabin Law. It outlawed "any play based upon antagonism alleged formerly to exist, between master and slave, or that excites race prejudice." An infraction of this law was punishable by fines and incarceration. In other words, the "darkies," as property of enslavers, had to be portrayed as living "gaily" and contentedly in the mythologized Old South. (Stephen Collins Foster's original lyrics depicted this in his "My Old Kentucky Home.") The intention was to outlaw the staging of the immensely popular "Uncle Tom's Cabin" plays.

At this time, any portrayal of discontented enslaved people—which could "excite race prejudice" against white people—ill-suited the neo-Confederate discourse that had captured the Commonwealth. On the other hand, white citizens thought that public performances of buffoonish "coon" characters—such as the regular entertainment in minstrels and vaudeville shows—did *not* excite racial prejudice against people of color. Consequently, in that historical moment, culturally based hypocrisy blatantly materialized.

Governor J. C. W. Beckham (1869-1940) presented the pen he used to sign the Uncle Tom's Cabin Bill to the Lexington chapter of the

United Daughters of the Confederacy, who had been instrumental in its passage. Then, he sent a framed copy to the Confederate Museum in Richmond, Kentucky. What was the provenance of the wood for the frame?—a tree at the Lexington family home of Confederate General John Hunt Morgan, the commander of Morgan's Raiders.[27] The symbolism was intentionally transparent.

Furthermore, the white public's arousal opposing these stage performances "acted as a catalyst for full adoption" of "the Confederate tradition," according to the Ohio River Valley historian Christopher Phillips.[28] Although the Commonwealth had not seceded from the Union some 45 years earlier, it continued the cultural process of neo-Confederatization that began during the Civil War. Overall, at this point, white Kentucky was thoroughly committed to maintaining the political, economic, and social order designed to benefit white people, even in its public entertainment.

This genre of racialized entertainment was long-lasting. In 1926 and for several decades, *Amos 'n' Andy* numbered among the nation's most popular radio shows. The programs starred two white men talking in Black idiolect with stereotypical malapropisms and comic misadventures. These radio shows finally ended around 1960.[29] Even Walt Disney's culturally neutral—or so it seemed—Mickey Mouse character had its roots in blackface.

For several years in the early 1950s, the Central City Lions Club produced a revival vaudeville-minstrel show with some entertainers in blackface in the Central City High School auditorium. Male and female emcees and twenty-three non-blackface performers wearing short white jackets and black bow ties took the stage. This show featured locally prominent professionals, business people, and the then-mayor. The seven people in blackface, wearing satin outfits, included a male in reverse "black eye" (i.e., a white circle on the black makeup) and a female "mammy" with a top-knotted headscarf carrying an infant doll.[30]

Program notes for this minstrelsy have not survived. Nonetheless, we can speculate that Black idiolect, stereotypical caricatures, and malapropisms of the *Amos 'n' Andy* variety constituted part of the fare. Furthermore, they most likely sang the nostalgic, tear-producing notes of Stephen Collins Foster's misunderstood "My Old Kentucky Home, Good Night." Kentucky historian Emily Bingham writes that this "[o]ne little song reproduced slavery's brutality for the sentimental and material benefit of white people." Would the Lions Club members have thought of how a "seductive" and "destructive" song "so memorable and also so formed by forgetting" would be inappropriate?[31] Imminent Kentucky historian Thomas D. Clark, writing in 1948, said he had not found a single criticism of this world-famous song.[32] Few people then understood the meaning of its lyrics.

Accurate historiography in the present commissions us to move beyond chastising past peoples for their cultural myopia. Instead, we should comprehend past events and people in their contemporary cultural contexts. With this view, we can understand that the Lions Club naively presented its shows as harmless and wholesome fun without their understanding of the impairment they exacted by the dominator culture. For at least a century, this racialized humor burrowed deeply into the American *cultural code*—or "cultural unconscious."

Condescending humor was a constituent of the general white attitude toward Black people.

Actor Hattie McDaniel (1895-1952) portrayed the most famous instance of mammyism in her award-winning role in the 1939 film *Gone with the Wind*. Yet, McDaniel could not sit inside the venue during the Academy of Motion Pictures awards night. Instead, the Academy required that she wait outside Coconut Grove until the last moment to enter to receive her award. Poet Rita Dove composed a poem about this scenario that included these lines: "What can she be/ thinking of, striding into the ballroom/ where no black face has ever showed itself/ except above a serving tray?/...your huge face a dark moon split/ by that spontaneous smile—your trademark,/ your curse. No matter, Hattie: it's a long, beautiful walk/ into that flower-smothered standing ovation,/ so go on/and make them wait."[34] Nevertheless, culturally, the wait was not over. The crusade that began in 1941 against the stereotypical mammyism in Hollywood films had not yet influenced the choice of entertainment in the nation's hinterlands, as in the Central City minstrel show depicted above.[33]

While Black people continued their struggles for advances in their work environment, others continued living ordinary lives. Even under the best circumstances, most people never get their proper historying—their *mnemonic restitution* (or "memory justice"). They forever remain erased and forgotten.[35]

An instance of this is the few scraps we know of Central Citian "Uncle" Winton Robinson and his wife, Caroline.[36] Robinson was born into racial enslavement in Virginia in 1822. His marriage to bondservant

Caroline Newton produced two enslaved children during their mutual bondage. After emancipation and the Civil War, the couple and children moved to Tennessee and, sometime around 1882, to Central City for an unknown reason. For about 60 years, Winton Robinson preached within the Primitive Baptist denomination. The couple produced ten more children, with four residing in Central City.

No one recorded an interview with the Robinsons about their past experiences in the Black lifeworld of Southern servitude, Civil War, Reconstruction, Redemption, and Jim Crowism. Regrettably, no biographer recorded the Robinsons' first-hand knowledge of the extreme social changes over the decades—experiences hard to imagine.

Winton Robinson lived 43 years in bondage. What unpaid work did he do? Was Robinson a skilled artisan, as were many of the bondservants? Robinson and his wife lived through the Civil War in Virginia—did he join the Union Army? Did he see Generals Lee (CSA) or Grant (US)? Next, the Robinsons lived through Reconstruction. Did vigilantes target their family? Then, they lived through post-Reconstruction in Tennessee. What kind of work did he and she do—sharecropping? Had lynchings occurred in their area? Finally, the Robinsons lived in Central City beginning in the late nineteenth century. Did he work in the coal mines, and she as a domestic?

In a remarkable circumstance, after the Robinsons moved to Central City, their former enslaver, Rev. McTear, traveled twice from Virginia to visit them. This action demonstrates the lifelong closeness of the threesome.[37] In a thought exercise, we could wonder about the Robinsons' human qualities, such that their former enslaver would visit them. Moreover, we might think, too, about the enslaver Rev. McTear. What was the nature of the relationship between him and the Robinsons? Did their relationship exhibit the racial paternalism that historian George Wright observed in postwar Louisville's white social and political establishment, except on an interpersonal basis?[38] Was Caroline a domestic "servant" for the McTear household? Did she nurse the McTear children?

Furthermore, in their conversations, what would they have talked about? Would the three have discussed the regime of racial bondage, such as whippings, rape on an industrial scale, forced couplings, and selling family members downriver? Would they have reviewed the Civil War's social and personal meanings and Black Americans' involvement? The false promises of emancipation? The unreconstructed outcome of Reconstruction? The power struggles and post-Reconstruction reassertions of white redemption—white social, economic, and political dominance? Second-class citizenship? The psychosexual meanings of the lynching epidemic? The racialization of spacings and places, such as "Colored Town," where the Robinsons lived in Central City?[39] Would they have conversed about how crucial it became, as the old folk song had it, to "keep your eyes on the prize?"

Alternatively, would the Robinsons have acknowledged how the far horizon—the prize—toward which one runs remains unchanged on the cultural landscape? Regardless, the "palace-of-justice promises" have long remained for America to fulfill in the coming day. While sitting together in Central City Colored Town, did the former enslaver and the formerly enslaved discuss their individual and mutual judgments of the American cultural character?

As recorded in his obituary, Winton Robinson kept excellent health until shortly before he died at age 110. Then, in the last week of 1932, his burial was in the nearly forgotten, weed-infested Crawford Cemetery in Central City.[40] The obituary in the Central City newspaper does not mention whether Caroline (Newton) Robinson died earlier or survived her husband. Probably she had already died because the paper claims that Winton Robinson was "the last slave negro residing in Central City."

Thousands of enslaved persons lived and died in Muhlenberg and tens of thousands in western Kentucky. The two Robinsons were examples of former bondservants who toiled without pay for much of their adult lives. But, unfortunately, along with many others, their life stories lie undisturbed in the musty silent archives.

With a degree of historical continuity, the "slavery question" of the Old South and Civil War eras continued after the war to become the "Negro question" or "problem" of the late nineteenth century. This conundrum materialized as the practical problem of conferring rights and citizenship for the millions of Black Americans well into the twentieth century. The great Frederick Douglass addressed this. "There is no negro problem," Douglass asserted. "The [real] problem is whether the American people have loyalty enough, honor enough, patriotism enough, to live up to their own constitution."[41]

Moreover, would they even remember? The obscuring of knowledge in the education system about the Jim Crow era has ill-prepared Americans for this current cultural moment, as much of the prevailing story has evasion at its heart. Schools teach triumph—America had many of these—but not the contextual evils that give the victories their meaning. For instance, Black Civil War veterans were not invited (except as laborers) to the gigantic 1913 Fourth of July celebrations at Gettysburg, attended by 53,407 Federal and Confederate veterans. President Woodrow Wilson spoke at this fiftieth anniversary "Peace Jubilee" reunion of the war that overthrew racial enslavery. Yet, he failed to mention either racial bondage, its overthrow, or the contributions of Black soldiers.

Historian David Blight labels this national convocation "a Jim Crow reunion," where "white supremacy might be said to have been the silent, invisible master of ceremonies."[42] Commenting on this gathering, the *Louisville Courier-Journal* proclaimed: "God bless us every one, alike the Blue and the Gray, the Gray and the Blue! Beholding, can we say happy is the nation that *hath no history*?"[43] To this, Blight remarks: "Glorious remembrance was all but overwhelmed by an even more glorious forgetting."[44] This species of selective forgetting—an intentional disremembrance—mirrors the standard Southern habit of myopically viewing the Civil War by re-creating its memory with self-serving meanings and goals in mind.

W. E. B. Du Bois, a scholar of the African American lifeworld, "looked out at the United States from the peak of a colossal mountain of racial facts."[45] Like Du Bois, this study gazes across the racialized historical events of the Commonwealth's cultural landscape. Unfortunately, the dearth of local primary accounts adds to the dungeon darkness. Nonetheless, the swirling outlines of the historical figures behind us in the dank corridors supply the essential facts of the continuing plight that point the way ahead.

Chapter 4

WORKING THE 'STEAMBOAT SUBLIME,' MAIN STREET, AND 'CAVERNS OF NIGHT'

Local historians must stand ready to connect their locales to both immediate and distant worlds.[1]

The post-Reconstruction-era vaudeville performances in blackface (like at the La Meade Opera House in Greenville) were standard entertainment in the nation's theaters. Traveling troupes of Black vaudevillians performed in land-based theaters and entertainment rooms on river steamer packets and showboats. Additionally, as second-class citizens, Black Americans supplied much menial labor on these steamboats.

Most cabin maids and roustabouts (deckhands or "rousters") on Green River steamer packets and showboats were Black Americans. "The roustabouts did most of the hard work on the boat[s]," Muhlenberger Agnes Harralson, an eyewitness, reports, "loading and unloading, shifting freight and caring for the animals." Who were they?

> They were usually transient black men who worked hard for an hour or two, then had nothing to do for another two or three hours. They had no [onboard living] quarters. In summer they slept wherever they happened to be [onboard] between the landings, but in winter the warmth of the

engines drew them to the lower deck. With their natural penchant for music, the rhythmic cadence of the paddlewheel furnished a beat for the rollicking tunes before they fell asleep. The theme song of the rousters on all the boats was, 'This ain't nothing but a monkey boat, don't do nothing but load and tote.'[2]

Black Americans worked on board in other roles, too. A photo of *Crescent City*'s dining cabin shows six Black servers, uniformed in white, standing at attention. They were ready to serve a dining crowd of twenty-four passengers, who legally had to be white.[3]

Another category of onboard staff, the cabin maids, worked in the recess section on the second deck, aft the staterooms, where they pressed passengers' clothes. A white Central Citian, traveling from Rockport to Evansville, talks about his presence in the recess when cabin maids (their race undisclosed) pressed his mother's dress for dinner that evening. This passenger relates a humorous anecdote about a maid's confusing the use of "to commemorate" with "to remember."[4] His anecdote falls within the cultural practice of minstrelsy.

Many Black laborers worked in the steamer-packet system as deckhands, boiler-room workers, and other interior staff, including waiters, cooks, maids, and entertainers. Black labor, first as enslaved and later as hired hands, proved instrumental for a century in creating the *steamboat sublime* on the Green, the Commonwealth's crown jewel.[5] Before the railroads came, Green River Country was already absorbed into the great Mississippian Empire. This incorporation formed the apex of nineteenth-century Muhlenbergian culture and commerce. Besides the Black laborers, many who worked in this grand commercial enterprise of the "steamboat sublime" were entertainers. A noteworthy example is Arnold Shultz (1886-1931), the peripatetic musician who influenced dozens of musician-miners in the Green River Valley, who, in turn, influenced Merle Travis. Shultz played the showboats up and down the Green from 1905 to 1918.[6]

However, work as a rouster entailed little sublimity and no grandeur or beauty. On the contrary, rousting entailed arduous, dangerous work: loading and unloading cattle, 1,000-pound hogsheads of tobacco, and barrels and boxes of various other products. Two rousters who worked the steamboats on the Ohio and Green described the life of this worker class before World War II when most of the labor was done by hand and on their backs. The two confirmed that they had no beds on board and used wheat and corn kernel bags for sleeping spots.

However (contra Harralson, above), when the boats came to a port, the rousters labored until they loaded and unloaded every item, sometimes without breaks for 10 to 12 hours. In describing the brutal work, a rouster recalled this event: "A man [a Black rouster] fell dead at South Carrollton, Kentucky, in line walking. He had a heart attack and fell with a load on his shoulders. I taken care of him, he died. Worked out! He was overworked. Fell out."[7]

Before the turn of the twentieth century, several Black enterprises operated in Muhlenberg amid the burdensome Jim Crow social order, with at least two in South Carrollton (as noted earlier) and several in Greenville. The notorious outlaw Jesse James (1847-1882) sat for a shave and had his horse shod in Greenville (probably in June 1881). The barber, "Uncle" Green Stuart, and the farrier, "Uncle" Noah Mathis, were Black men. After these two commercial transactions, the famous robber and his diminished gang of three (without the reformed Frank James) robbed the store at Dovey. After the robbery, Greenvillians realized that Jesse James had freely roamed the town. Although the details are incomplete, this story points to a Black barber and a Black farrier open for business in Greenville ca. 1881.[8]

Many thriving Black establishments operated in the larger Muhlenberg towns in the first quarter of the twentieth century. These Black enterprises, primarily but not entirely serving Black patrons, opened in Central City, Bevier-Cleaton, Drakesboro, Greenville, and South Carrollton.[9] One can sketch an intriguing picture with a substantial list of prosperous Black business enterprises in or near the business district of Central City that existed until at least the 1930s. Three businesses served the public in a building along the Illinois Central Railroad (ICRR) tracks, facing the LuRay Hotel, including a pool hall and restaurant, a second restaurant, and a clothes cleaning and pressing business. A second clothes-pressing shop was operating nearby on the northeast corner of Broad Street and the Louisville & Nashville Railroad (L&N) tracks.

Other Black-owned enterprises located in downtown Central City: a boarding house on Locust Street, south of the ICRR tracks; a third restaurant and a barbershop in the Jenkins Building on South Locust Street; and a funeral home (operated by Blake Finch of Drakesboro) on Newman Street. Like many railway depots, a Black man located a shoe-shine stand at the Central City depot. At more locations in Colored Town, hairdressers opened for business.[10]

Other scattered Central City Black business establishments included a second boarding house (on Reservoir Avenue), a second undertaker and a fourth restaurant (both on Railroad Street), and a fifth restaurant (on North First Street). Additional Black businesses included a third boarding house and a welding shop (both on Front Street), a grocery (on Pendleton), and a coal hauler who owned and drove his wagon team (on Sandusky Avenue).[11]

Also located in downtown Central City were three Black physicians' clinics. First, James S. May (from Arkansas), a National Medical College (Louisville) graduate, registered to practice medicine in Muhlenberg in 1908. Second, Robert T. Bailey, originally from Shelbyville (his medical schooling is unknown), registered in Muhlenberg in 1919. He treated patients in his Bailey Clinic in downtown Central City, where he died in 1934 (see Chapter 8). Third, King E. O'Neal, a graduate of the prestigious Meharry Medical College, Nashville, registered to practice in Muhlenberg in 1923, with his office on Sandusky Street.[12] No sources indicate whether these three physicians' medical practices overlapped in time or how long doctors May and O'Neal remained in the county. However, it is remarkable that three doctors, mostly or entirely, treated Black patients in Central City.

The Sanborn Map Company displays on its 1910 map of Greenville that a "Roller Skating Rink (Negro)" operated a block off Main Street near the courthouse.[13] If Greenville supported a roller rink, undoubtedly, it had many other Black businesses in 1910 and later, such as restaurants and others like those in Central City. For instance, Greenville supported a Black-owned taxi-cab service, several hairdressers, a movie theater (Bailey's on Court Row in the 1920s), and a sawmill south of town.[14] One of these Black Greenville enterprises included the barbershop owned by Jack Mathis (1870-1952). His business closed in 1947 when he retired after 50 years of barbering.[15] Bevier-Cleaton supported some of the same Black business activities as in Central City: ice delivery, a restaurant, pool hall, restaurant/pool hall, and a coal mine. In business in Drakesboro were four Black restaurants, a pool hall, and a boarding house.[16]

In the 1930s, B. Mathis, a Black entrepreneur, owned and operated one of the most popular restaurants in Greenville and the county. Mathis located it in a highly trafficked site on Main Street, close to the county courthouse. For this reason, citizens conducting business and attending to legal matters in Greenville, locally and from surrounding counties, often frequented the Mathis restaurant. This dining establishment so impressed a local historian that he recalled prices and menu items—for example, fried corn cake. Contrary to the theme of invisibility, he contends that Mathis was the most remembered person in Greenville 40 years after his death and "was a real part" of the town.[17] Yet, in his effusiveness about the Mathis restaurant, he neglects to mention that custom segregated it for white patrons only.

Drakesboro supported the first Black physician in the county—W. E. Cobb, who moved there in 1904. Like Central City, Greenville supported three Black physicians during the early twentieth century. The first was Amos Cornelius, from Logan County, a National Medical College graduate registered to practice in Muhlenberg in 1907. He located his office upstairs in downtown Greenville's old Bank

Building's back rooms. Dr. Cornelius relocated to Owensboro during World War I.[18]

The second physician was Ulysses Simpson Porter, from Warren County. He graduated from Meharry Medical College and registered to practice in Muhlenberg in 1915. Dr. Porter located his office at his home on East Campbell Street. Around this time, Dr. Porter also worked as the only Black doctor in Russellville—operating a dual medical practice.[19] The third Black physician was Eugene G. Lester, from Georgia, a graduate of Meharry Medical College, who maintained practices in Madisonville and Greenville.[20] In the first quarter of the twentieth century, it is remarkable that many Black physicians with recognized medical training flourished in the county when Black public schools were inadequate.

The above shows that several dozen Black-owned businesses must have operated in Muhlenberg in the first four decades of the twentieth century. These business-owning Black families moved into middle-class status. Their various enterprises also signaled a threshold of Black citizens of Central City, Bevier-Cleaton, Drakesboro, Greenville, South Carrollton, and others living near these towns who possessed enough expendable income to make these businesses commercially viable. What was the source of this Black income? The base of the local Black spending came from Muhlenberg's most significant local industry: coal mining. In 1914, a quarter of Muhlenberg miners were Black men.

In addition to these professionals and Black-owned businesses, Black Muhlenbergers worked in the three primary extractive industries—farming, logging, and coal mining, as already noted. They also found jobs in the Greenville tobacco factories and sawmills scattered throughout the county.[21] Others found employment as skilled craftspeople. For example, the death certificate of A. J. Robinson, Greenville, who died in September 1914, listed his occupation as a brick mason.[22]

Black Muhlenbergers also worked as service workers in various establishments. Others worked in hotels (primarily as maids and valets), on steamboats (as maids, rousters, and boiler room attendants, as noted above), and for the railroads as porters and section hands. For instance, Peter Vanlandingham worked as a section hand because a newspaper reported that he died in December 1892 at South Carrollton after falling from a handcar.[23]

Additionally, substantial numbers labored long hours in white homes. They worked with little pay as domestic servants, child nurses, caregivers, and "washerwomen," toiling on their employers' clothes and linens in their own homes so that they could take care of their own children. Muhlenberg's occupational division of labor matched Bowling Green in its employment types. In the latter city in 1928, 85 percent of gainfully employed Black people worked as low-paying domestic servants in white homes or as common laborers in, for example, tobacco factories.[24]

This employment structure persisted from past times. In the South, beginning in the 1870s, single Black women were three times more likely—six times for married Black women—to participate in the labor force than their white counterparts.[25] These race, class, and gender traits disadvantaged these women. An interlocking order of oppression resulted from this tripartite intersectionality. Recognizing this, Imani Perry, writer and professor of American civilization at Princeton University, writes of the "long-standing American habit of making Black women the mules of the world." [26]

As noted above, many Black men worked on the railroads. A frequent traveler from Kuttawa, Lyon County, rode the passenger trains in western Kentucky in the 1920s, lodging often at the LuRay Hotel (a "quite famous… fine hotel") in Central City. "In memory," he recalls, "I can still hear the negro porter, standing on the platform, yell out: 'LuRay Hotel! LuRay Hotel!'"[27]

That Central City depot platform must have had separate Black and white waiting rooms, restrooms, and water fountains. A Black Owensboran remembers the segregated setting at the Owensboro L&N depot in the 1940s.[28] Poet, playwright, novelist, and brilliant member of the Harlem Renaissance Langston Hughes (1901-1967) wondered in 1943: "Where is freedom going on a Jim Crow train?"[29] Indeed, separate facilities were in place from at least 1892 until the 1960s up and down the ICRR and L&N lines. (The General Assembly finally rendered null the 1892 Separate Coach Law when it passed the Kentucky Civil Rights Act of 1966.)

To be clear, the "petty apartheid" of segregated facilities—restrooms, takeout windows, and others—was never trivial to those forced to endure them. Instead, it represented the tip of the iceberg of the systemic racism of the social order. This order was the overarching system of Jim Crowism that "included denial of due process and equal protection under the law and the extremes of economic exploitation made possible by elimination of citizenship rights." [30]

While the legal structure curtailed rights, the numerous Black businesses created relative prosperity for many Black Muhlenbergers in the first four decades of the twentieth century. With this evidence of Black businesses, especially between the First and Second World Wars, that era rates as a heyday of flourishing Black culture in Muhlenberg.[31] Hopkinsville had its thriving Virginia Street; Lexington had its central hub of Deweese Street. For several decades until after World War II, Louisville had the prosperous Walnut Street district in West End with hundreds of Black-owned businesses.[32]

Similar zones of economic empowerment existed in many other cities across the nation. These Black commercial zones included the Fourth Avenue district in Birmingham, the Hayti community in Durham, the 18th and Vine neighborhood (the Jazz District) in Kansas City, Black Bottom in Philadelphia, Jackson Ward in Richmond, the U Street corridor in Washington, DC, and, of course, Harlem in New York. In Tulsa, the Greenwood neighborhood—the so-called Black Wall Street—flourished before the white populace burned, dynamited, and aerially bombed it out of existence in a racial pogrom on June 1, 1921.

As noted above, in the early twentieth century, Central City, Greenville, and the other Muhlenberg towns, when downtowns were the centers of everyday life, had thriving thresholds of Black-owned businesses. They would soon disappear, however, beginning in the Depression years. In a historical irony, the few firms that survived those lean times closed when integration came in the 1960s and negated the need for separate businesses.[33] Hence, in a long reversal, remarkably few Black-owned businesses survive in Muhlenberg and elsewhere in small towns today.

Black Americans had always been integral to the Western Coalfield's most important economic activity as laborers in coal mines. They had worked in enforced servitude in mines since its beginnings before the Civil War. However, for Muhlenberg and western Kentucky, starting in the 1870s, Black workers, despite Jim Crow discrimination, were increasingly employed in mining due to labor shortages in the industry. Their hiring also resulted from coal operators' prevailing belief that Black workers would not join labor unions or engage in labor strife.[34] At times, coal operators imported Black workers from the Deep South to replace striking white miners, as in Hopkins County in 1900. This hiring practice exerted downward pressure on all miners' wages, a development that white miners naturally resented.

Foreshadowing later migrations, many Black citizens moved to Muhlenberg from 1901 to 1910 to find work. Subsequently, the county's coal production increased 535 percent in that decade, from 532,581 tons (1901) to 2,849,690 tons (1910).[35] Thus, while coal production soared by more than 2.3 million tons, so did Black immigration. As a result, in the decade after 1900, Muhlenberg's Black population increased by 34 percent, many migrating for jobs in the mines.

Soon, with the beginning of World War I, the northward and westward flood of Southern Black workers increased. In 1916, the next migratory trend—the so-named Great Migration out of the South (1916-1970), when millions of Black Southerners, including Kentuckians and some Muhlenbergers, moved northward and westward—helped fill northern cities' needs for rapidly expanding industries (a migratory pull factor) due to the increased industrial demands of World War I. Besides jobs, Black Americans' fundamental reason for leaving the South was to escape Jim Crow marginalization, dispossession, and racial intimidation and violence (a push factor). Part of this marginalization persisted because half of Kentucky's Black farmers (49.1%) were vulnerable tenants.[36] These dual migratory push-pull factors promoted outmigration and deepened the labor vacuum in the source areas from where the workers vacated.

Then, in 1916, to further help satisfy their needs for workers, coal companies in the Western Coalfield imported seven hundred Black Alabamians to work in the mines.[37] Obviously, the industry created a labor shortage, as, in the decade after 1910, Muhlenberg lost 5 percent of its Black population even with the importation of workers. This decrease formed yet another demographic swing in a series of swings.

Miners may voice complaints about "owing their souls to the company store," as the coal-mining blues lyrics by Merle Travis fatalistically paint it. Nonetheless, many lost their *lives* at punctuated tragic moments to the company mine. An instance is the Moody Mine disaster at South Carrollton in February 1908, when ten miners died.[38] Two years later, in February 1910, the deadliest mining tragedy in Muhlenberg happened at the Browder Mine, where an underground gas explosion killed thirty-four miners.[39] In January 1912, a third multiple-victim mine mishap occurred close to downtown Central City in the DuPont Central Mine (for which Central City took its name) when five died.[40] A fourth disaster shocked the county on February 16, 1926, in the Nelson Creek Coal Co. mine, eight miles north of Central City. This catastrophe killed eight miners, five as members of the rescue team. Two or three of these dead rescuers were sons of two of the three who died in the initial explosion.[41] A fifth mining calamity happened near Drakesboro on December 19, 1928, in the Black Diamond Mine, when a gas explosion that "shattered the shaft" caused a slate fall that killed six miners.[42]

Three decades would pass until the most recent multi-casualty mining disaster in Muhlenberg. On August 7, 1968, this sixth accident occurred at the River Queen underground mine between Central City and Greenville. This explosion killed nine miners.[43]

However, through more than 150 years of coal mining in Muhlenberg, most accidental mining deaths came about as single fatalities. For example, the year after Otto Rothert's 1913 book, the death certificate of Willie Render—a "colored" miner, married, age 28, of South Carrollton—documents that he was "mashed by slate in Crescent Mines."[44]

The many single-fatality accidents and the six multiple-fatality mining disasters above affirm that coal mining has been exceedingly dangerous. It became an even more heightened deadly business, especially after coal companies introduced more mechanization into their underground operations ca. 1895. Unfortunately, the mining machinery produced higher coal dust levels, leading to more coal dust explosions—much more than the individual miners laboring with picks and shovels.[45] Thus, the carnage continued. For instance, the explosion at a mine in Webster County in August 1917 took sixty-two lives.[46] From 1964 to 1980, forty-nine mining fatalities occurred in Muhlenberg. Forty-four of these accidental deaths happened in underground mines, while strip mines accounted for five.[47]

For the entire nation, from 1901 to 1908, a staggering number of miners—16,734—lost their lives in the nation's mines, with another 37,017 seriously injured.[48] For the state, in the century from the 1890s to the 1990s, more than 7,100 work-related fatalities occurred at coal mines.[49] For Muhlenberg, for the 108 years from 1872 to 1980, more than three hundred miners died in coal mines.[50] "No industrial state," Kentuckian Harry Caudill lamented, "has ever permitted such carnage in its mines as has marked America's coal pits."[51]

The coal-mining death toll is immense when including those who have died due to the slow death of black lung disease (coal workers' pneumoconiosis). For Muhlenberg, the estimated number of mining deaths, including black lung, amounts to more than 1,300 miners who died over the long arc of mining in Muhlenberg (see endnote 50). The Muhlenberg mining deaths began early in its mining history. An instance of a nineteenth-century death (no year given) is that of Lonnie Stroud, a member of an original family (along with the Moreheads) who settled in pre-Central City's environs.[52]

What was the Black presence in the coal industry? One way to arrive at the number of Black workers in local mining is to consider the number of those who lost their lives in the mine tragedies in the early twentieth century. From the beginning, as did mines all over Kentucky and other states, Muhlenberg's mines integrated Black men into their workforces—enslaved people initially, free labor afterward.

The number of Black miners must have been substantial, as indicated by the proportion of their fatalities in the first three disasters. In the 1908 South Carrollton mishap, eight of the ten deaths were Black miners (80%). At Browder in 1910, nineteen of the thirty-four deaths were Black (56%), and at Central City in 1912, one of the five (20%). When averaged, Black miners accounted for about 55 percent of the deaths in these first three multiple-casualty disasters before World War I. Nonetheless, in the accidents at Nelson Creek (1926) and Drakesboro (1928), none of the casualties was Black (otherwise, the news articles would have listed them as such). However, two of the five miners who "crawled to safety" in the Drakesboro accident were Black Americans—George Killgrew [*sic*] and E. Cunningham.[53]

These casualty data show substantial Black involvement in Muhlenberg's coal mining until 1928. Moreover, significantly, as an elderly Black Kansan coal miner recalled (ca. 1900): "[T]he damps [explosive and noxious mine gases] and rock falls didn't care what color you were."[54] Stalking the mine corridors, Death did not discriminate on race.

Finally, Otto Rothert's authoritative 1914 data (in *Coal Age*) established that one-quarter of the 3,500 men employed "in and around" Muhlenberg's mines were Black workers when the county's total percentage of people of color was 10.2 percent.[55] Based on these 1914 figures, 875 Black men (out of a total Black 1910 population of 2,911) may have worked in Muhlenberg mines. If accurate, this number represented a large percentage of the working-age Black males in the county who were 14 years and older. (With the 1902 child labor law, children under 14 were not *legally* allowed to work in mines in Kentucky.)[56] These data confirm two socioeconomic phenomena: the crucial economic importance of Black miners to Muhlenberg's coal economy and the vital dependence on labor in the coal mines for Black families.

This account should add another point. In the 1920s, mechanization in the coal mining industry reduced the workforce's numerical demands. As a result, although this economic sector added more than 10,000 jobs in Kentucky between 1920 and 1930 (a 23% increase), Black Kentucky miners decreased slightly. Thereafter, year after year, the number and percentage of Black miners dropped (Table 1).

Table 1: Black Kentucky Miners, 1900-1980

Year	Total Miners	Total Black Miners	Black Miners as Percent of Total
1900	9,299	2,206	23.7
1910	18,310	3,888	21.2
1920	44,269	7,407	16.7
1930	54,307	7,346	13.5
1940	54,676	5,473	10.0
1950	64,074	2,965	4.6
1960	37,519	1,135	3.0
1970	21,470	445	2.1
1980	50,572	804	1.6

Source: Adapted from Ronald L. Lewis, *Black Coal Miners in America: Race, Class, and Community Conflict, 1780-1980*, 191-193, Appendix.

The introduction of technology proved partly responsible for this decrease. It reduced the need for the traditional, unskilled pick-and-shovel miner and increased machinery training. Mine managers trained white workers more often than Black employees in this work environment. A Black miner working in West Virginia from 1935 to 1957 observed: "[A]utomation and the race thing" caused Black miners' demise.[57] "They [coal operators] don't bother to train black men to operate modern equipment," a Black miner in eastern Kentucky claimed.[58] Thus, the broader society's racial caste order extended into hiring and promoting miners as mechanization and occupational segregation came to the coalfields.

As a final example of the miners' plight, John O'Malley, the head "shot firer" at Central Mine in Central City, took a day off on January 17, 1912. That was the day of the fatal disaster when those five ill-fated miners replaced him at the mine. O'Malley lived extraordinarily optimistically with the daily prospect of sudden death, claiming he had been "knocked down" seventeen times by firing blasts. Nonetheless, he believed he was "providentially cared for."[59] O'Malley lived and worked as a man prideful but somber, independent, and hardened. Since his Irish name hints at Catholicism, shot-firer O'Malley regularly carried his steely, doom-laden beliefs to Mass less than a half-mile away at St. Joseph Catholic Church (completed that same year).

When working underground in Muhlenberg's mines, belief in the protection of Providence bolstered the workers while tramping in the dark, damp corridors deep underground—the "caverns of night."[60] While trudging the coal corridors with their fatalistic faith, each Black and white miner lived what we could label the *coal miners' blues*.[61] This blues outlook acknowledged that mining threw a lifeline with desperately needed jobs. However, it continually and capriciously endangered these same lives, sometimes snatching them without warning. As Merle Travis sang: "Where the demons of death often come as a surprise/ One fall of the slate and you're buried alive."[62] Additionally, with black lung disease, a wasting death lingered at other times. A local historian lamented the cost accounting: "Every lump [of coal] extracted carries a human price."[63]

However, livelihood and mortality were not the only storylines. Creative expression rose from the seams of number nine coal: the music of Muhlenbergers Ike Everly, Kennedy Jones, Mose Rager, Merle Travis, and the itinerant Black musician Arnold Shultz. This culturally based music, often doleful yet spirited, materialized as a cultural form, born of the miners' lifeworld of hardships and the threat of instant maiming, obliteration, or prolonged, choking death. As the musicologists say, these sounds were *autochthonous*—arising from the same flesh-devouring earth that yielded the hard living in the caverns of night that claimed too many precious lives.

"Danger was double" for all coal miners, as Travis lyricized. However, for Black miners, like all Americans of color, other experiential, "dangerous doublings" existed with which to contend. As examples of these dangerous doublings, one could recall this chapter's events and social background, including Du Bois's concept of double consciousness.

Nonetheless, in the Muhlenbergian cultural landscape, joy, hope, dedication, and sacrifice were also consistently present along with the fatalistic coal miners' blues. A mining historian comments on the hard life of physical labor that coal mining necessitated and its less-than-ideal status: "So what they [miners] do is reverse that matter and they take pride in the fact that they can actually survive in such a place. That makes 'em hard, and they stand on their own, and they don't care what the public thinks."[64] The grim lyrics of Merle Travis's "Nine Pound Hammer" express the irony: "Well, when I'm long gone you can make my tombstone/ Outta number nine coal, outta number nine coal."[65]

Chapter 5

TRIAL AND EXECUTION OF HARRISON ALEXANDER

Each place lives with the burden of its own history.[1]

Besides work and entertainment, the white Redemptionist political ideology of the post-Reconstruction period materialized in the criminal justice system. This setup, as designed, sometimes intimidated Black citizens into submission, as illustrated by the 1906-1907 legal proceedings and public execution of Harrison Alexander. The white jury sentenced the accused to a public hanging until dead.[2]

But first, a time-out for the reader. Trauma scholar Mari N. Crabtree speaks of the unsteady ground of historians' responsibility and ethics of depicting violence through images and the written word. Crabtree relates two impulses in direct conflict: the historian's desire to unearth and reveal stories and the need to preserve the dignity of the victims and survivors. She notes that the NAACP published lynching photographs from the 1920s to the 1940s to push for anti-lynching legislation. "I have grappled" with this dilemma, says Crabtree (as has the author of this book). She believes that not writing about the mistreatment might give the impression that it did not have a significant impact or was not as horrible as it was. Additionally, she recognizes the political and educational contributions of a realistic rendering of actual, even dreadful, historical events.[3] With this as a caveat and guide, the present report pushes on.

In August 1907, in an extraordinary move, seventy-six of the most illustrious men in Central City signed a petition to the governor, J. C. W. Beckham (1869-1940). They wanted his commutation of Harrison Alexander's death sentence to the legal maximum of twenty years in the state prison. Compelling reasons and motivations must have underlain their request to spare the life of a 16-year-old Black youth whom an all-white jury found guilty of raping a white woman. Nevertheless, their proposal—the "Petition of Seventy-Six" (my term)—did not move the governor.[4]

We know the affair's sordid denouement. Local officers publicly executed Alexander on the county jail grounds on August 9, 1907. That summer was one of the coldest in memory, with August temperatures in the area plunging to 52 degrees F. Nevertheless, a crowd estimated at six hundred witnessed the execution, guarded by a 35-member detachment of the State Guard. For these hundreds of people in the middle of Greenville in the unseasonably chilly early August morning, it was not too discomfiting to witness the death of a Black Central City youth of 16 years. "[T]he drop fell at 5:32 o'clock," 33 minutes after sunrise.[5] Unfortunately, records do not show whether any signers of the Petition of Seventy-Six were present at the execution. However, attendance was probable for many of these not-disinterested people. Nonetheless, it instilled a cold, disturbing memory in the witnesses, one they would never forget.

How so? The Alexander hanging turned out to be a travesty of justice and a public-relations calamity in more ways than the officials severely mishandling the execution and requiring an agonizing half-hour to finish. What happened? The authorities incompetently measured the rope too long, enabling the hanging adolescent to touch the ground with his toes.[6] Then, rather than releasing the condemned from his noose and hauling him up the thirteen steps to the scaffold platform for another attempt at a quick re-hanging with a readjusted rope, Sheriff J. A. Shaver inexplicably chose a different method. The sheriff ordered his deputies to tug the rope from above, resulting in a protracted 32-minute ordeal.[7]

The curious attendees thought they would witness the professional near-instantaneous death by state-sanctioned hanging. Instead, if they stayed, six hundred onlookers, including children, watched a harrowing half-hour ordeal. Eyewitness documents discovered in Roark Funeral Home described the bungled hanging as "very gruesome."[8] Many probably fled the nightmarish scene as the executioners tortured Alexander to death by slow strangulation in the rising sunlight.

This trial and execution is another moment of violence that allows a delving into the political and cultural milieu and discourse of the first decade of the twentieth century. Who were these distinguished signers of the Petition of Seventy-Six? This ad hoc group included four doctors, a dentist, and the Central Coal & Iron General Store manager. It also had a jeweler, a second general store owner, a former postmaster, a future postmaster, the owner of marble works (the current postmaster), and the editor of the *Central City Farmers' and Miners' Advocate*. Not least, the lot included two future police-court judges. These were all influential men.[9]

One more man of distinction, the first to sign the petition, was William D. McElhinny, the mayor of Central City from 1905 to 1909. Mayor McElhinny was powerful as vice president and treasurer (1899-1911) of Central Coal & Iron Co., the county's largest employer.[10] Among this set of seventy-six, we can imagine other men of rank and means and at least several church elders and deacons. This bloc of leading citizens, composed of the town's top political and business leaders, publicly pleaded for a lesser, non-capital sentence for young Harrison Alexander.

This list of illustrious citizens demonstrates that serious doubt must have roiled their minds and consciences, as it did others, including the town's women. They voiced concerns about the evidence, proper handling of the case (the prosecution and defense), the verdict, and sentencing. These seventy-six men risked their reputations with their official request to the Commonwealth's highest officeholder. Their urgent plea was that a 16-year-old Muhlenberger of color from the Black Galilee section of Central City should not face hanging from the Greenville gallows.

What did these seventy-six men know or presume about this case? Their petition's prefatory text addresses two problems with the legal proceedings. First, they argue: "There were but two witnesses who testified to the commission of this crime, Florence Whitehouse [the white accuser] and a Negro named Joe Dulin" Second, Dulin, a friend or acquaintance of the accused, accompanied him on the afternoon of the alleged rape. For this reason and others, many citizens suspected Dulin to be, at minimum, an accomplice to the crime.

Moreover, suppose there were two initial parties of interest: Alexander and Dulin. In this case, before the court charged Alexander as the sole perpetrator, the police must have eliminated the other party as a suspect. However, the case documents do not reveal how the authorities dismissed the possibility of Dulin's criminal complicity.

Florence Whitehouse, the victim of the alleged violation, was the plaintiff. The Petition of Seventy-Six chronicles that Whitehouse had been evaluated medically as mentally deficient and committed three times to the Western Lunatic Asylum at Hopkinsville. Incredibly, Alexander's defense lawyer never introduced this crucial detail at trial. "Florence Whitehouse had prior to the commission of the offense been confined in an Asylum two or three times," the petition argued, "and many people believed that the Negro Dulin was the guilty party or at least as guilty as Alexander." Furthermore, "to our minds," the petitioners reckoned, "the unsatisfactory evidence in the case" warranted imprisonment rather than capital punishment. These leading citizens concluded this about the crime's sole witnesses: The court should have judged Whitehouse, the plaintiff, as highly unreliable and Dulin, the "friend," as patently suspect.[11]

Another avenue of defense for Alexander would have been to play on the prevalent color prejudice of the early twentieth century. Defense attorney John Feland knew that he could sully and even destroy Florence Whitehouse's reputation, hence the status of her testimony in the eyes of the all-white jury. Imagine the reverse of this scenario: If the victim had accused a white man of rape, his defense, as was the practice in American jurisprudence (inherited from English common law), would have made her sexual history, thus her character, fair game for besmirching. This procedure permitted the exposure of women's carnal records as part of their relevant moral character and, in effect, put the accusers, the women, on trial.[12]

With this tactic, attorney Feland, who was white, could have exploited white bigotry by introducing evidence that Whitehouse had lived with several Black families in Bevier-Cleaton. She seemed not to have had a permanent home, going back and forth several times from the asylum in Hopkinsville to the home of one Black family or another. Dulin himself testified that Whitehouse occasionally stayed at his mother's house, where Dulin also lived.[13] If the criminal justice system used implicit color prejudice against Alexander as the feared "black menace," then his defense attorney could have exploited white prejudices, in reverse, to his benefit. Undoubtedly, attorney Feland thought of this. Why did he not use it? Did his "white conscience" prevent his attacking a white woman with allegations of consorting with Black people? For this reason, Alexander's legal defense appears to have been highly incompetent and professionally negligent.

Here is defense attorney Feland's July 29, 1907, letter, verbatim, addressed to Governor Beckham only 11 days before the scheduled execution. His letter requests a stay (delay) of carrying out the sentence:

> In the matter of Harrison Alexander convicted in the Muhlenberg Circuit Court for assault and punishment fixed at death. I want to call your [the governor's] attention to the record disclosing that this prosecuting witness Florence

> Whitehouse has been three times incarcerated in the Asylum of our state, and this was not brought out until it was too late [for] the defense to take it up. I now learn that she was never discharged as cured of her insanity, and that she was only paroled on account of the crowded condition of the Institution. You will notice upon an examination of the record that she testified like a crazy woman and I was so impressed with this when she spoke of my client as a Pop-eyed S— of a B—— [*sic*], that I did not even try to cross-examine her.

Next, after his misstep, Feland tries to recoup some squandered time:

> I am sure that no possible harm can come of an investigation and I would like to have enough time in which to get the records copied and to take some dispositions of physicians who treated her and tell about her mental responsibility. It's hard indeed to give up life at Fifteen [the age of Alexander], but it looks especially hard to be called on to do this upon the testimony of a lunatic, subject as they always are to harmful influences. I can't help but believe that the Negro Dulin is the real culprit and that his corroboration of the crazy woman is but an effort to unload on my client. I respectfully request that you stay this execution for sixty days in order that we may be absolutely sure that the punishment is deserved.[14]

It is difficult to explain why the defense attorney chose not to cross-examine Whitehouse. Feland could have easily made the case that she was mentally incompetent, even deranged, or at least an unreliable witness. As the court-appointed attorney, part of the problem was that Feland lived in Hopkinsville when transportation was difficult. Perhaps he chose not to make the necessary efforts that would have accrued more expenses to conduct a competent defense. Furthermore, an additional disadvantage resulted from the undeniable problem of presenting a Black man's testimony against a white woman. This testimonial situation was still in play even though, under pressure from the federal government, in 1872, the General Assembly rescinded the 1866 law prohibiting Black testimony in state courts.[15] But in 1907 Kentucky, Black testimony against white people would have fractured deep social norms.

Governor Beckham chose not to grant the stay of execution to allow time to prepare this relevant and reliable line of defense. Beckham was the same political figure previously noted who sent the pen he used to sign the Uncle Tom's Cabin legislation to the United Daughters of the Confederacy. He also sent a copy of this bill to the Confederate Museum in Richmond, Kentucky, framed by wood from a tree in the yard of Confederate General John Hunt Morgan. These actions reveal something of the ideals and sympathies of the governor. Unfortunately, the absence of his signature on the stay of execution prevented the proper investigation that would have been crucial to the legal defense and life of the accused young Black man. Instead, its absence sent Harrison Alexander to the Greenville gallows.

Concerning the local white public's collective consciousness: What should we make of this statement by the Commonwealth's most influential newspaper? The *Courier-Journal* reported that after the crime against Whitehouse on July 2, 1906, a "race war" occurred in Central City and Bevier.[16] What did the paper mean by "race war?" Who was involved—Blacks, whites, or both? How did the purported fighting proceed? The choice of wording about a "race war"—was it *code language* that worked as cover for white hotheads seeking immediate retribution for a crime, in other words, clamoring for a lynching? Was this paper's statement a journalistic euphemism to gloss over what might have been the actual events? That is to say, did white agitators want to lynch Alexander and anyone they found resisting their aggression? Moreover, how did the prevailing racial doctrine of white supremacy fit in? With unanswered questions, this story remains shrouded in silent archives like an abandoned coal mine corridor.

Furthermore, valid questions arise about the manner of jury selection and the potential for a fair trial in Muhlenberg. If the court accepted that proper legal action could proceed locally, then a change of venue was unnecessary. Nonetheless, the need for the armed State Guard indicates the intense public agitation surrounding the Alexander rape case. Moreover, after his arrest, circumstances forced local authorities to send the accused to neighboring county jails, first to Elkton and then to Hopkinsville, to prevent vigilante violence against him.

On August 18, 1906 (a Saturday), State Guard companies from Hopkinsville and Earlington encamped on the county jail grounds to protect the accused and maintain order on the first day of the court proceedings. The impassioned public interest necessitated the soldiers' presence, as evidenced by the crowd of 3,000 gathered in Greenville for the trial. A maximum throng of four hundred interested onlookers packed the courtroom (in the La Meade Opera House because the present county courthouse was under construction).[17]

On this first day, the Commonwealth's attorney, Robert Young Thomas, Jr. (1859-1925), needed to establish the crucial point that Alexander would get a fair trial in Muhlenberg. Thomas called fifteen well-known white men who opined that a jury (albeit all-white) could furnish the defendant a fair hearing. The court proceedings then carried over to Monday, the second and final day.[18]

Was this trial of Harrison Alexander a legal lynching? In *legal lynchings*, authorities severely streamlined the hearings of capital cases (sometimes lasting for mere minutes). They retained some forms (thereby the legality) but not the substance of fairness and due process. Guilty verdicts were preordained. In the Alexander case, the semblance of a bona fide legal process partially negates the label of legal lynching. At least three juridical procedures support this conclusion. The Commonwealth furnished Alexander with legal counsel, and the county kept the features and effects of a typical courtroom. Moreover, the court followed the barest of standard procedures for the two days of the trial.

Nonetheless, the defense counsel's competency and effort were sorely lacking, a deficiency that the judge could have rectified. However, none of the principal stakeholders (the prosecutor, law officers, judge, jury, and the white public) demonstrated any interest in a competent defense. Interest in skilled representation came from Alexander, his family, the Black community, and the seventy-six petition signers. A reasonable conclusion holds that the Alexander trial skirted close to a legal lynching. Despite the legal trappings, the Commonwealth and defense attorney Feland did not provide adequate representation or reasonable due process. After the defense's deficiencies, the jury returned a guilty verdict after deliberating an unconscionably brief 19 minutes.[19]

Defense attorney Feland appealed the conviction. While awaiting the Appeals Court decision, the Muhlenberg court again suspected white mob action as a genuine threat. Accordingly, it sent the condemned youth back to Hopkinsville (with a new, more secure jail). However, if vigilante virulence were an imminent concern before and after the trial, does this not cast doubt on the likelihood of a fair legal process? Crucially, why was there no change of venue? Alexander's defense attorney, living in Hopkinsville, could have given him better representation there. Prosecutors, though, may always oppose such a move. Still, we should not forget that the flamboyant R. Y. Thomas, Jr., wanted his day in the local court, an event he would not get with a change of venue.

According to prosecutor Thomas's letter to the Court of Appeals, Feland failed to file a "bill of exceptions." Therefore, the court could not consider further court instructions or transcripts of testimony. Thomas wanted the appeal thrown out on this technicality. However, the court did not mention this point of law or the substance of Feland's request in its brief decision. Instead, it judged the evidence "conclusive of his [Alexander's] guilt beyond a shadow of a doubt" and that the trial "was conducted throughout in an orderly and regular way." The Court of Appeals pronounced that the punishment (death by hanging) was "extreme, but deserved." [20]

Local authorities worried about unrest before the execution, so they appealed to Governor Beckham to consider the matter. Beckham assigned State Adjutant General Henry Lawrence to determine the need for a military presence to maintain order. The press reported that tension came from two sides: rumors of a "possible attempt by negroes to release Alexander" and the "excited white people of the county."[21] However, an attempted rescue by Black citizens ranked as highly dubious. Perhaps Adjutant General Lawrence considered the more likely scenario of white vigilantes bent on lynching, especially if the governor granted a stay of execution. Lawrence responded by again encamping the State Guard detachment on the courthouse lawn. He had a historically valid reason to weigh this potentiality. For decades throughout Kentucky and the South, in many instances, the racially agitated white public did not wait for the slow gears of the judicial process to turn in its course. Instead, they lynched.

The date of Alexander's execution took on added significance for public order. Each year for the four decades before 1907, an appreciable percentage of Black western Kentuckians celebrated Emancipation Day on August 8 (a date unique to western Kentucky, with Juneteenth in other parts of the nation). Henderson, Hopkinsville, and Paducah (since 1886) held the biggest festivities—all within easy reach of Black western Kentuckians.[22] For instance, in 1906, 12,000 people attended the event in Paducah. Many traveled via railroads and river steamer packets from Chicago, Louisville, St. Louis, and Memphis.[23] Consider the numbers. Besides those large crowds in Paducah, add the thousands who attended festivities in Henderson, Russellville, Hopkinsville, Crofton in Christian County, and Allensville in southeastern Todd (the oldest since 1868).

The Alexander execution occurred early on Friday, August 9, 1907, the next day after Emancipation Day. Many local people of color were away from Muhlenberg at one of these multi-day gatherings. The choice of this execution time and date by the authorities could have been a strategic maneuver to ensure public order, at least vis-à-vis Black Muhlenbergers. To wit: Local people of color were elsewhere at a culturally significant celebration of Black liberation and would not have been at the execution scene to foment trouble. So, the authorities might have reasoned.

Besides, it stretches credulity to think that local Black citizens contemplated absconding with the condemned prisoner. Just as no general "negro uprising" of the enslaved occurred in the "Christmas Scare" of 1856, neither was it likely for any citizen jailbreak of Harrison Alexander. Grumbles against perceived injustices likely happened, but, as with slave rebellion, the problematic logistics of prisoner jailbreak militated against any attempt. An insurrectionary threat looked exceedingly unrealistic. Where and how would they go?

For this reason, the real reason the State Guard contingent encamped on the jailhouse lawn for the trial and execution was to prevent another lynching by white actors. The travesty of an inadequate defense of Alexander signified one thing. However, the notoriety of an extrajudicial lynching, with the extensive publicity in the state and national press, meant another matter entirely. Undoubtedly, many white officeholders recalled the "seditious, barbarous, disgraceful scenes" surrounding the 1870 lynching of Bob Gray in Greenville 37 years previously.[24] This time, the authorities must have wanted to avoid a messy scene at all costs. Besides, the prosecuting attorney had his political career to advance and protect. To wit: Robert Young Thomas, Jr., was then running for Congress. Thus, he was simultaneously the prosecutor and aspiring politician seeking to boost his standing among his electoral constituency in this highly publicized case.

Undoubtedly, Thomas was the most colorful and widely known public figure in Muhlenberg in that era.[25] It helped that his father, Robert Young Thomas, Sr., was a well-known Methodist minister who dedicated the present Central City church at Second and Broad Streets. In 1878, Thomas, Jr., began practicing law in the town after obtaining a bachelor's degree from Bethel College, Russellville. (He also earned a master's degree in 1881.) In 1884, Thomas mixed the legal profession with journalism when he started the *Argus*, the first Central City newspaper.[26] Then, in 1885, Thomas served as the county representative in the Kentucky General Assembly.

During Alexander's legal proceedings, Commonwealth's Attorney Thomas campaigned as a Democrat for a seat in the U.S. House. His party controlled governments throughout the South and the Kentucky General Assembly. How would white voters react if the Commonwealth's attorney could not convict a "black menace" (even if he was an adolescent)—thereby "saving white womanhood?"

A powerful, "extremely aggressive" prosecutor, whom local historian Paul Camplin called a "fire and brimstone orator," Thomas must also have had considerable political influence.[27] Because sometime earlier, in a paradoxical legal episode with an odd twist, he obtained a pardon from Governor Beckham for a Greenville man found guilty of murder, whom Thomas, himself, had successfully prosecuted.[28] His subsequent securing of a release for this defendant he had convicted displayed prowess as a prosecutor (the man found guilty was probably innocent of the crime) and influencer in high places. Was it indicative of a political stratagem that Governor Beckham—the officeholder who refused to sign the stay of execution to allow the admission of crucial evidence—was also a fellow Democrat? The following year, 1908, R. Y. Thomas, Jr., the fiery preacher's son, was on his way to the nation's capital as a career congressman (and close colleague of Kentucky representative, later senator, and vice president Alben Barkley) for his first of nine consecutive terms representing the Third District.

R. Y. Thomas, Jr.'s., political aspirations explain why the governor denied the request to stay the execution. His refusal prevented the defense attorney from belatedly introducing the facts of the plaintiff's alleged insanity. The governor's refusal also preserved his colleague Thomas's further desire for political office. Beckham probably reasoned that Alexander was at least somewhat implicated, and the Black youth wielded no political power or influence. Besides, Beckham had his own political career to consider: How would it look if he, as governor, refused to execute a culturally labeled "black menace" whom a jury (but not of his peers) had found guilty? Had the Court of Appeals not approved the execution? After his governorship, the state's voters sent Beckham, in 1915, to the U.S. Senate.

Moreover, why did Otto Rothert—that close observer of Muhlenberg's social environment, who undoubtedly knew about this ugly affair in detail—not include anything in his historical narrative about these legal proceedings? The answer must be that he lived too close to the events and knew many participants still living when he published. Rothert dedicates his 1913 book to the "Pioneers of Muhlenberg who by their resolute deeds and heroic lives made possible the achievements of a later day."[29] From his vantage, Rothert gazes back on "heroic lives" and the latter-day "achievements" they foreordained. His intention dictated that such an untoward spectacle as the questionable legal proceedings and public execution of 16-year-old Harrison Alexander would not be suitable for inclusion in his general history.

The recent hanging, with its incompetent, excruciating final enactment, and all the proceedings leading to it were too awful and so expressly unjust, in Rothert's judgment, for his public comment. In short, these events did not fit historiographically into his primarily positive, intentionally *contributionist* narrative. Rothert and most countians wished the Alexander affair to recede into no more than a forgotten footnote in a fading history. Indeed, his textual placement of the event represents an act of historiographical obscurantism. Rothert relegated it to the silent archives in an extremely short one-sentence footnote, with both the year and the dead boy's name incorrect.[30]

This analysis has featured the seventy-six high-positioned white Central Citians who questioned Alexander's guilt, the incompetent legal defense, the circumstantial evidence, the date set for the execution, and the careers of two politicians. But what of the denizens of Muhlenberg, people of color, especially? What were their thoughts? How did they respond? Did they plot a hopeless jailbreak and rescue? With the Alexander execution, to what degree did Black Muhlenbergers—as they remembered the lynching of Bob Gray a generation earlier—again endure collective trauma in August 1907?

Ernest Gaines explores this topic in his acclaimed 1993 novel, *A Lesson Before Dying*.[31] Did Black Muhlenbergers instinctually know before the court handed it down, like the plantation quarter dwellers in the novel, that the sentence would be hanging until dead? The Alexander trial jurors deliberated for only 19 minutes. Does this confirm this belief? Did Black and white Greenvillians think the gallows looked as gruesome as the Gaines's characters when they saw workers unloading the electric chair (Gruesome Gerty) from a truck? Did Greenvillians, Black and white, react to testing the scaffold's trap door the way the fictional townspeople responded to the generator's noisy hum when workers checked it for the electric current?

In the broader setting, Alexander's public execution occurred just two months after the nation's largest post-Civil War Confederate celebration. Two hundred thousand attendees, including eighteen thousand Confederate veterans, gathered for five days in Richmond, Virginia, to dedicate an elaborate monument to Jefferson Davis on his ninety-ninth birthdate. Moreover, as previously described, the United Daughters of the Confederacy were collecting funds to erect a memorial to the "Confederate fallen" in Madisonville.

Did the Greenville gallows, erected to execute this son or grandson of enslaved people, face metaphorically toward the South? After all, in this affair, were the Muhlenberg white public, the state's governor, and the Commonwealth's attorney more interested in the exercise and symbolism of their power? Yes, probably. Nevertheless, the Petition of Seventy-Six white men complicates this story. Still, that they were unsuccessful points to the underlying racial ideology that won out and ultimately administered death. But a question remains: What is the burden of this history on this place?

Chapter 6

ENDEMIC VIOLENCE

*Death lifts a bony hand/
and Madness makes a wild demand.*[1]

Bloodlust in western Kentucky has a historically entrenched pedigree. A more extensive geographical entity than a county but smaller than a state, a *violence-prone region* has a "unique history of turmoil" and "impact far beyond its own boundaries."[2] Western Kentucky historically has existed as such a place. A historian of vigilantism recorded nine distinct violent vigilante resurgences, both minor and significant, in the western region. The large ones happened in Todd, Christian, Hopkins, and Muhlenberg in 1845 and Paducah in 1846-1850. More minor episodes occurred in the Green and Little Barren rivers area in the 1790s, Russellville in 1793, various sites in the western region in 1798, Henderson County in 1816-1817, Hopkins and Henderson counties in 1820-1822, and a protracted period in Muhlenberg from 1825 to 1850.[3]

But first, a word about societal animosity. Social violence is best understood not as a universal social form, an act done by all people, but "as something that unfolds through [particular] political, economic, and social processes."[4] These structural operations have specific histories, emplacements, and cultural influences and can thus be analyzed. As with the historiography of enslavery, this section attempts to elucidate one type of inhumanity in its geohistorical specificities.

At least one historian argues that white cruelty against the enslaved in the nineteenth century contributed to the region's continuing cultural pattern of endemic lawlessness.[5] The milieu of post-emancipation lynchings differed from chattel bondage since enslavers had held their bondservants as valuable investment property and profitable sources of income. For this reason, enslavers protected their human chattel in some fundamental, utilitarian fashion, as they would a useful horse or mule. However, in the post-Civil War periods, terroristic threats, floggings, house burnings, and lynchings became commonplace.

Furthermore, Kentucky historical folklorist William Lynnwood Montell examined bloodlust in an undesignated four-county area (two in each state) along the Tennessee-Kentucky border midway between Nashville and Knoxville. He believes the widespread guerilla activity during the Civil War created a persistent environment of ongoing animosity because neighbors, friends, and relatives opposed and fought each other.[6] If historically accurate, most of the Commonwealth would be prone to postwar bloodletting. From the long racial enslavery era to the vigilante Regulators of 1830-1850, the bloody Civil War, the Regulator agitation immediately after the war, the vortex of Reconstruction, the frenzy of the 1870 Negro Equality Panic, and the post-Reconstruction virulence of white "redemption" and reunion—endemic lawlessness sullied the region.[7]

Although severely understudied, another festering backstory may have contributed to the postwar agitation. Scholars increasingly recognize that the entire post-Civil War society was in the throes of generalized postwar traumatic stress. A holocaust of 750,000 dead and 460,000 wounded (plus 50,000 civilian deaths) must have produced an unimaginable lingering psychic malaise. Historian Diann Miller Sommerville has studied the dramatic increase in suicides and admissions to insane asylums in the postwar South. She concludes: "The historical record reveals a pattern of post-traumatic psychopathology among [Civil War] veterans."[8] Moreover, the traumatized may have transferred their mental wounds outwardly to convenient targets.[9] "Man had been at once agent and victim of war's destruction," historian Drew Gilpin Faust argues. "Both as butcher and butchered, he had shown himself far closer to the beasts than to the angels."[10] For some, the bestiality continued after the war in other guises.

The dysfunctional white conduct during Reconstruction and the following Readjustment period supplemented a mental retreat into the invented and vanished Old South. This sentimental revisionism gathered strength around the time of the centennial celebrations of the American Revolution in 1876, when people compared the nation negatively to the supposed Golden Age of the colonial and Revolutionary War eras.[11] The imagined heroic time of the American founding and the dreamlike "moonlight and magnolias" South must have beckoned emotionally to white Kentuckians. Moreover, how many white Southerners longed for the plantation South's mythologized enslavery days when "darkies" knew their place? And the time when white people were sure of theirs?

These momentous, even revolutionary, political, and cultural changes created by the Civil War and emancipation instigated a subsequent ideological neo-Confederatizing process. Although it had already begun imagining itself as a Southern border state, white Kentucky grew more sentimentally Southern after the war. At this point, it set on a path of unjust legal and customary Jim Crow discrimination, lynchings, and terroristic intimidation. White Confederate Southerners lost their disunionist military struggle for a separate political nation, replacing that political dream with a racial and cultural vision. Henceforward, as examined in Chapter 2, a Southern white identity and distorted Southern history would prevail.[12]

Although the Confederacy suffered military defeat, "only by the most specific, immediate definition," as journalist-historian Jelani Cobb remarks, "can we consider the Confederacy to have lost the Civil War."[13] Instead, the racial causes and consequences of the war were jettisoned to emphasize the mutual North-South valor and even chivalry on the battlefield. "In the moment of death, the Confederacy entered upon its immortality," Robert Penn Warren observed.[14] Why is this important? "Its legacy has defined a great deal of our history since then," Jelani Cobb explains.[15] In essential ways, political and cultural, the nation remains ensnared in the continuation of the postbellum period's influence, itself conditioned by the prior era of antebellum race-based enslavement.

We are still living with many of the failures of Reconstruction, historian Allen Guelzo concludes, "in the shape of our persistent inability to achieve satisfactory racial harmony." These failures are "like a massive national hangover, which prevents us from clearly remembering just why the war happened in the first place."[16] Alexander Stephens, the vice-president of the Confederacy, was not unsure when he declared forcefully that those eleven rebelling states fought the war in defense of racial enslavery. We are yet in a hangover stage.

The 1866 McRoberts lynching in Danville and the hundreds of other anti-Black brutalities reported by the Freedmen's Bureau comprised just the beginning of an intensely violent phase in the Kentucky past when inhumanity "surfaced like angry boils."[17] These same racialized attitudes in Danville in 1865 and 1866 were at work in Muhlenberg, evidenced by the 1870 Gray lynching and another in 1874.

Apropos this, "[i]t is charity and wisdom to keep in mind the two hundred years' *schooling in prejudice* against the Negro which the ex-slaveholders are called upon to conquer," advised the always charitable Booker T. Washington in 1884.[18] Almost a half-century earlier, Alexis de Tocqueville, the keen French observer of early nineteenth-century American democracy and lifeways, remarked: "The law may abolish slavery, [but] God alone can obliterate the traces of its existence."[19]

Writing three decades before the freeing of the last enslaved Americans, Tocqueville proved prescient that an institution deeply rooted in society for two centuries would require efforts more concerted than merely passing laws and issuing proclamations (as did President Lincoln). Neither would the bloodiest, most deadly war in American history eradicate the influences of hereditary bondage on social institutions and the hearts and minds of the American people. The subsequent events of the Reconstruction period bore this out. Moreover, during this period, the late war's central meaning for white people changed from Black emancipation to white reconciliation and national reunion. As part of this centrality, racial enslavement was mythologized and intentionally whitewashed.

During Reconstruction, Redemption, and the approaching Jim Crow regime, "[w]hite violence, or its threat, lay like a fog over the black [tobacco] patch communities" of middle Tennessee and western Kentucky, according to historian Suzanne Marshall.[20] The sheer number of lynchings in Kentucky speaks to the validity of Tocqueville's pessimistic observation that socioeconomic and psychic traces of bondage would perdure for a long time.

These social vestiges of bondage remained because people fixed them in cultural habits, social institutions, and human memories, public and private. Importantly, these sedimented traces, many as everyday racialized practices, would form the template for the subsequent rapidly developing American modernity. For these reasons, the Reconstruction period continued the racial practices, conflicts, and ideologies from earlier decades and set these along with racial identities and class and social hierarchy for the decades to come.

The overthrow of racial bondage in the Civil War and the lingering postwar dilemmas of the "Negro question" must have mentally and morally roiled white Kentuckians. As already explained, "the place of blacks in the postwar world" became the "single most crucial issue" in public discourse.[21] A telling resolution of the "question" of Black Kentuckians' position in the larger society is that churches across the Commonwealth segregated themselves soon after the war into Black and white congregations.[22] In Muhlenberg, by 1867, the newly liberated congregants of color left the Unity Baptist Church. They had attended with their enslavers for decades, sitting in a segregated space at the back of the chapel.[23] Across the United States, not only in the South, the "Negro question" was answered by implementing Jim Crow apartheid, hierarchy, and oppression.

Nonetheless, we should not forget that as social agents, Black Americans busied themselves with answering their own questions about their place in society. Their "emancipationist vision" of the legacy of the Civil War entailed seeing themselves clothed in liberation, citizenship, and Constitutional equality. To them, the war reinvented the republic.[24] In this reinvention after the war's destruction, they played a vital role in rebuilding the nation—infrastructurally, socially, and spiritually.[25]

As newly liberated people, they designed the architecture of a new life from meager resources but substantial cultural reserves. As examples of this social infrastructure, they created new institutions of religion, politics, marriage, family, and education. Historian Vincent Harding explains that "there is a river" of vital Black cultural reserves flowing through three centuries. This deep-flowing stream carries the Black—and American—dreams of freedom.[26]

The dreams and struggle for Black liberty and reparative justice would be long and arduous. Because, as historian David Blight explains, unfortunately, the "forces of [white] reconciliation overwhelmed the emancipationist vision in the national culture."[27] For this reason, as delineated in the following chapters, the people of Kentucky and the United States found themselves in a lingering, seemingly nonending stage of racial "readjustment." Such that after the Civil War, through the Reconstruction period, and for a long time afterward, an unfading fog of white terror lay over the land.

The original impetus of the saga of the Night Riders sought to organize tobacco growers in western Kentucky and middle Tennessee to oppose the monopolistic power of the American Tobacco Company (aka the "Trust," headed by James Duke).[28] In 1904, farmers organized the Planters' Protective Association (PPA) at a meeting in Guthrie in southern Todd County. Some 5,000 farmers joined the cooperative (eventually reaching 30,000) or signed the PPA's pledge not to sell their tobacco to the Trust, effectively countering its monopolistic marketing. The ensuing social strife of the so-called Tobacco Wars, or the Black Patch Wars, involved much rage, intimidation, coercion, and inhumanity.

Within the PPA, a white vigilante subset formed—the so-called Night Riders (but known in some areas as Possum Hunters)—to keep its members in line by threatening and punishing those farmers who refused to join or sold their crops surreptitiously to the Trust. Individuals and groups in the PPA directed some of this violent activity— amounting to agrarian guerrilla warfare—against the region's Black farmers, especially toward the end of the period. An apt description is that the Night Riders were "the guerillas of the tobacco war." [29]

Although Muhlenberg sits squarely within the 30-county dark-leaf tobacco agricultural region known as the Black Patch, only a thin record of any PPA activities in the county exists. However, Night Rider sabotage came to Muhlenberg as early as June 1907 when unknown, possibly "rash" persons made "depredations." In other words, they "scraped" several growers' tobacco seedling beds.

Inevitably, the PPA became more active in the county, even if only by threat or example. In December 1908, the depredations grew more serious when vigilantes torched Lewis Kirkpatrick's tobacco barn near Penrod. Some 13,000 pounds of the leaf, belonging to Hugh N. Martin (a tobacco buyer from Greenville and Louisville), lit up the night sky. Martin had purchased the crop from a local growers' union, but this did not satisfy the demands of a faction of the PPA.[30]

That same year, State Guard detachments were called out to twenty-three Kentucky counties to quell Night Rider activities. Among these counties, twelve were in the western region, including Christian, Logan, Todd, and Muhlenberg. The Commonwealth positioned mounted infantry patrols in some of these counties—including Christian, Crittenden, and Logan, but which of the others is unclear.[31] Furthermore, by January 1909, the PPA had leased a factory from the influential Martin & Puryear firm to handle the crop pledged by local growers. The *Greenville Record* authored an article encouraging this development.[32]

Unlike surrounding counties, no sources have surfaced about further Night Rider activity in Muhlenberg. However, as they rode away from the burning barn in Penrod, perhaps these vigilantes sang the same sardonic song as the horde in 1906 who torched two large tobacco warehouses in Princeton. They sang, "The fires shine bright on my old Kentucky home."[33] The barn burning in Muhlenberg accomplished its intended intimidation.

In July 1908, less than a year after the Alexander execution, Jim Crow virulence resurfaced in Logan County. Authorities arrested Rufus Browder, a young Black sharecropper near Olmstead, for killing white overseer James S. Cunningham, who many believed was the leader of the local Night Riders. Browder had argued with Cunningham over the terms of his labor contract.[34] After the precipitating argument, Cunningham cursed the Browder family as they left the property, struck Rufus Browder with a whip, and shot him in the chest. The wounded Browder returned fire and killed Cunningham. The authorities could have acknowledged Browder's reasonable claim that the killing was justifiable self-defense. Instead, they charged him with murder. At trial, his all-white jury sentenced him to death by hanging. Subsequently, the state Court of Appeals reviewed the case and ordered a second trial. The venue of this second hearing moved to the Simpson County Court in Franklin.

This time, the prosecution and the all-white jury, aware of the Appeals Court's potential second intervention, again found Browder guilty but sentenced him to life imprisonment. Browder went to the state penitentiary. In November 1911, Browder's defense attorneys requested executive clemency for the remainder of his prison term. However, the Simpson County attorney, C. B. Moore, wrote the Republican governor, Augustus E. Willson (1846-1935), not to vacate the remaining years of Browder's sentence. "My opinion is that the pardon of this negro," the county attorney offered, "would have a strong tendency to incite [white?] mobs in the future in this section and be an inspiration to the lawless [white?] element to do their bloody deeds of violence."[35] In doubt of the justness of the charge of first-degree murder, Governor Willson intervened and commuted Browder's sentence to ten years. Unfortunately, Browder died in prison in his twenties before completing this reduced term.[36]

Not satisfied with the court proceedings, white Logan Countians sought to send a direct terroristic message. A mob of a hundred men extracted—"with guns leveled at the jailer"— four men associated with Browder (but who had nothing to do with the self-defense killing of Cunningham) from the Russellville jail. The gang lynched Robert Boyer, John Jones, Virgil Jones, and Joseph Riley on the edge of Russellville on August 2, 1908, from the same tree used to hang the Proctor brothers on December 18, 1896. The unnamed reporter for the *Courier-Journal* was most likely a local person who witnessed the atrocity. He emphasized the quiet, orderly rapidity of the jailhouse capture and lynchings, with no shouts or gunshots. The reporter gives an insight into the orderly rabble: It was "under the leadership of some capable disciplinarian." The reporter knew this leader—most likely a prominent person in the community who could command such quietly efficient discipline. The criminal horde finished by pinning a placard to one of the hanging bodies warning Black Logan Countians to "let white people alone or you will go the same way." The murderous mob dispersed silently, returning to their sleeping families.[37]

Jim Crow still flew over the landscape while Rufus Browder wasted away in prison. A particularly dreadful event in Livermore (McLean County) on April 20, 1911, illustrates the continuity of this racial regime, garnering state, national, and international press coverage.[38] After an argument, Will Potter (age not given in any of the accounts), a Black employee of a poolroom, shot 22-year-old Frank Mitchell, a white man. That night, citizens assumed that Mitchell would not recover from his wound.

In the meantime, the shooting news spread rapidly. The local citizens grew "infuriated" and organized a lynch mob of fifty men. The town marshal learned of the lynchers' plans, deputized a half-dozen associates to protect Potter, and quickly moved him to safety in the basement under the stage floor of the town Opera House.[39] However, the lynchers broke in before the marshal could reinforce the theater, with the county sheriff and his posse arriving by boat via Green River. The mob dragged Potter to the stage and roped him. "His captors then ranged themselves in the orchestra pit," explains the *Courier-Journal*, "and at a pre-arranged signal began to shoot. For a minute or more the auditorium reverberated with the roar of the pistols and rifles." The crowd fired two hundred shots at the body of Potter.[40] In a second version, as reported in several newspapers, the conspirators hanged the body over the stage and charged admission. Men in the closer and higher-priced orchestra pit paid to fire their weapons multiple times into the live body, hanging like a piñata. Those in the cheaper gallery seats were allowed only a single shot.[41]

"The better element of citizens of McLean County deeply deplored the action of the mob," the *Courier-Journal* reported in its follow-up article, "and were strong in their calls for the indictment of the members of the lawless band."[42] It was unclear whether McLean Countians had been "strong in their calls" before or after the NAACP issued its May 2 resolution condemning the lynching. Furthermore, the NAACP had sent letters to Congress, President William Howard Taft, and Kentucky Governor Willson requesting official condemnation.[43] Also, the story went national when the *New York Times* printed an account of the event, which, in turn, put increased pressure for action on state and local officeholders. Soon, this incident acquired international notoriety when *Le Petit Journal*, a Parisian newspaper, published an article headlined "Story of Vengeance." It ran with a nearly full-page artistic rendering (with caption) of the target shooting of Potter.[44]

Within a few days, authorities arrested eighteen men in Livermore due to the intense outside public pressure. They charged three leaders with murder. The result? The jury hastily acquitted each of the eighteen defendants of all charges. Perhaps no one came forward to testify against them. Moreover, by the time of the *Courier-Journal* article of May 13, with the bullet-riddled body of Will Potter three weeks in its grave, Frank Mitchell was well on his way to recovering from his wound.

Chapter 7

POSSUM HUNTER REIGN OF TERROR

The facts of the world are sometimes more imaginative than the productions of our imagination.[1]

After the Tobacco Wars Night Riders, the so-called Possum Hunters appeared in January 1914, centering on five counties in the Western Coalfield: Hopkins, McLean, Ohio, Butler, and Muhlenberg.[2] Local historian Paul Camplin explains that the Possum Hunters were a "self-appointed [white] vigilante group [who] had assumed the power to punish selected citizens for supposed wrongs. They appeared at night, robed and wearing masks and carried out unlawful acts at will."[3]

The Possum Hunters mimicked the Night Riders, at least initially. A few years after the Night Riders faded into the countryside, the Possum Hunters attempted to use the same strategies and tactics to the coal industry that the Night Riders had applied to the corporate powers controlling the marketing of tobacco and their cooperating farmers. Initially, many Possum Hunters may have been unemployed or disgruntled miners, so they targeted coal companies. However, the objects of their attacks rapidly began to parallel those of the Night Riders and the much earlier Regulators of 1830-1850 and again in the years immediately after the Civil War: those whom they deemed had transgressed community morality, including clergymen, teachers, cohabiting unmarried couples, and, in a sometimes planned, sometimes random fashion, citizens of color.[4]

According to the first news report in early April 1914: "Fear stalks at the heels of men, women and children in the coal-mining district of Muhlenberg county." The article continued: "It is ever present, the menace being a band of silent men who ride at night, wreaking vengeance for real or fancied grievances. The situation has all but paralyzed business, and work at the Gibraltar Coal Co. has been entirely suspended."[5] The Possum Hunter intimidation and the stalking fears of spring 1914 were but the beginning. The area soon became rampant with rumors, distrust, and suspicion of neighbors, co-workers, government officers, and law enforcement. The contemporary news reports came from outside the immediate area since the local newspapers feared printing details of the terrorist activities.[6]

The social environment would worsen with death threats, severe lashings, and beatings, causing numerous natives to flee the area. The agitation took several forms: coal tipples destroyed, coal mines shut down, witnesses intimidated, authorities threatened, and neighborhoods traumatized by gunshots from dozens or even hundreds of guns. The primary method was severe beatings: "Scores of people, men, women, and children, have been dragged from their homes and beaten almost to death."[7]

From this, it is easy to imagine that "hitherto peaceful homes have been converted into arsenals. Men sleep with six-shooters under their pillows and Winchester rifles on chairs near their beds."[8] Possum Hunter bands threatened entire towns with destruction, such as Morgantown (Butler County).[9] Some Possum Hunters even burned the car and garage of former county judge Richard O. Pace because he allowed his vehicle to assist local officials in their investigations.[10] Moreover, multiple murders occurred.

The news reports were clear that many of the victims were mid-level employees of coal companies; for example, those whom the Possum Hunters thought exerted some power over hiring and firing. However, after aiming at mine managers and supposed transgressors of morality, the Possum Hunter vigilantes targeted people of color, although probably not as numerically often as the white victims.

A local eyewitness acknowledges Black residents as this third targeted group: "Their [Possum Hunters'] vengeance was especially directed toward the coal operators and the negroes."[11] A federal judge from Madisonville records that the Possum Hunters "were dedicated to driving black labor out of the coal mines."[12] A reporter confirms the Possum Hunters' goals: "The outlawry is directed especially at negroes and those employed in non-union coal mines. In this section of Kentucky there are a number of mines which have refused to allow their [work] forces to become unionized, and to do this they have employed constantly increasing numbers of negroes. But negroes outside of the immediate mining districts have also been victims of the 'possum hunters.'"[13] The mix of labor struggles and color prejudice concocted the recipe for intense rage. In this case, the "wild demand" made by this madness entailed some degree of ethnic cleansing.

Scattered news reports tell of the anti-Black brutality. For example, a court found a Butler Countian guilty of flogging Jim Ray, a Black man of Rochester, on November 7, 1914.[14] Less than a week later, on the same night as the hanging of the local leader of the Possum Hunters (see below), with the sulfurous smoke of home coal fires drifting in the air, a gang of two hundred men approached from the north (from the Hillside area) and "shot up" in a "reign of terror" the Galilee section of Central City. Black workers built the Galilee neighborhood, where the parents of the publicly executed Harrison Alexander lived.[15]

This lawless band fired a thousand gunshots, yet a reporter declared, "[N]o serious damage was done."[16] This newsman points to the lack of physical harm to bodies and homes. However, considering the perduring virulence in the region: "All suffered damage," a historian observes, "but paradoxically, few considered violence inherently damaging."[17] Hers is a general view of a violent culture. Moreover, the damage, of course, manifested as both physical and mental. Nonetheless, a longstanding racially dehumanizing belief was enunciated by Thomas Jefferson in 1787: "Their [enslaved people's] griefs are transient. Those numberless afflictions…are less felt, and sooner forgotten with them."[18] In December, vigilantes killed "a negro boy who strayed too close to a window."[19] No one published a word of how the suffering family or traumatized community felt.

From a perch in the twenty-first century, we perceive that cruelty can induce psychic damage. For example, in 1915, the word "shell shock(ed)" appeared in print for the first time just a few months after the above events due to the early casualty reports from World War I combat. Today, we know this (and "battle fatigue" and "combat fatigue") as clinical post-traumatic stress disorder (PTSD). Considering the 1914-1916 period of the Possum Hunter terror, we can imagine that many Muhlenbergers and others in the region experienced these events with some residual trauma.

On April 28, 1915, a gang of twenty men raided the Black "settlement" outside Rockport on the Green River in Ohio County. White residents had harbored "considerable feelings against" their Black neighbors. They sent warnings to several, including Ben Moppins, to leave. Some Black residents did, indeed, move out of the settlement. However, not a sufficient number moved, so the dissatisfied mob swarmed to the house of Frank Short, at home with his brother Albert (a local lawyer), Harrison Maddox, and a preacher named Hayes. The four were flogged and marched off, but Albert and Maddox broke away and entered another house. The crowd fired a "general fusillade" of bullets into the house, but Maddox was the only person wounded. "The attack last night," according to a newspaper, "has caused the greatest alarm among the blacks, and it is thought that practically the entire colony will leave the section."[20]

No label was attached to this white gang, but its purpose was to rid the area of Black residents. Oddly, the larger *Owensboro Messenger*, labeling the group "Possum Hunters," did not carry this story until

Maddox died several days later. Afterward, Ohio County authorities convened at Rockport in an atmosphere where "excitement is high."[21] No reports of their deliberations or criminal charges have surfaced.

We can apply the familiar term *ethnic cleansing* to these events. Although authorities assured protection to Black citizens in a few places in Hopkins County, nearly all fled from several other districts, including Carbondale.[22] But even with this evidence, the degree to which the Possum Hunters (and unlabeled others) targeted people of color is difficult to assess. However, national publications usually recorded that Possum Hunters attacked Black communities. Additionally, they harassed those white mine managers who hired them.

Hundreds of men, possibly thousands, were involved in this crusade. For instance, on a full-moon summer night (probably in 1915), as she and her husband sat on their porch in Drakesboro, the daughter of Drakesboro's founder remembers seeing two hordes of Possum Hunters:

> [W]hen suddenly out of the stillness there seemed to emerge a dark cloud, so noiseless at first that we did not realize what was happening. As the 'cloud' advanced from a thickly shaded grove from the west and the tramp of feet in marshal [*sic*] tread came nearer and louder, a thousand men marching two by two passed within sixty feet of our front gate. At the depot they turned to the south and marched up the railroad about two hundred yards to the intersection of Main Street or the Greenville Road, when they turned east and on toward Paradise into dark woods. We sat almost petrified. 'What was that?' I said. 'Possum Hunters' came the answer. In five minutes another group of as many men came from out of the 'Nowhere' from the north, on the railroad [tracks], turned east and joined the first group as

they marched out of sight into the night. Not a sound was heard except the sound of the tramp of marching feet.[23]

Her astonishing story is surreal, and her numbers perhaps unbelievably exaggerated: two groups of one thousand men each. Nevertheless, notwithstanding that, consider another account. In late 1914, a "carefully planned raid" of three hundred men attacked an unnamed mine store in Muhlenberg.[24] These numbers and others from surrounding counties point to several thousand dedicated men involved and organized in the underground Possum Hunter movement.

In the first two decades of the twentieth century, it is unclear whether the perpetrators of the various gang activities were Night Riders, Possum Hunters, or, beginning in 1915, the newly resurgent Klan. Moreover, it might not matter, especially to its victims. However, not all the mistreatment emanated from these groups. Instead, the endemic historical and cultural pattern of violent behavior in western Kentucky maintained the longstanding climate for random acts of racial animosity.

For instance, on December 30, 1914, near Trenton in Todd County, a band of men labeled "possum hunters" killed Edmund Christian—"an aged and law-abiding negro"—at his home. Governor James B. McCreary, a Confederate veteran who had been a lieutenant colonel under John Hunt Morgan (CSA), offered a $200 reward for the perpetrators' arrest. In a letter accompanying a protest petition signed by "leading citizens," the reward announcement came from the Todd County judge's statement that "the murder was atrocious and unprovoked."[25]

No motives surfaced for the Edmund Christian murder. However, in another instance, the reasons were transparent and understood. In Henderson, a "mob of masked men" held the county jailer prisoner while they snatched an accused Black man from his jail cell. Ellis Buckner (no age given) had been "charged with having attempted to criminally assault" a 15-year-old girl. On Sunday morning, November 26, 1915, the masked gang hanged Buckner from "a tree overlooking the [Ohio] river."[26] The Possum Hunters carefully planned the more momentous events, but the Buckner lynching happened as a spontaneous mob action. Regardless, dominator culture needed to demonstrate its control, even if randomly. This same creed also applied to the unprovoked murder of the law-abiding Edmund Christian.

Several origins of the Possum Hunter movement are evident, although none is sufficient or conclusive. In any case, the attribution of historical causation is always risky. However, investigators could examine this extralegal mass movement's various goals, if not the causes.

A few years earlier, the Night Riders focused on controlling tobacco marketing and its selling price. With time, though, some of their activities became more like a "regulating party." As related above, this term referred to the nineteenth-century vigilante Regulators, 1825-1850, who punished offenders who transgressed their conceptions of community norms.[27] "Now, they [the Possum Hunters] took care of what evil was going on in the county," a resident of Horse Branch in Ohio County recalled. "They whipped people that didn't do right. If they didn't do that, what they would do, they would fix a bundle of switches, and leave it at the doors" as a threatening symbol of impending peril.[28]

The Possum Hunters, argues a Kentucky folklorist, "seem to have morphed from fighting in the Tobacco Wars to a 'whatever goes' vigilante group."[29] Some Possum Hunters' targets were mine managers who influenced hiring, as already noted. A reporter, though, was perplexed: "Why the men banded themselves together originally is merely a matter of conjecture, so far as the uninitiated are concerned, but at present the organization seems to have no definite aim or purpose, it being merely an instrument for avenging personal grievances." [30]

This contemporary reporter offered two origin theories of the Possum Hunter movement that he gathered from "among those who dare [to] have a theory." First, the Possum Hunters modeled their aims and organization after a similar group formed in Hopkins County in 1913. Its purpose was to force coal miners to organize a labor union.[31] Perhaps this took pressuring individuals to join existing unions since the United Mine Workers of America was already operating in the Western Coalfield.

The second theory was nebulous and garnered a sketchy explanation from the Louisville newspaper reporter. "[T]he secret organization in Muhlenberg county," he maintains, "is the result of *socialistic doctrine* that had been preached among the miners and others from time to time."[32] The historian cannot entirely dismiss this theory because unionization rapidly became prevalent in the Western Coalfield and nation. A few years before, in 1912, the textile workers' strike in

Lowell, Massachusetts, led by the Industrial Workers of the World (the IWW, or Wobblies), helped spread labor disquiet.

At this time, many Americans believed the future would entail profound social unrest, even class warfare. This widespread dread cropped up before the Red Scare began in 1919 over political anarchism and the Bolshevism emanating from the Russian Revolution. Further back in time, workers organized nationwide strikes in the 1870s and 1880s, with pitched battles breaking out between workers and their capitalist overlords. Then, moving into the Gilded Age, "the Civil War gave way to class war," historian Jackson Lears remarks.[33] All this shows that miners in the Western Coalfield must have been familiar with and possibly sympathetic to the principles of unionism and socialism.

However, no primary source materials have surfaced about socialistic doctrine in Muhlenberg until the 1930s (and the organizing efforts, in 1938, of the Workers Alliance of America), other than the regular union organizing among the miners.[34] Testimony in an April 1915 Butler County trial of a Possum Hunter revealed that a prosecution's witness had attended the first meeting of the Amalgamated Workers of the World Organization (AWWO).[35] This was probably a local name created by a faction of the Possum Hunters in Butler since no evidence of a national union by this name has surfaced.

Nonetheless, the AWWO resembles the name of the Industrial Workers of the World (IWW). With connections to socialist and anarchist unionism, the IWW was founded in 1905 and reached its peak influence in 1917. The Possum Hunter ring in Butler probably chose the term "amalgamated" to show that it was not constituted solely by a single type of worker—in this case, coal miners.

The region was not unfamiliar with organized labor actions. For instance, in 1887, the Greenville Tobacco Works employees began a work stoppage. They were most likely Black workers, some of whom were adolescent boys and girls. "The hands who wrap the Greenville brand of plug tobacco" demanded more pay than their current 12 cents per hundred pounds. The company then advertised in the *Owensboro Messenger* for new workers to replace the strikers.[36]

In the same year, the joint-ownership Co-operative Coal Co. organized in what became the village of Powderly, between Greenville and Central City, perhaps the only place in the United States named after a labor leader. This cooperative endeavor reflected a "socialistic doctrine" in which shareholders invested cash or labor. Furthermore, as was typical, individual miners owned their housing rather than the company. Moreover, they collectively built their school. Hence, Powderly was initially not a company town like the other coal camps but a "cooperative settlement."[37]

These worker-owners chose the toponym Powderly for their camp to honor national labor leader Terrence Vincent Powderly (1849-1924), originally from Carbondale, Pennsylvania, and then Scranton. He was a three-term Progressive Party mayor of the latter city. By the founding of the Powderly cooperative coal camp in 1887, Terrence Powderly held the top position of Grand Master Workman in the Knights of Labor, just then peaking as the nation's largest union. Moreover, the entire labor movement recognized Powderly as its foremost spokesman. The Cooperative Coal Co.—with its workers as owners—was probably in solidarity with the Knights' labor and social programs.

Several instances might be relevant for assessing whether Terrence V. Powderly and the Powderly coal camp's cooperative community could serve as some explanation of the etiology of the Possum Hunters. As the union leader, Powderly promoted a "cooperative brotherhood of workers" at one end of the spectrum, with the Knights' anarchist and socialist members at the other.[38] The more militant labor leaders condemned Powderly for avoiding conflict and reluctance to call strikes. He also enacted union policies that promoted Black and female membership and leadership (although scholars have criticized its effectiveness). In 1887, when the miner-owners founded the Co-operative Coal Co. and the Powderly camp, the Knights of Labor added 30,000 new Black members nationwide. This effort increased Black membership by a third.[39]

None of the cooperative mine's policies in Powderly would have been a model for the Possum Hunters. However, one trait is relevant: The Knights were secretive and ritualistic. They incorporated some Masonic-like structure and rituals and required an oath of secrecy. Likewise, secret hand signs and lapel pins also identified Possum Hunters to each other. They swore allegiance on bended knees at an altar of "pistols, rope halter and strap."[40] Moreover, they exacted promises from their members and coerced many others into joining. The leaders who administered the oaths informed the new initiates that they intended the guns and ropes to punish members for disloyalty and the strap for "outside work" when they lashed their selected community victims.[41]

As already noted, historians cannot entirely dismiss the influence of the vague notion of a "socialistic doctrine" that might have existed within the mining unions in the Western Coalfield. For instance, in the summer of 1911, for seven days and nights at Viola in Graves County, a Christian socialist camp meeting attracted 500 to 800 attendees. Speakers came from Montana and Chicago.[42] To be sure, after the abuses of laborers in the Gilded Age, many workers, unionists, and intellectuals believed in class struggle and the need for an active workers' party. Before 1920, the latter included Charlie Chaplin, Clarence Darrow, John Dewey, W. E. B. Du Bois, Helen Keller, Jack London, Eugene O'Neill, Carl Sandburg, and Upton Sinclair, among many others.

The 1912 presidential election pitted the incumbent Republican William Howard Taft against Democrat Woodrow Wilson and former president Theodore Roosevelt on the Progressive Party ticket. Also running was Eugene V. Debs, the Socialist Party candidate, on a platform advocating women's suffrage, ending child labor, and improving workers' conditions. With an astounding 14 percent of its vote (766 for 13.7%), Muhlenberg led the state in voting for Debs—more than double the national share (6%, with more than 900,000 votes) and more than quintuple the state (2.6%). Ballard and McCracken gave Debs 7.6 percent of their respective tallies (Debs had spoken in Paducah), with Calloway at 7.2 percent, Union 6.8, Henderson 6.7, Ohio 6.1, Hopkins 5.9, Trigg 5.7, and McLean 4.2. Compare these to Todd's 2.5 percent, Christian's 2.3, Logan's 1.9, Butler's 1.8, and Daviess's 1.1. Many other counties were similar to Warren's minute 0.83 percent for Debs. Hence, something in Muhlenberg and most Western Coalfield counties led to solid voting for the socialist presidential candidate. To be sure, coal miner unionism drove the high socialist turnout.

Then, in late November 1915, the Kentucky Socialist Party organized a chapter in Owensboro with members from the Second Congressional District, including Henderson, Nortonville, and Livermore. (Muhlenberg was in the Third District.) The state party secretary spoke for its 12,000 Kentucky socialists (he claimed) when he advocated for "a greater civilization built upon the solid rock of humanity first."[43] So, western Kentuckians generally understood socialist ideas, even if they were not dominant in the region.

However, several historical models for the Possum Hunters' vigilantism were more relevant than workers' political ideology. These included the local slave patrols and citizen militias—the Home Guard—before and during the Civil War. Besides those, the most fitting model was the nineteenth-century Regulators, noted above, with nine distinct violent resurgences in the western region beginning in the 1830s.[44] Moreover, we cannot dismiss the impact of the more recent "regulating" Night Riders, whose intimidation and coercive exploits were well-known and probably copied. Historian Suzanne Marshall concludes that a "culture of violence" was created after initial settlement in the 1790s in the 54-county Black Patch region (thirty-six counties in Kentucky, eighteen in middle and western Tennessee) that depended on farming dark-fired tobacco. Marshall contends that this culture of lawlessness was created primarily by white men to "maintain their power over their families, blacks, and the community."[45]

Accordingly, a better explanation for the advent of the Possum Hunters lies in the backlash to the social and demographic changes that roiled the region in the late nineteenth century. One of these salient changes was the post-Civil War breakdown of the control maintained by internal church discipline. Churches were allowed and expected to adjudicate and discipline their congregants in the first half of the nineteenth century. For example, during the Civil War, the Hazel Creek Missionary Baptist Church formed an investigating committee, drawing from three nearby congregations, to help decide what to do about a member who had murdered a fellow congregant. Subsequently, Hazel Creek ruled that the killing was "not justified" and, for this reason, expelled the accused men.[46] Records do not mention anyone filing formal criminal charges against these men because of the breakdown of law enforcement during the war.

Historian Christopher Waldrep examined church discipline in Trigg County and the Black Patch tobacco region as representative of the demise of localism engendered by the social changes that swept the U.S. due to rapid industrialization, wage labor growth, urbanization, and the bureaucratization of society. He posited that the decline in church discipline led to vigilantism when the judicial system could not enter the moral vacuum. Thus, the enforcement of community behavior passed from churches to vigilante groups seeking to maintain community standards of morality. "There was a surge in vigilante activity all across the South," according to Waldrip, "as church discipline declined."[47]

Unfortunately, these post-Civil War changes called forth the traditional white animosities toward people of color and the culture of violence that used mistreatment as a tool to maintain the racial order. Whites sought more of this order as the Black population increased. In the decade after 1901, Muhlenberg's Black population increased by 744, more than 34 percent. Tobacco prices dropped precipitously in 1904, pushing Black laborers to migrate from the surrounding farming areas. For example, that year, Christian County experienced a net loss of fifty-two school children, primarily Black pupils. This population loss was due to workers moving to Missouri to work in mines and to Mississippi to pick cotton.[48]

Some of these Black laborers must have migrated the short distance to Muhlenberg, where coal mining was booming with its 535 percent increase in produced tonnage during that decade. But, no matter whence the Black newcomers came, many white residents were troubled by their growing numbers. If so, the increasing Black demographic and social presence supplies at least partial causation for the origin of the vigilantism of 1914-1916. In brief, the rapidly growing Black population challenged the Jim Crow racial caste order imposed by white locals. Moreover, the latter responded in the violent ways of tradition.

Furthermore, numerous historians have argued that the bondage practices of 1795-1865 instilled the cultural pattern of lawlessness in the western region. As noted above, the early twentieth-century Possum Hunters' coercion and the slightly earlier Night Riders were reminiscent of the Old South slave-patrolling surveillance. In this system, each county administration, including Muhlenberg, officially hired these armed patrollers to guard roads, surveille the countryside, and capture fleeing refugees or even local bondservants traveling without permission papers.[49] In 1914-1916, the chief weapons of the Possum Hunter movement—like the Regulators, slave patrollers, and Night Riders before them—were threats, intimidation, guns, whips, and fear.

In summary, several motives seem to have propelled the Possum Hunter movement. First, it was an effort to unionize the coalfield. Second, they often pressured specific mine managers to hire (or not lay off) workers. Third, like the nineteenth-century Regulators, the Possum Hunters functioned as morality police. Fourth, in the arena of the encompassing dominator culture, anti-Black brutality raised its threatening head. Finally, the Possum Hunters established a shadow police state to accomplish these goals. The following section shows why this revolutionary goal eventually failed.

Many inhabitants of Muhlenberg and surrounding counties did not support the Possum Hunters due to their penchant for viciousness. As did the Night Riders (and the even earlier nineteenth-century Regulators), they faced the tactical problem of instilling intra-group discipline while gaining support among the general populace. Much of the venom was directed internally as reprisals at their own members. However, a countervailing extralegal citizen association quickly appeared: Those who directly opposed the Possum Hunter vigilantism.

Even though it is unclear how to apportion the several possible causes of the Possum Hunters' advent, some evidence surfaced about the beginning of their demise. This information came from the attestation of two people strategically positioned to hold some secret knowledge. It began with the murder of the Possum Hunters' alleged local leader by the top of the official power structure. This group is where the evidence points.

The problem for law enforcement in bringing the Possum Hunters to justice was that witnesses were mortally afraid to testify against them or even be seen talking to law officers. The public knew of the credible threats circulating in the community and the many horrendous beatings and whippings that had already occurred. Authorities in several counties had gathered intelligence on some participants, the various bands, and their inner workings.

However, prosecutors had to present the testimony to grand juries to obtain indictments. To stop the commotion and terrorism, law enforcement officials—the judge, county attorney, sheriff, and other law officers—required proof, and they needed names. But how could they obtain names and evidence? Authorities offered rewards. For instance, by request of the circuit judge with jurisdiction over Caldwell and Hopkins counties, Governor James B. McCreary (1911-1915) set a $200 reward for information leading to the arrest and conviction of any Possum Hunter.[50] In Muhlenberg, though, the authorities found another way.

More than a half-century after these events, two countians occupying critical positions shared their strategic knowledge about the culmination of the Possum Hunter era. The first local informant was Elmer Cornette, who had worked, in 1914, as a weighmaster and outside foreman for Hillside Coal Co., near Powderly. Cornette broke his half-century silence when he sent his inside version of events to Agnes

Harralson, local historian and columnist of the *Central City Times-Argus*.[51]

The key event was that Henry Allen, the alleged leader of the Muhlenberger band of the Possum Hunters, white and about 30 years old, was found hanging from a tree near Oakland Mine, near Hillside, early on November 13, 1914. At that time, as were at least five others, Allen was under indictment for "unlawfully confederating," in other words, for conspiracy to terrorize. Two weeks earlier, in an unmistakably direct challenge to authorities, Allen led a sizeable contingent numbering in the hundreds to Greenville, where they marched menacingly around the county courthouse. Allen held a red banner that displayed an image of a possum.[52]

Cornette divulged that his brother, who worked for the *Greenville Record*, telephoned him at the Hillside Mine office, requesting that he investigate the hanging that morning. He ascertained that those who found the body had taken it to a local house. Furthermore, the county attorney, sheriff, and coroner were on their way to begin their official examination. W. H. Gray served as the county attorney; Robert Wickliffe held the sheriff's office. Although the coroner remained unnamed by Cornette and several news accounts, he was George Young.

Cornette, arriving before the three officials, observed the body. He concluded that Allen had not died by hanging, as the eyes did not bulge nor the tongue protrude. Also, the corpse did not show a broken neck, as could occur (but not always) in a hanging.[53] For his part, Cornette spoke to no one, allowing the three officials to perform their inquiry without his input.[54]

Among coroners' few duties in Kentucky was the preliminary investigation of instances of sudden death, whether accidental or otherwise. The coroner was obligated to present his assessment to a quickly impaneled jury, often on the spot, who usually endorsed the coroner's conclusions. Physicians rarely occupied this office since the state did not require it.[55] And something else to consider: In the early part of the twentieth century, law enforcement in the state was still the local authorities' bailiwick, as the Commonwealth did not form the Kentucky State Police, with statewide jurisdiction, until 1948.[56]

In the inquest into the death of Henry Allen, the Muhlenberg coroner George Young ruled death came by hanging, contra the observation of Cornette. However, the local law officers found no additional facts on his death besides Allen staying the previous night with his father-in-law and someone calling him by name out of the house. "Hanging by persons unknown" is where the Henry Allen murder mystery remained for almost a half-century when Elmer Cornette disclosed his story to Agnes Harralson in 1962.

In 1915, however, the local Possum Hunters suspected an opposing ring had murdered Allen. They were ready for retaliation, including revenge killing. A local news account reported: "Tonight [Nov. 13, the night after the hanging] there is much lurid feeling in the county. The possum hunters are claiming that Allen was hanged by *an organization opposed to their own*. They say that they are 3,300 strong in Muhlenberg county and that they will stretch up every one who is suspicioned of having taken part in the hanging of Allen."[57]

Even though some Possum Hunters must have held suspicions about the true identities of the murderers of Henry Allen, these conspirators were never discovered or revealed, at least by the authorities. Moreover, reports show no one committed any revenge reprisals due to the Allen murder, which remained unsolved.

Five more years passed before Elmer Cornette knew of the circumstances of the kidnapping and murder of Henry Allen. Two informants, whom he does not name, confided to him. He learned that "some very outstanding men in the county" had organized a secret "posse" to force Allen to divulge the names and activities of his comrades-in-arms. With this, Cornette confirmed the suspicions of the Possum Hunters.

In effect, whoever they were, these well-positioned people conspired to use the same vigilante tactics as the Possum Hunters to destroy the vigilantes. This secret ring surveilled Allen for the opportune time when it could kidnap him while away from his house. Their chance came on November 12, when Allen stayed the night at his father-in-law's home. At about 9 p.m., the posse called Allen out of this house—wearing just night clothes and shoes—accosted him, threw him into their mule-drawn buggy, and drove away.[58]

With their captive, the posse of prominent men rode to the sooty tipple of Woodson Mine, a half-mile away, and entered the "dynamo room" containing an electric generator. They demanded that Allen disclose names, dates, and activities. Through his two informants, Cornette writes that the posse had no intention of harming Allen. Instead, they wanted to "bring him to his senses" and extract information, albeit coerced.[59] When Allen refused to talk, they applied a "light shock" to his body. Allen then begged them to turn off the electricity and blurted that he would tell them what they wanted. However, after stopping the current, he again refused to talk.

At this point, the interrogators intended to repeat the process with another shock. But, tragically, they had not realized that the still-running dynamo had built up a lethal current. The high voltage instantly electrocuted Allen when they again applied the electric wires to him.

This vigilante posse of prominent men now had a dead body on their hands. Frantically searching for a solution, they hanged the body from a tree near the Oakland Motor Road at Hillside. They wanted it to appear as a hanging death resulting from an internal, fratricidal dispute within the Possum Hunters. Cornette underscores his conclusion: "So, my theory that Allen was [already] dead when hanged proved to be true." [60]

Nearly a half-century after this crime, Elmer Cornette completes his story:

> I have never divulged the names of the men who participated in this tragedy and I have never written it down. I have all the names in my memory. The last survivor died about four years ago. It would serve no good purpose to divulge them now. The death of Henry Allen was an accident, probably a criminal one, but as his death put an end to a reign of terror and brought law and order back to Muhlenberg County, I feel that in the main it was a good thing.[61]

So, Cornette never disclosed the names of those he knew to have comprised the anti-Possum Hunter posse of prominent men. However, he strongly hinted at who they were and revealed "some very outstanding men in the county" as participants. In one way or another, this group involved several local people in serious crimes: homicide, coverup, or both.

First, for the concealment: Attention must focus on Robert Wickliffe, the sheriff (and probably some of his deputies who accompanied him to the coroner's inquest). The deputies, or others, might have been involved in the prolonged surveillance of Allen's movements. Next, W. H. Gray, the county attorney, appeared on the scene. Third, the coroner, George Young, was responsible for determining the cause of death. Cornette concluded categorically that Henry Allen had not died by hanging. Nonetheless, the law officers and the coroner ruled that his death was precisely that: death by hanging.

The inescapable conclusion from a close textual reading of Cornette's letter is that these officials took part in a criminal coverup. That is, if a history sleuth can credit a single informant, albeit one in a position to know. In time, though, a second source and another conspirator surfaced. They both were highly placed men.

This second informant was the former county attorney, circuit judge, and Assistant State Attorney General Arthur Triplett Iler (1900-1997).[62] Judge Iler penned his periodic history column in the *Central City Times-Argus* under the nom de plume of "The Old Timer." In these pieces, Iler did not write of the alleged coverup. Instead, in a 1970 interview, he implicated four well-known countians in the murder. First, Iler pointed to J. P. Cox, superintendent of the Bevier Mine and leader of the anti-Possum Hunter vigilantes. Second, he identified J. D.

Langley, the Central City police chief. The third conspirator was Charlie Heltsley, the "best blacksmith in Muhlenberg," who worked at a mine in Bevier-Cleaton and later served as the Greenville police chief. Iler reported that four or five men participated.[63] Logic dictated that one or more men at the Woodson Mine who could operate the "dynamo," or generator, may also have been involved.

In his 1970 interview, Judge Iler corroborated much of the same scenario as Cornette. First, he contended that the vigilantes accidentally electrocuted Allen when they attempted to extract information about the Possum Hunters. Then, stunningly, Iler pointed directly to a fourth person involved in the murder: his former law partner and later a high-profile state attorney general, Hubert Meredith.

Besides Judge Iler's decades-long law partner, the powerful, widely-known Hubert Meredith (1880-1957) was his close friend. Meredith served as the Commonwealth's attorney and, later, state attorney general, 1937-1944, under governors Happy Chandler and Keen Johnson.[64] At that dire time of proliferating Possum Hunter lawlessness, authorities appointed Meredith as a special prosecutor to take on the vigilantes. For this, Special Prosecutor Meredith wanted inside information and testimonial evidence. He needed an informant.

Judge Iler revealed how "Meredith got some of the evidence":

> They [the anti-Possum Hunter group] took a man [he does not name Allen] to a coal mine out about Hillside. They took him in the power house and over to the generator. It was run by steam. Who ever was operating it didn't know much about electricity. They told him they were going to electrocute him if he didn't give them some information. He

gave some of it. They asked him about particular people and other things and he refused to tell them so they put two raw wires to him and turned the generator on. They electrocuted him, accidentally. The generator had been left on and the power built up. They decided they had better take him to the woods near Woodson and hang him. I have always believed that *Hubert Meredith was with the group too*.[65]

Why did Cornette tarry for almost a half-century to publicize his knowledge of the story (and Iler until 1970)? Cornette offers a critical clue: "The last survivor died about four years ago."[66] The Harralson-Cornette article appeared in late January 1962. Hubert Meredith died on December 31, 1957, within one month of four years before Cornette's letter.

Why the coverup? With Allen's unintended death, the law officers themselves were illegally involved in "unlawfully confederating" and "conspiring to intimidate"—the criminal charges against the Possum Hunters. Then, this murder by the law officers and well-known men necessitated a diversionary tactic: the decision to hang Allen's dead body from a tree. This strategy helped create the rumor that other Possum Hunters had executed Allen in an internal dispute. After all, the Possum Hunters exacted a blood oath of secrecy from its members to never betray the organization. A national publication repeated the common belief that the Allen murder was a revenge killing by the Possum Hunters.

What motivation could the Possum Hunters have had for a revenge killing? They may have suspected that the then-indicted Allen would confess or had already.[67] This storyline of vengeance and retribution had the ring of plausibility to the local public. "Just why he [Allen] should have been hanged and by whom is a mystery," reported an Ohio County newspaper. "The only suggestion heard is that he may have had trouble with the others of the organization which resulted in their inflicting the extreme penalty. No other explanation appears possible at this time."[68] The "suggestion heard" could well have been started and spread by law enforcement and other highly placed perpetrators of the crime.

Finally, it is instructive how the rest of the Bluegrass State looked at Muhlenberg during this period. On the front page of its November 17, 1914 edition, the *Earlington Bee* reprinted an editorial by the *Courier-Journal*. This editorial called for more significant efforts to combat illiteracy. It also invoked the Commonwealth's obligation to deal with the "savagery in Muhlenberg." The largest newspaper in the state headlined its editorial "Savagery and Ignorance" in addressing the county as the "section from which comes recurrent bad advertising for the state as a whole":

> While the Women's Forward movement is setting out to raise funds to fight and conquer adult illiteracy in Kentucky, Muhlenberg county continues to provide ample proof of the need of the philanthropic work that is to be undertaken by the Kentucky Illiteracy Commission with the money that will be raised.
>
> Such conditions as those existing in Muhlenberg indicate more degradation than that which has from time to time been made evident by the outrages in the mountainous counties [of eastern Kentucky]. Apparently the savagery in Muhlenberg is not superinduced by, or dependent upon, the political conditions which nourished the so-called Hargis-

Cockrill feud in Breathitt [County] a dozen years ago. The Muhlenberg outlaws are, apparently, ignorant yokels whose immunity is provided by their numeric strength plus the comprehensible timidity of a law-abiding minority in rural sections infested with ruffians and assassins.[69]

This *Courier-Journal* editorial connects Muhlenberg's "savagery" to poverty and illiteracy in contrast to eastern Kentucky's familial and factional feuding. It then curiously assigns some responsibility for the "century of neglect [that] is reflected in Muhlenberg county" on the "wealthier sections of the State" and even "democratic government." Perhaps this comment points to a perceived inadequate state funding for education. For its part, the *Earlington Bee*'s editors might have felt some *schadenfreude* with the Louisville newspaper's pointing to Muhlenberg's misery.

However, from our present perspective, blaming Allen's death on "ignorant yokels" is a historical error rich in irony. Because we now know that leading citizens, law enforcement officials, and the future state attorney general perpetrated the crime. Imagine Special Prosecutor Hubert Meredith and his co-conspirators reading this editorial castigating the savagery committed by "ignorant yokel" Muhlenberger outlaws. As a result, Central City Police Chief J. D. Langley suffered a reported "nervous breakdown" and eventually left the county.[70]

The Possum Hunters came to a sputtering, judicial end with several criminal court cases in a few counties in 1915-1916. Notwithstanding the demise of this vigilante movement, racial oppression continued in the Bluegrass State between the two World Wars, exemplified by several violent, episodic events. An instance is the infamous ethnic cleansing of people of color from Corbin, in eastern Kentucky, on October 30, 1919.[71]

Moreover, in 1923, some Klan presence appeared in Muhlenberg (when Indiana was the center of Klan activity). The mayor of Central City, Lannie Jackson, also served as president of the local District 23 of the UMWA. A set of local citizens requested that the mayor prohibit a Klan meeting. Jackson declined, citing the freedoms of speech and assembly, but vowed to intervene if they wore masks. Nonetheless, Jackson roundly condemned the Klan. As an official of the UMWA, he observed that the Klan destroys the union, "as our membership is composed of Methodists, Baptists, Catholics, Negroes, Jews and many other nationalities." Per its bylaws, he vowed to expel any union members if they joined the Klan. "I am convinced they are a menace," he continued, "to the American principles, to society, to organized labor and the advancement of Christianity."[72]

As this chapter has shown, the greater menace has been the culture of violence in western Kentucky. This cultural landscape has included the inherently violent institution of racial, hereditary enslavement. As noted above, the western region experienced periodic upheavals of Regulatory lawlessness. Barbarity reached prodigious proportions during the Civil War when border-state Kentucky became a terrain for intense irregular warfare. The Commonwealth was primarily an undefended space for incursions by freebooting guerrilla bands—the so-called *bushwhackers*—who scoured, robbed, murdered, and traumatized the countryside. Next, the intense rage and fanaticism continued during

Reconstruction against Black Kentuckians and their white Republican supporters. These dozen postwar years of turbulence segued into the post-Reconstruction era when lawlessness was widespread in all parts of the Bluegrass State. For instance, reported homicides in 1890 in the state ranked second in the nation only after the 3.75 times larger New York.[73] The post-Reconstruction era also saw the rise of Jim Crowism with continuing racial virulence and the institutionalization of legal segregation that continued unstopped into the 1960s.

Admittedly, the historical events presented in this chapter stretch the imagination. But this is why we investigate, study, and produce historical accounts. As it turns out, the events of history, as this chapter's epigraph says, might be more imaginative than fiction. Writer James Baldwin—a keen observer of history, violence, democracy, and the American identity and character—ties these cultural elements together: "Violence has been the American daily bread since we heard of America.," he writes. "This violence, furthermore, is not merely literal and actual but appears to be admired and lusted after." What else? "It is "the key to the American imagination." [74]

Chapter 8

THE STRANGE CASE OF DR. R. T. BAILEY

*We are never as steeped in history
as when we pretend not to be.*[1]

"Making history," explains a historian, "is as much about burrowing into secret places with fewer facts as it is about simply creating order from records of the past."[2] Given this, we are restricted in ordering the few known facts about Dr. Robert Thomas Bailey's strange case. These include serving as a Methodist minister in Powderly and a physician in downtown Central City for several decades. In 1920, he headed the drive to build a Black public school in that town.[3] However, this slice of yore offers a compelling opportunity to "burrow into a secret place," where documented events are few and questions are many.

We know how the case ends. R. T. Bailey, the Black doctor, ingested carbolic acid (aka "phenol") on April 17, 1934 (according to his death certificate), just before entering the chambers of the circuit court in the Muhlenberg County Courthouse. The 55-year-old defendant collapsed in the courtroom chair with acid dissolving his innards. He faced the judge's bench, sitting again for the drawn-out legal proceedings continuing against him. The criminal charge? The court documents specify that, without noting the patient's race, the county attorney indicted Bailey for performing an illegal abortion.[4] However, the local newspaper declared: "Operating on a white woman."

The Bailey abortion case, now sensationalized by the paper, first appeared on the court docket in the 1933 April Term as *Commonwealth of Kentucky v. Dr. R. T. Bailey*, Order 6075, with bail set at $1,000. However, for unknown reasons, the court held the case over for the September term, then the January term, 1934, and then again for the April term.

Dr. William Stringer, a white Central City dentist, testified as a key witness for the prosecution. Records do not yield the rationale for his testimony or its content. Nonetheless, his previous civic work might suggest his role. Eighteen years earlier, beginning in 1916, Stringer served as the Central City Law and Order League president. This citizens' group offered rewards for information leading to prosecutions and convictions based on the city's Prohibition liquor laws. For evidence contributing to a successful first prosecution, the league paid $50 for a white violator's conviction and $25 for a Black violator. In addition, the association offered $100 for a white and $50 for a Black perpetrator on a second and subsequent guilty verdict.[5] As a leading citizen and moral "regulator," Stringer may have given investigative evidence on Bailey's medical practice.

Ora Lee Bailey was the widow left behind. (The *Central City Messenger* obituary omitted her name, age, and profession.) We know that the Baileys and Pauline Johnson, the widowed mother of Ora Lee, were originally from Shelby County, Kentucky. The three resided in Central City's Colored Town, on the "Alley between First and Second

Streets."[6] Ora Lee worked as a veteran public-school teacher at Powderly (first?), Rhodes School (by 1922-1923), and Central City Colored School (sometime after 1928).[7]

Her husband's suicide left a gaping hole, exposing a place of silence since no further details about the Baileys' lives have surfaced. However, we can ask: What were R. T. Bailey's motives for suicide? What were his thoughts that led to his demise? Was Bailey's action a deadly demonstration against the state statute that made abortion illegal or perhaps against how authorities unjustly enforced it? Was his provision of abortion healthcare a regular part of his practice? Who were his clientele? Were they Black and white patients?

What was the historical context of this 1934 Bailey abortion-suicide case? It occurred during the Great Depression when men, women, and families were under intense economic pressure. Jobs disappeared, wages fell, people lost homes, owners booted tenants out, and people starved, including in Muhlenberg.[8] This precarity drove more women to seek abortions—legal and illegal—reaching a new high during these years, including women's self-administered acts. As a result of the increased number of self-abortions and frequent sepsis among poor women, many hospitals had to treat them in special septic wards. For example, Chicago's Cook County Hospital not only performed dozens of abortions each week but also maintained a separate septic ward for many of those who self-aborted.

Due to the large numbers, medical practitioners and public health officials began recognizing the results of self-abortions to maternal mortality. For instance, a large study in the late 1920s found that an astounding 14 percent of maternal mortalities were due to illegal abortions. Accordingly, physicians began including women's social conditions as a component of their medical decisions, thus adding to the "therapeutic" abortions that doctors had performed for years in clinics and hospitals for middle-class women.

Unfortunately for R. T. Bailey, abortions were illegal in Kentucky. However, it is not hard to imagine physicians performing these "therapeutic" abortions in the clinics and even homes in the towns and cities of the state, as they did across the country. Authorities typically looked the other way by leaving medical decisions for middle-class women to the patients and medical practitioners. But Dr. Bailey was Black, and the patient was white.[9]

Several questions surround the Bailey case. One of the central conundrums concerns the evidence against him. What was it? Moreover, we can wonder how the authorities obtained this evidence. Why was a dentist a chief witness for the prosecution? Usually, the prosecution called a woman for whom the doctor had performed an abortion to testify in these cases. Was there one? Did some influential Muhlenbergers want to rid the county of one of its few physicians of color? Was the main problem that Dr. Bailey performed the procedure on a white woman? Possibly.

After ingesting the poison, someone transported the dying Bailey to his Central City office, where he quickly succumbed. Why was he not administered critical emergency treatment in Greenville (besides the stomach pump given him) rather than carrying the dying man to his office in another town? Was there a suicide note? If not, why? Finally, will this tragic incident ever be accorded a full historying?

Without more evidence, we can presume that the criminal case was going badly against Bailey. However, with the prospect of losing his state medical license and facing two to twenty-one years in the state penitentiary, we could reason that this doctor was dramatically protesting what he considered an unjust racialized application of the criminal code.[10] To wit: Authorities may have charged him for breaking the abortion law only after operating on a white woman. If correct, his drama was a self-murdering act of sociopolitical protest against the dominator culture. Moreover, he conducted it as physically embodied and sardonically symbolic as is imaginable.

R. T. Bailey's choice of the county courtroom for his suicide discloses his comprehension of the local power structure. The Nobel Prize-winning Southern novelist William Faulkner understood it. He seems to have been writing about the Muhlenberg County Courthouse, crowning a hill and visible from miles away, when describing a fictional setting in his mythologized Jefferson, Yoknapatawpha County, Mississippi. "But [towering] above all, the courthouse: the center, the focus, the hub; sitting looming in the center of the county's circumference like a single cloud in its ring of horizon," Faulkner wrote, "laying its vast shadow to the uttermost rim of horizon; musing, brooding, symbolic and ponderable, tall as a cloud, solid as rock, dominating all."[11] This is where Bailey chose to die: at the looming, brooding, symbolic center facing the judge.

R. T. Bailey chose the site of his final self-destruction well. He wanted to physically face the personification of political power in 1934, at the seat, the hub, the locus of the local authority. Facing the judge, Bailey pondered the carbolic acid corroding his innards. He might have brooded on the sites of historical shock just beyond the courthouse walls. In or near these same precincts, a horde lynched Bob Gray in 1870, and a mob lynched Dudley White in 1874. Moreover, in 1907, the county executed 16-year-old Harrison Alexander by public hanging.

Suppose R. T. Bailey was vomiting the phenol-denatured tissues of his esophagus and stomach lining onto the courthouse hallway floors. In this case, he passed the segregated restrooms and separate drinking fountains for "Coloreds" that persisted in the Muhlenberg County Courthouse until 1964 or 1965.[12] Then, perhaps, Bailey perversely staged his suicide—a self-lynching—to wrest control from the historical master narrative of "separate but equal." In effect, Bailey played this deadly drama by writing his own script.

Not only the place but the timing may also be instructive. In 1934, the protracted travesty and ordeal of the Scottsboro Boys case of Alabama still made headlines whenever a new development appeared. In the U.S. Congress, the sole Black lawmaker, Oscar De Priest (Republican, Illinois), was still trying unsuccessfully to desegregate the Capitol's public cafeteria for the House of Representatives. Moreover, two days before Dr. Bailey's death, a U.S. senator announced the belated beginning of the debate on the Costigan-Wagner Anti-Lynching Bill. This legislation would have penalized local jurisdictions monetarily and fixed federal charges on local sheriffs for failure to protect prisoners. In other words, local sheriffs would be held responsible for any more lynchings, and they would cost local taxpayers money. However, the solid bloc of Southern Congressional members immediately organized resistance, claiming the primacy of states' rights. As a result, leaders never reported the bill out of committee.

Since R. T. Bailey left no suicide note, he perhaps thought that posterity would ignore a Black man's verbal death throes. The "secret place" of Bailey's motivations, thoughts, and beliefs will never come to light. What he did leave, instead, is his embodied, final enactment, a type of *guerrilla theater*, a politically enacted performance art of the most lethal kind. He may have thought that denizens of the future would not consider his absence of words but, instead, the sociopolitical circumstances and meanings of his life and chosen death.

Relevant here is Ralph Ellison's interpretation of Richard Wright's 1944 memoir *Black Boy*.[13] "[Wright] has converted the American Negro impulse toward self-annihilation and 'going underground' into a will to confront the world," Ellison observed, "to evaluate his experience honestly and throw his findings unashamedly into the guilty conscience of America."[14] Similarly, R. T. Bailey, who had no chance to read Wright and thus might have taken another approach, used his self-annihilation as his stark statement for posterity, throwing it into the consciousness, if not the conscience, of Muhlenberg and America.

Chapter 9

BLACK SOLDIERS IN THE WORLD WARS

All history in some ways wishes to say something about its own present time.[1]

Black Americans fought in every American war, from the Revolutionary to the Civil War, the Spanish-American, World Wars I and II, Korea, Vietnam, and beyond and between. Historians widely recognize that their participation as soldiers in the Civil War was critical for the Union Army and turned the tide for winning that conflict. Out of 41,935 African American males of military age (18 to 45 years) in Kentucky in the early 1860s, government officials credited the state with 23,703 Union Army and Navy enlistees. This number of Black enlistees represented a remarkably high 57 percent of the total possible for the state.[2]

America entered World War I when anti-Black hostility was at its post-Civil War peak. The apartheid of Jim Crowism and the ideology of the Lost Cause continued its cultural march. President Woodrow Wilson, an avowed segregationist, occupied the White House, where he screened *The Birth of a Nation*, directed by Kentuckian D. W. Griffith. In May and July 1917, a few hundred miles to the west, "race riots" occurred in East St. Louis. That same year, Mayfield and Murray erected Confederate monuments. Furthermore, construction began on the 351-foot obelisk honoring Confederate Jefferson Davis—"a Southern Shrine, a spot forever dear to the heart of Dixie."[3]

What was the wartime white attitude toward Black Muhlenbergers? If the opinion of Congressman R. Y. Thomas, Jr.—in his fourth of nine terms in Congress—represented broader attitudes, then long-term prejudicial beliefs prevailed. In a letter to President Wilson, Thomas complained: "[T]he negroes are permitted to stay at home and hang around the towns and steal, while the white boys are taken from the farms and sent into the army."[4] Rep. Thomas did not know that Black Muhlenbergers would serve at a higher rate (at 3.9%) than white countians (3.1%) when using their total populations.

In World War I, the U.S. military sent many Black soldiers overseas with the American Expeditionary Force. Eighty-three were Muhlenbergers.[5] The largest number of these Black Muhlenbergers were members of the various regiments (64th, 809th, 813th, but mostly the 801st) of the Pioneer Infantry, an all-Black unit.

Eight or more Black Muhlenbergers participated in combat units. At least six of these served with the 369th Infantry Regiment in the 93rd Infantry Division, an all-Black division. These soldiers were Pete Duncan, Bevier-Cleaton; Ernest Morton, Graham (born in Drakesboro); Will M. Reynolds, Greenville; O'Hara Simons, Greenville; and two Saulsberry brothers, David and Shelby, Greenville.[6]

White officers commanded the Black 369th Infantry Regiment (like in the Civil War). Since white soldiers refused to serve with Black troops (as also happened in the Civil War), the American command attached the 369th to the French Army. This combat unit fought with French weapons and wore American uniforms with French helmets and other accouterments. German troops across the no man's land respectfully labeled the Black 369th the "Harlem Hellfighters" for never losing ground or a captured man. The French labeled them the "Men of Bronze" and extended better treatment to this unit than that coming from white American soldiers. The French government awarded the entire regiment and 171 individuals of the 369th with either the Croix de Guerre or the Legion of Honor.[7]

The 369th participated in the Second Battle of the Marne and the Second Battle of the Argonne Forest. Its overseas deployment ranked the longest of any American unit. When the 369th returned home, New York City gave the regiment a heroes' parade, including (one would like to imagine) the Muhlenbergers Duncan, Morton, Reynolds, Simons, and the two Saulsberrys.[8]

After World War I, some white citizens directed their racial animus against those returning Black veterans. For example, Rufus B. Atwood, a native of Hickman (Fulton County), later served for 33 years as president of Kentucky State University (1929-1962). When he returned from Army service, Atwood's father cautioned that many would not greet him as a war hero. For this reason, his father advised Atwood to avoid wearing his uniform in public.[9] In fact, mobs lynched at least ten World War I Black veterans, with five occurring in Georgia. In addition, some white folks in Kentucky and other states were aghast that Black soldiers returning from war held democratic ideas of social equality and proudly wore their uniforms and medals.

"If blacks thought [that] fighting for their country meant that the [racial] caste system would be abolished, they were mistaken," Georgia historian Donald Grant observes. "Discrimination against Black troops did not let up after the fighting stopped—if anything, it increased."[10] Before the war, citizens of color tended to see their ill-treatment as part of the "global color line." This discrimination had long encircled Europe, plunged into Africa with European colonialism, snaked across the Atlantic with captives to the United States, and in 1918, with Jim Crow social hierarchy and ostracization.[11]

Nonetheless, soldiers of color fought overseas with hopes of a more authentic democracy at home. Historian Donald Grant underscored the attitude back home: "Whites were horrified that black soldiers had learned 'social equality' from the French and would expect better treatment."[12] Unfortunately, when the war ended with the Allied victory, dismantling domestic racial apartheid and hierarchy did not materialize.

In World War II, over one million Black American men and women served, a fact often overlooked. Indeed, the nation's white press maintained a near-complete silence on the Black units unless racial strife arose. Nonetheless, as in the Civil War, the United States could not have won the war without the essential effort of these patriotic citizens. Later generations of Americans think of these war years as a time of unity. But this unity was directed at the war effort. Socially, this time was far from peaceful, especially on the labor and racial fronts.[13]

At least 224 Black Muhlenbergers served in the Armed Forces during World War II. Within two months after the first peacetime conscription in November 1940 and before the war began, twenty countians, including twelve Black Muhlenbergers, volunteered and were inducted into the U.S. Army. Another 214 or more Black countians served at the onset of action: 181 in the Army, forty in the Navy, and three as navy marines. Out of these, eighteen attained the rank of Army sergeant. As many as five Black Muhlenberger women served in the Armed Forces: four in the Army and one in the Navy.[14]

Black women did more than join the armed services during the war years. Six hundred thousand found jobs in ship and rail yards and industrial plants manufacturing army vehicles, tanks, airplanes, and munitions.[15] They, too, were integral members of the Rosie the Riveters corps.

An even earlier local Black enlistee was Charles E. Baker of Central City. He enlisted in the Navy in 1939 and was assigned to the *USS West Virginia*, a *Colorado*-class battleship and the battle-fleet flagship stationed by late 1940 at the U.S. Naval Base at Pearl Harbor. Baker was aboard on December 7, 1941, when two Japanese bombs and six aerial torpedoes targeted it. The *West Virginia* sank, engulfed in a conflagration of flaming fuel oil leaking from it and the nearby *USS Arizona*. He swam to safety, badly burned.[16]

In addition to the injured Baker, two Black countians who served during the war lost their lives. Steward's Mate 1st Class Harry Thomas Allison (probably from Central City) was the first casualty. The Navy assigned him to the destroyer *USS Morrison*, which saw action all over the Pacific, including the Battle of Leyte Gulf.[17] Allison died during the invasion of Okinawa on May 4, 1945. After several attempts, his ship was hit by a Japanese suicide plane and three others, suffering massive damage and heavy casualties.

The second Black casualty was Army Private 1st Class Paul Blasengane of Drakesboro, assigned to the 92nd Infantry—the heralded Buffalo Soldiers Division—a unit of the Fifth Army. The 92nd participated in the Italian Campaign, the only Black infantry division to serve in the European Theater. The death of PFC Blasengane on November 5, 1945, happened in the Mediterranean area a few months after the war ended.[18]

Even though Black Muhlenbergers endured second-class citizenship and worse, they still admirably performed their part in these conflicts bookended by the Civil War and the two world wars, but not overlooking the Korean Campaign, the Vietnam War, and beyond. Thus, we should recognize that Americans of color, like others in these wars, including the "Greatest Generation," sacrificed for their country. However, Black soldiers also were "fighting for hope"—their hope for the promises of democracy.[19]

Black Americans had long used military service to gain access to fuller citizenship. Not only did they tackle discrimination within the military, but they also took the struggle to adjacent civilian communities.[20] But perhaps the Double V Campaign best represents the aspirations of Black Americans during World War II. This initiative began with a letter to the editor of the *Pittsburgh Courier*, a leading Black newspaper, by a 26-year-old Kansan on January 31, 1942. He asked whether he should sacrifice his life to live "half-American." Along with the fight against fascism abroad, he wondered "if another victory could be achieved at the same time," in effect, promoting a double victory—overseas while also not "los[ing] sight of our fight for true democracy at home."[21]

Inspired by his letter, on February 7, the *Courier* launched its Double V (i.e., double victory) campaign. This idea rapidly disseminated as a national patriotic effort that encouraged buying war bonds and stamps, contributing to blood banks, and conserving and collecting materials. On the domestic front, the campaign focused on fighting discrimination, especially voter disfranchisement, pushing for equal education, and demanding better job opportunities in the defense industries.

Langston Hughes's famous wartime poem expresses the "double" perspective of American citizens of color during the war. In his "Beaumont to Detroit: 1943," he muses:

> You tell me hitler
> Is a mighty bad man,
> I guess he took his lessons
> From the ku klux klan.
>
> You Jim Crowed me
> Before hitler rose to power—
> And you're STILL jim crowing me
> Right now, this very hour.
>
> Yet you say we're fighting
> For democracy.
> Then why don't democracy
> Include me?
>
> I ask you this question
> Cause I want to know
> How long I got to fight
> BOTH HITLER—AND JIM CROW.[22]

The Double V campaign and other wartime efforts set the stage for the postwar civil rights movement. Moreover, the global military conflict constructed a broader platform for the Black freedom struggle. Consequently, these world events internationalized the thinking of Black intellectuals, as reflected in the national Black press. For instance, in February 1943, Horace Cayton, Jr. (1903-1970), a Black sociologist and newspaper columnist for the *Pittsburgh Courier*, wrote: "The Negro is developing an international point of view more rapidly than the rest of the [American] population." The historical terms had shifted. "The basis of the Negro's struggle has changed," Cayton continued. "Where at first his demands were simply for Negro rights, now they are for democratic rights for all people throughout the world."[23] Furthermore, these wartime actions evidenced that Black citizens did not give up on their country, even though they met "Jim Crow in uniform" at almost every turn.[24] Henceforward, the struggle would continue into a new phase.

Chapter 10

COMPLEXITY, CONTINUITY, AND RACIALIZED SPACES

Black matters are spatial matters.[1]

Kentucky ratified the Nineteenth Amendment to the U.S. Constitution on January 6, 1920, prohibiting denying the right to vote to citizens based on sex. Without question, the passage of this amendment by the General Assembly would have fallen by the wayside without suffrage leaders'—both men's and women's—immense organizational efforts. In August of that year, Tennessee became the last of the required thirty-six states to approve this amendment. With its passage, Black and white women could vote for the first time in a presidential election. However, they had only a brief time to register before the November election day. Nevertheless, if Muhlenberg proceeded like other places, nearly all Black and white women enthusiastically performed this citizenship duty.

The history of women's suffrage is a story of the fight for equality. Nonetheless, the broader society's color prejudice deeply embedded itself in the women's suffrage campaign but without the Jim Crow virulence. Instead, it encompassed the soft violence of studiously denying the Black voice in the mainstream suffrage struggle. During the seven decades of the campaign, American women of color made significant contributions to passing the Nineteenth Amendment. Nevertheless, they had to do it on a separate track. Yet, Black women's "transfiguration in status and identity" from the antebellum era to post-World War I helped transform the broader women's movement.[2] As Black American poet and suffragist Bettiola Heloise Fortson (1890-1917) of Hopkinsville advised: "Carve out your own career/ Pray don't wait to be led:/ Then you won't feel the sneer/ Or have briny tears to shed."[3] This proactivity leading to careers and public activism is precisely what American women increasingly sought, whether Black or white.

Black women did more than register to vote. NAACP branches in eleven or more states, including Kentucky, organized women's political education and training classes. As a result, the state's women of color quickly became involved in the Republican Party. In March 1920, a Winchester teacher, Annie Simms Banks, won an appointment to the state party convention, the first for a Southern Black woman. She also sat on the party rules committee. Banks announced, "[B]efore long, we are going to make ourselves felt."[4]

Republican leaders across the country alluded to the emancipationist symbolism of the "Party of Lincoln." With this electoral strategy, they appealed directly to women of color by encouraging them, as daughters and granddaughters of bondservants, to vote Republican. It must have worked in Muhlenberg since it was among the only twenty-five Kentucky counties voting a majority for Republican Warren G. Harding. Black women may have made a difference locally. The remaining counties went for Democrat James M. Cox (giving him all the state's thirteen electoral votes), as did the entire South except Tennessee. However, Harding won the election by a substantial popular majority nationwide and in thirty-seven of the forty-eight states.

The dedication ceremonies for the Lincoln Memorial on May 30, 1922, in the nation's capital illustrate cultural change and historical continuity. President Harding, former president William H. Taft (then chief justice of the Supreme Court), and the frail Robert Todd Lincoln, the only surviving child of Abraham and Mary Todd Lincoln, attended. Robert Russa Moton (1867-1940), son of enslaved people and president of the Tuskegee Institute (replacing Booker T. Washington), presented the keynote address.

"With malice toward none, with charity for all," Moton offered, repeating Lincoln's words. "[W]e dedicate ourselves and our posterity, with you and yours, to finish the work which he [Lincoln] so nobly began," Moton announced to the nation. To do what? "[T]o make America an example for all the world of equal justice and equal opportunity for all." This event formed a striking tableau with the Lincoln Memorial as the backdrop, symbolizing the hope of an American society free from prejudice and open to opportunity for everyone. This son of enslaved people spoke to the crowd with eloquent words about opportunity and equal justice echoing over the scene. Not to be overlooked, the setting also included eager Black attendees. In keeping with the times and illustrating a degree of continuity, the organizers confined them to an area of segregated seating.

An anecdote from the guitarist and Country Music Hall of Fame singer and songwriter Merle Travis (1917-1983) illustrates historical complexity, continuity, and change over time. His story relates an instance of manumission and the bequeathing of real estate to bondservants. Among his earliest memories was living on the "old Littlepage place" between Beech Creek and Browder. (Travis does not give the year, but ca. 1922-1924.) Before the Civil War, the Littlepages, an English family, owned the land and its resident enslaved people.

When the war came, the landowning Littlepages moved to England and left their land to their bondservants. Some seven decades later, the Travis family rented a pre-Civil War house on that same property, then owned by the formerly enslaved "Aunt" Rowena E. (Smith) Littlepage (1860-1948) and "Uncle" Rufus Littlepage (1858-1928). Travis recalled that when it came time to collect the rent, "Uncle" Rufus would come to his backdoor. He would "take his hat off, you know, and say: 'Mizz Travis, I believe it's time for the rent, Ma'am.' And my momma would say, 'Would juh come in?' And he would say, 'No, Ma'am, I'll just wait out here.'"[5]

Travis understood his story's historical irony and its reversal of the norms of the power of whiteness. Namely, his white family paid rent to a Black "landlord and landlady" formerly enslaved on that same property. Nonetheless, the historical inertia and practical power of whiteness were still paramount, at least socially and symbolically. To wit: Landlord "Uncle" Rufus always stood politely at the backdoor with his hat in hand.

Writing in 1933, acclaimed Black historian Carter G. Woodson understood this cultural milieu and seemed to be speaking directly to this event. "If you make a man think that he is justly an outcast, you do not have to order him to the back door," Woodson observed. The Travises were perhaps as courteous as they could be toward "Uncle" Rufus. But, no matter: "He will go without being told," Woodson underscored, "and if there is no back door, his very nature will demand one."[6]

Even with some advances in race relations, this era continued with ongoing social and political struggles. Oppression arose against the Black construction workers who helped build the massive dam on Kentucky Lake from 1938 to 1944. After the Tennessee Valley Authority completed its construction phase, it razed the workers' segregated "Negro Village" and kicked them out. Marshall County (county seat: Benton) subsequently continued as a "sundown county"—a county purposely kept all-white.[7]

From World War I through World War II, millions of Black citizens streamed north and west to escape the social, economic, and political marginalization of the Jim Crow South. They filled the vacuum in manufacturing jobs in those regions' cities. Unknown numbers left Muhlenberg and western Kentucky during this migration. Some volunteered from their new home states to join the two war mobilizations. This exodus of Black Muhlenbergers and other Kentuckians helped change the nation's regional geography as they transformed the urban racial geography in Kentucky, the West, Midwest, and North. Take Harold Washington (1922-1987), elected mayor of Chicago in 1983, as one example among millions. His father was born in Ballard County, Kentucky, before his family migrated to Massac County, Illinois.[8]

As the racial geography changed in the early twentieth century, Kentuckians' mental geography continued its decades-long reorientation. Kentucky, the Civil War "border state," gave way to its new regionalization in the "Border South."[9] Not merely a middle state between the North and South, the Commonwealth reoriented its outlook and relative location. In other words, by the early twentieth century, white Kentuckians completed the process, begun during the Civil War, of de-placing themselves in their geographic imaginations from a neutral or even pro-Union between-state position. They then re-emplaced themselves as the northern cultural zone of the South. Many of the events in this chapter mirror this Southern cultural-cognitive self-emplacement.

In 1948, President Harry S. Truman integrated the U.S. military and established the Commission on Civil Rights. These developments occurred amid Black citizens' endeavors to advance the American democratic project. Later, their struggle to obtain civil, legal, and political rights peaked in the 1960s. Southern historian C. Vann Woodward understood this era as a Second Reconstruction to regain the lost civil and political liberties that the three Reconstruction Amendments had constitutionally conferred. Woodward described the hazardous flow of these changes, including economic, as "precipitous rapids."[10]

In the post-war social setting, the color line—drawn symbolically, politically, and materially—was alive and well. For example, Langston Hughes reported this in March 1947:

> I went to a Marian Anderson concert the other day, and they had the audience divided into white and colored, dead down the middle and nobody dared to cross that line. That did not look civilized to me, because the same music went in all ears. Marian Anderson had a white accompanist and she kept taking bows with him and holding him by the hand while they both took bows. But if a white person and a colored person in the audience had held hands across the dividing aisle, evidently it would have been against Georgia law, and they could be put in jail.[11]

Representative of the local cultural landscape after World War II, Greenville held a costumed Confederate re-enactment as late as 1948. This event celebrated Confederate General Simon Bolivar Buckner's attendance (possibly with 6,000 soldiers) at the 1861 funeral wake of his friend Charles Fox Wing (1779-1861), for 57 years, the Muhlenberg court clerk.[12] C. Vann Woodward labels this idealizing, "nostalgic vision of the past" as "archaic romanticism." It was enabled because "[o]ne of the most significant inventions of the New South was the 'Old South.'"[13] Greenville was reinventing itself as a place in the Old South.

Beginning in 1948 and continuing the nostalgic vision of the mythical Old South, the white Hopkinsville Kiwanis Club presented a blackface minstrel show for eight or nine years to raise funds for a segregated swimming pool. Each year, the shows ran for three or four nights to packed houses in the auditorium of Hopkinsville High.

Christian County historian William Turner spoke of "the paradox of this whole thing": white people in blackface caricaturing Black folk to raise funds for a white establishment that Blacks could not enter.[14] The practice of racial exclusion had its absurdities. Then, the pool quietly closed unceremoniously due to the 1966 state civil rights law pushed by Governor Ned Breathitt (from Hopkinsville). In contrast, after integration came in the mid-1960s, Central City kept its municipal swimming pool open until ca. 1995-1996.[15]

In 1951, referring to the fight against totalitarianism in World War II and the Cold War, Rufus B. Atwood, president of Kentucky State University, observed: "We [Americans] cannot afford, the world cannot afford, to have this nation made ineffective by the taunt: 'Your undemocratic deeds speak so loudly that your democratic professions cannot be heard.'"[16] Atwood's comment prefigured those of Rev. M. L. King, Jr., imploring the nation to live up to its democratic ideals.

The 1950s political establishment moved to support the struggle against the racial caste system because Black rights emerged as Cold War propaganda and competition between the Communist Bloc and the democratic West. Legal scholar Derrick Bell's "interest convergence principle" applies here. Bell's analysis of the Supreme Court's 1954 *Brown v. Board of Education* decision posited: "The interest of blacks in achieving racial equality will be accommodated only when it converges with the interests of whites."[17] In this scenario, the aspirations of an effective national foreign policy coincided with the calls for a rational approach to domestic racial policy. So, American leaders began to see civil rights laws as favorable to the image they wanted to present to the world.

Also symptomatic of this period was the billboard erected in 1958-1962 by local citizens outside Central City on Highway U.S. 431 that read: "Save Our Republic! Impeach Earl Warren."[18] One major gripe against Warren, the U.S. Supreme Court chief justice, was the court decisions of 1954-1955 that integrated schools.

The nation also advanced with a growing Black middle class but continuing stagnation in the less privileged socioeconomic strata, including the Black and white underclass. A telling symptom was the *racial wealth gap*. In early 2023, *Forbes* reported (using data from the Federal Reserve) that the average Black household earned half that of the average white home. The wealth ownership was even more skewed: Black families owned only between 15 to 20 percent as much net wealth as white families.[19] Social and economic policy expert Heather McGhee reminds us that this type of wealth (primarily based on homeownership) was self-perpetuating, and government decisions had shaped its acquisition. Furthermore, the gap has widened over the last three decades.[20]

Several markers of economic well-being, or lack thereof, show this same Black precarity, much of it class-based. For example, non-Hispanic Black women, as compared to non-Hispanic white women, are three to four times more likely to die from a pregnancy-related death.[21] Another indicator is the number of children living in *extreme poverty* (the share under 18 who live in families with incomes less than 50 percent of the federal poverty level). In 2008, 23 percent of Black

Kentucky children lived in extreme poverty, but only 11 percent of non-Hispanic white children. By 2015, the extreme-poverty numbers had dipped slightly to 21 percent of Black children and 10 percent of white children in both cohorts.[22] Therefore, white children were less than half as likely to live in extreme poverty as Black children. As Ta-Nehisi Coates remarked, "[T]he concentration of poverty has been paired with a concentration of melanin."[23] Furthermore, the record has been problematic in other critical areas, such as policing practices and criminal justice.

Essentialized, manufactured "Black criminality"—beginning in colonial times and continuing through the Jim Crow era—has had dire and dreadful ramifications for the Black American experience. For instance, historian Jonathan Scott Holloway relates that for an extended period of the twentieth century, "by opening their newspaper to the crime blotter," readers understood that "'colored' really meant criminal."[24]

In these matters, not only did white society criminalize Blackness, but it also created the existential quality of a wholesome whiteness in binary opposition. Legal scholar Kimberlé Williams Crenshaw succinctly characterizes *whiteness* as "not a simplistic racial characterization, but a deeply structural relationship to social coercion and group entitlement."[25] Whiteness does not necessarily apply to or coincide with a racial group. On the contrary, it is a social *property* that a racially designated person or group may possess—a measurable holding that relates closely to class and the exercise of privilege and power. This quality—and its absence—is displayed throughout this volume.

Besides personal welfare, we should keep in mind that "[a]nyone born [in the U.S.] before 1964 was not born into a democracy, because blacks could not vote."[26] (In Kentucky, though, Black men have voted legally since 1870.) Disparate mortality rates and nonvoting due to felony disfranchisement laws hide much of this non-voting behavior. For example, researchers estimated 2.7 million excess Black deaths between 1970 and 2004 (due to higher infant mortality rates and other health issues), totaling 1 million lost Black votes in the 2004 election. Of these, 900,000 votes would have gone to the defeated Democratic presidential nominee. These potential Black voters who lost their franchise through death or disfranchisement amounted to 15 percent of the Black vote. Furthermore, at the state level, they estimated that in this same period, these hypothetical survivors (and not counting the disfranchised) would have reversed the outcomes—from Republican to Democratic candidates—of seven close senatorial and eleven gubernatorial elections.[27] These researchers conclude about this "Black missingness":

> Although less spectacular or overtly intentional than the noose, the culture of impunity that allows us to escape accountability for the structural violence that disproportionately cuts black lives short—whether through acute injury, a discriminatory and militarized criminal justice system, or the accumulated physiological insults inherent to everyday life at the margins of a race-conscious society—remains a moral failure and a threat to democracy.[28]

In a similar study in 2010, a team of researchers found that 3.9 million Black men and women lost their right to vote due to early death or incarceration, amounting to a national African American disfranchisement rate of 13.2 percent. The Bluegrass State was among five southeastern states with the highest rates: Alabama, Florida, Kentucky, Tennessee, and Virginia. Most of these people were "literally missing" from their home communities because they were incarcerated or had died prematurely. The Black "missingness rate" of potential Black voters in these five states—counting premature deaths and incarceration—ranges from 20.7 to 24.3 percent. [29] As a significant contributor, the Black infant mortality rate (IMR) is twice that of the white IMR. The researchers conclude: "Since racial disparities in health and incarceration result in such a large number of missing black voters, an observer might ask: How truly representative is American democracy?"[30]

Nevertheless, most people acknowledge that the nation has lurched toward racial equality, at least legally and, in many ways, politically. These successful changes and troublesome stagnations point to this historical conclusion by a long-time journalist: "Kentucky actually didn't know what to do about the civil rights movement. It had always been wishy-washy on the black question." He continued, "[the state] had been unable to make up its mind about slavery." As a result, in the 1950s and 1960s, "it was having a hard time deciding how to view protesting blacks."[31] In other ways, as this book shows, the Commonwealth had not settled its mind about racial matters into the 1960s. However, it went much deeper than mere white ambivalence. Color prejudice and living amid inequality exacted psychic costs on everyone.[32]

Social constructs, mental formations, institutional practices, and the unwieldy weight of history have engendered and maintained massive social inertia that seems perennially locked in place, even if often hidden. Perhaps these words of the University of Kentucky agriculture professor James A. Jackson, who grew up on a farm near Pembroke in southern Christian County in the 1950s, can adequately, or at least partially, illuminate the circumstances of that place-world:

> There was no real outward overt type of discrimination [in the 1950s southern Christian County]. Mostly the blacks worked for the whites. It was *just the way things were set up* and no one bucked the system. And on the sides of the whites they didn't really come overtly anti-black type things. It was just more of a thing that having the blacks work for them and having them to continue to work for them and hopefully be happy.[33]

Jackson's view reflects the experience of one man of color recalling his lifeworld in a small area of the western region, a situation we could label "quiet racism."[34] His statement is presented here not as a "whitewash" of the history of the blatant racial behaviors of the past that this book has described. Instead, his words form one bookend on a shelf that ranges from systemic, institutionalized racism on one end to color-prejudicial thoughts and actions of individuals, on the other. Jackson continues: "Even though there were no overt signs of racism...the general theme was always there. In other words, as long as you were black you were second." Jackson spoke of a "general theme"—

pervasive, pernicious, often subtle, and generally accepted as "just the way things were set up." Similarly, Annie Bard of Central City recalled the restrictions in local restaurants where she was not allowed to sit at tables and was required to order food only for take-out.[35]

However, in the longer view, "Without question, when using 1865 as a starting point," as Black historian George Wright argues, "there have been numerous positive changes in virtually every area for [Kentucky] blacks."[36] It is worth noting that the state Democratic Party never instituted the "white primary" of whites-only voting, as did eight states across the Deep South. Nonetheless, as it appeared in 1955, a year after the landmark *Brown v. Board of Education*, any political advances would necessitate a fight against white resistance.

The Jim Crow system placed indelible traces on the physical and social landscape. Writer bell hooks spent her early formative years in the 1950s in the hills of Christian County before her family moved into Hopkinsville to make it easier for hooks and her Watkins siblings to attend all-Black Attucks High School. Hooks recalled her life in Hopkinsville that paralleled in meaningful ways some of the Black lifeworlds in Muhlenberg:

> For black Americans living in a small Kentucky town, the rail-road tracks were a daily reminder of our marginality. Across those tracks were paved streets, stores we could not enter, restaurants we could not eat in, and people we could not look directly in the face. Across those tracks was a world we could work in as maids, as janitors, as prostitutes, as long as it was in a service capacity. We could enter that world, but we could not live there. We had always to return to the

margin, to beyond the tracks, to shacks and abandoned houses on the edge of town.[37]

These recollections by bell hooks mirror a similar social and material reality in the cultural landscape of Central City. This town, too, had railroad tracks that once intersected downtown, along which Black Central Citians, to reach downtown, walked from their residences in so-called (by whites) Colored Town.

Activity space is the physical area where an individual circulates in regular, daily activity. The activity space of Black Central Citians had a permeable social boundary line drawn around it that limited Black movement. As a general rule, we should note this: All humans make spatial choices limited by their sociopolitical constraints in timespace. In tangible ways, what should have been free spatial choices of Black Central Citians were informal spatial constraints placed on them. A resident on Morehead Street in the 1960s recalled only once seeing any Black person walking on that street. This observer remembered staring at the strangeness of the Black man's movement within the cultural landscape of that white section of town. The incongruousness of the Black body moving in segregated white space was noticeable. Due to the unspoken rules of local Jim Crow segregation, the Black man's activity space was supposed to be elsewhere. This scenario demonstrates that cultural landscapes work to include and exclude particular people. It also illustrates that the problem of color in the twentieth century was "the line": "the line of demarcation, the boundary line, the undrawn but universally felt line between neighborhoods" and other places, "the line one must toe but never cross"—in other words, the "color line" that Du Bois wrote about.[38]

The racial boundary lines also demarcated the interior of restaurants. Jeff Taylor, a Black Central Citian, recalled when his father took him downtown to the Peerless Café in 1964 or 1965 when he was about six. "I thought it was so cool that we were sitting in the kitchen with the hustle and bustle [of the restaurant workers] and all the great food," Taylor related. "Through a set of swinging saloon-type doors, I could see all of these [white] people sitting up front. I thought how stupid of them to be sitting way up there when they could be back here with the cooks, waitresses, and food." The young Taylor questioned his father about why the white patrons were all in the front. His father "blew it off" with no answer. "For years, I thought the white patrons were just dumb," Taylor remembered. "It was a while before I found out why we were really in the kitchen. But at six years old and as innocent as an angel, I thought how cool [to be sitting in the kitchen]."[39] The elder Taylor may have momentarily considered breaking the news to his son about a subdominant status in the American caste system. Pulitzer Prize-winning author Isabel Wilkerson related a similar story about a Black college professor and his young son in a restaurant in Oakland, California. "The boy [his son] was so sweet-faced, innocent, and free. How could he [the father] tell him that the world, his country, saw him as a threat? When exactly is the best time to break a child's heart?"[40]

The comments above by several people also illustrate the thematic perspective of the present study: that *race manifests in space* and creates a particular cultural landscape. Even the designation, by white townspeople, of the neighborhood known as Colored Town as a supposedly distinct "town" (instead, it was a set-off neighborhood) served to segregate Colored Town symbolically, if not entirely physically, from the rest of the townscape. (Black Central Citians referred to the white part of town as the "white section."[41])

Spatially, Colored Town was set at the edge of Central City, just as hooks describes Hopkinsville. To the east of the Colored Town neighborhood, on the opposite side of the line of white houses, is Little Cypress Creek's marshy bottomland, running northwestward from downtown. To the north, at least formerly, the town itself terminated at the end of the Colored Town neighborhood. Because of the low land and the L&N railroad tracks bordering the vicinity, Colored Town properties were less desirable for residences than elsewhere.

Also, the Colored Town neighborhood was situated contiguous to only a single row of houses occupied by whites (along North Second Street). Important both spatially and symbolically, this row of white houses faced away from Colored Town, with only the backyards of white residences bordering the Black neighborhood. Also significant is that the row of white houses along North Second Street was intersected by only three streets leading into the Black area, particularly at both ends. This isolation gave Central City Colored Town a configuration somewhat like an extended cul-de-sac.

The neighborhood location and cul-de-sac configuration of Colored Town showed the restrictive quality of this cultural landscape that exhibited a "geography of containment." Historian Stephanie Camp uses this term to describe a kind of proto-apartheid control in enslavery times. "At the heart of enslavement," Camp writes, "was a spatial impulse: to locate bondpeople in plantation space and to control, indeed to determine, their movements and activities."[42] Similarly, the concept of *geographic containment* can be applied to the twentieth century to see that white domination always had, at its core, different kinds of racialized social control, especially regarding space.

In the 1870s, when people of color first moved to Central City—earlier in Greenville and South Carrollton (as already patterned in the early coal camps)—mine operators set up a kind of exclusionary racial apartheid. In this transhistorical racialized geography, moving from coal camps to segregated towns, Blackness became spatialized—and due to this—so did whiteness. In other words, Black and white people lived in their respective, separated places.

Albeit at a microscale, hooks describes more than spatial marginality. She also speaks of social marginality: the types of jobs allowed (mostly service jobs), the enforced racialized behaviors (segregation in businesses), and an imposed psychic marginality (the avoidance of gaze). This constellation of spatial behaviors enacts *othering in space* that translates into psychosocial othering. That is to say, the forces that create physical spaces also materialize as spatialities of psychology and sociality. In other words, social forces construct places and profoundly influence minds and social relationships. And the reverse is true, too, with these working in both directions. If these forces are racially based, the outcomes will reflect these influences.

In other words, this social ordering across external space reflects the interior (mental) distance of the white self from the *other*. The arrangement manifests as a psychological distancing from an external other and an interior distancing from oneself. As James Baldwin spelled out: "One can measure very neatly the white American's distance from his conscious—from himself—by observing the distance between white America and black America."[43] White Southern writer Lillian Smith, in her controversial 1949 memoir about her childhood in a small Deep South town in northern Florida, observed this about its stark segregation: "A little white town rimmed by Negroes, making a deep shadow on the whiteness. There it lies, broken in two by one strange idea."[44] The historical existence of Central City's Colored Town, and all the others in the nation, represented the mental and physical brokenness of this distance and strange idea.

Chapter 11

JIM CROW EDUCATION

It is easy to proclaim all souls equal in the sight of God; it is hard to make men equal on earth in the sight of men.[1]

As described previously, through the income gained by employment in coal mining, the aggregate of families of color reached a spending threshold that supported large numbers of Black Muhlenberg businesses. Income, though, is not the same as wealth. One aspect of wealth is the command of human capital. Conceptually, *human capital* underscores that education, training, skills, experience, health, and connections manifest as nonmonetary investments, assets, and costs for persons, organizations, and society that usually produce monetary outcomes.[2] It is as real as business investment in equipment or other physical, productive means. For this reason, people strive to acquire, maintain, and pass these assets down to their children.[3] And, crucially, the initial input of this "capital" creates positive or adverse effects in a reverberating generational feedback loop through time.

A critical avenue for pursuing life, liberty, and happiness is the freedom and opportunity to achieve meaningful and practical knowledge. These human assets, especially education, forestall socioeconomic exploitation. Unfortunately, the existing power structure often prevented people of color from attaining literacy, gaining a basic education, and accruing this species of capital. The Southern slavocracy had blocked this fundamental human pursuit for most enslaved people. However, the Bluegrass State was one of the few slave states without laws against slave literacy. Nevertheless, across the Old South, "Black People," poet Nikky Finney reminds us, "were the only people in the United States ever explicitly forbidden to become literate." [4]

During Reconstruction, Black education leaders in the Bluegrass State met at several regional conventions. They applied considerable pressure on the General Assembly. Moreover, they threatened to take the state to court if it did not create an equitable statewide education program for Black Kentuckians. The legislature eventually heeded this call and was partially persuaded to act due to the possibility of losing federal funds earmarked for improving Southern Black public schools. Thus, Black Kentuckians deserve much of the credit for catalyzing a more adequately funded statewide public school system for Blacks and whites that the Commonwealth was previously reluctant to implement for either. Consequently, in early 1874, the General Assembly finally passed a law creating the structure of statewide Black public education. The result was that this legislation set up a separately administered, segregated, and unequal Black school system. For example, segregation laws required agents to locate Black schools a suitable distance from white schools—one mile in rural areas and 600 feet in towns and cities.[5]

Like ninety-two other Commonwealth counties, Muhlenberg established a Black public school following the 1874 legislation requiring each county to set up at least one, with exceptions. The following year, ninety-three counties were operating about six hundred Black schools. Muhlenberg set up a Black school system for the 1874-1875 school year. A document (dated July 1, 1874) of the Muhlenberg commissioner of common schools lists the trustees (as required by state law) for nine Black school districts in the county. By 1878, the remaining eight Black districts—each one an elementary one-room school with a single teacher—had 255 students. A Greenvillian recalled that she and other Black schoolmates attended, in 1884, a "house school" behind the Wesley Chapel AME Zion Church.[6] As corroborating evidence, William Henry Ross, a young Black American teacher from Hopkins County, taught in Muhlenberg in the 1885-1886 school year.[7]

In 1882, independent of the state laws governing education, a special act of the General Assembly created separate white schools for Owensboro. The charter for this district required that the "German language be taught, and that no colored pupils shall be admitted into these schools." At the same time, state funds supported a Black school in Owensboro, separate from the whites-only school district's local support. That same year, five hundred Black children of school age lived in Owensboro. Their brick school, erected in 1879 on Poplar Street, measured 30 feet by 40 feet. An unlikely two hundred students (the average attendance) crammed into 1,200 square feet of school space.[8]

In the previous generation, most formerly enslaved individuals and families struggled to create capital resources without reading and writing skills. This educational situation, along with other social barriers, obstructed the passing forward of multigenerational human capital. Nevertheless, despite the forces arrayed against them, Black Americans realized surprising educational success. In the five and a half decades after the Civil War, Black education in Muhlenberg advanced from near nonexistent literacy just after the war to a rate that soared to 81.2 percent in 1920.[9] This more than a substantial increase in literacy among Black Muhlenbergers offers evidence of Black agency and self-empowerment.

For instance, a local Black educator immersed herself in the Kentucky Moonlight Schools campaign begun in 1911 by white social reformer Cora Wilson Stewart, who launched her adult literacy campaign in eastern Kentucky that grew into a national grassroots literacy movement.[10] This Black Muhlenberger educator, Esther Nall, taught night school for adults in a barn at McNary Corners and a day school for children in the same structure. This teacher remembers: "I went to McNary to teach in 1919 and boarded with Mr. and Mrs. Houston Bard. There was no school building, so I taught in a tobacco barn. I do not remember the roll but I do remember that I taught Adult Education at night. The parents of the children came and it was interesting to see them studying."[11]

This advance in Black educational attainment shows the proactive efforts of Black Muhlenbergers to provide for their education and act as architects of their self-liberation. They understood that literacy formed the basis of education and the foundation for economic advancement. Thus, it is telling that, by 1892, a higher percentage of Black countians, based on enrollment, were attending school than were white children:

60 percent versus 56 percent.[12] For the entire state, by 1907, if not before, a higher rate of Black Kentuckians attended high school than white children.[13] In Muhlenberg, though, in schoolyear 1910-1911, no Black students attended high school in the county because the county had no Black high school (and few white children attended high school before World War I).[14]

An instance of the Commonwealth self-creating as a "sentimental Confederacy" appears when an officer at the United Daughters of the Confederacy's (UDC) 1904 Louisville convention downplayed the publicly visible stone and bronze monuments. Instead, the officer pronounced the UDC's "greatest of all monuments" was its educational work. This education program—its *thought monument*, the UDC called it—sought to indoctrinate the "pulsing hearts and active brains" of Southern white youth.[15] Thus, in 1920, Mildred Lewis Rutherford, the UDC's "historian general," composed a "measuring rod" pamphlet to assess school textbooks. Her list included these guidelines:

- [R]eject a book that speaks of the Constitution other than a Compact between Sovereign States.
- Reject a book that says the South fought to hold her slaves.
- Reject a text-book that…does not clearly outline the interferences with the rights guaranteed to the South by the Constitution, and which caused secession.
- Reject a book that speaks of the slaveholder of the South as cruel and unjust.
- Reject a text-book that glorifies Abraham Lincoln and vilifies Jefferson Davis.[16]

The UDC's education program, symbolism, mythology, rituals, and monuments created a positive interpretation and future memory favorable to the Confederacy's role in the late war. Moreover, these educators were adamant. Rutherford advised: "Don't say you *believe* that the South was right; say you *know* she was right.[17]

On another matter, the provision of library services to Black western Kentuckians offers insight into the institutional barriers against which they struggled. In 1892, Christian County distinguished itself with the first recorded instance of assembling a library in a "colored common school," with a reported worth of $96. Until 1908, officials set up school district libraries for Black students in Daviess, Henderson, Hopkins, Logan, McCracken, Todd, Trigg, and Muhlenberg (probably in Greenville) counties. In 1901, however, with 800 Black school districts in the state, only fifty-five had school libraries. (In 1908, Muhlenberg had eleven Black districts, each usually consisting of a single school.) The number of volumes reported for these school libraries averaged 410, valued at $257.[18]

Besides school libraries, the Commonwealth built twenty-four public libraries with tax monies and funds from the Carnegie Corporation. These public facilities faced the tactical problem of what to do with the Black public (another instance of the perennial "Negro question" or the "Negro problem" of the nineteenth century). Moreover, no Kentucky laws mandated separate libraries, unlike schools. Accordingly, since Carnegie offered no guidelines, local ordinances and customs determined the various practices across the Commonwealth.

In 1902, the city of Henderson obtained Carnegie funds for constructing two separate libraries, one for Black citizens and the other for their white neighbors. Although Memphis had the South's first public library for Black citizens, Henderson became the nation's first city (in 1904) to build a separate library structure for people of color. The two Henderson institutions—Black and white—were dedicated on the same day at different hours by some of the same city officials, including the mayor. In 1908, Louisville also obtained a grant to build a Black library.

Owensboro's main public library offered no library services for its citizens of color. In late 1914, this city opened its first public library for Black townspeople as a branch library inside Western High School (the Black high school in Daviess County). In 1918, the librarian at the main library reported that patrons at the "colored branch" used it as a reading room, preferring not to take reading materials home.[19]

In 1930, thirty-five Kentucky counties, with ten in the western region, including Muhlenberg (probably the Greenville Training School and the new, all-Black Drakesboro Community High), took advantage of the book program of the Julius Rosenwald Fund. This endeavor began in 1917 as a social project of businessman and philanthropist Julius Rosenwald (president and later board chairman of Sears, Roebuck & Co.). This program provided money for, among other projects, constructing 4,978 Black schools all over the South, including three in Muhlenberg, others in western Kentucky, and 155 across the state.[20] Rosenwald first worked with Dr. Booker T. Washington of the Tuskegee Normal and Industrial Institute (later Tuskegee University) to initiate the Rosenwald Schools project. The Rosenwald Fund paid the freight costs and a third of the collection expenses in its library program that sent texts to Black schools. These library collections cost $90 for elementary and $120 for high schools.[21]

The Commonwealth's white education bureaucracy actively ensured socialization based on racial hierarchy. After all, this was the era of Jim Crow. By 1937, the State Board of Education approved a reading list for public schools, as did all the Southern states. However, along with Florida and Louisiana, Kentucky's approved reading list was extensive, with annotations for each book. In addition, the Commonwealth was the only state with separate recommendations for Black and white schools. Literature for white students sometimes featured Black children speaking in southern dialect, such as A. V. Weaver's 1930 *Frawg*, an "amusing dialect story of Frawg, a little Alabama colored boy." Interestingly, the literature for Black students used the word "Negro," in place of "colored" in white texts.[22]

We can contrast the intentions of this school socialization program with mixed-raced poet and Vanderbilt University writer-in-residence Carolyn Randall Williams, who espouses a different idea about socialization in the not-too-distant past. Her verdict is that her body and light complexion are potent witnesses to the sexual practices of racial enslavery. She brings the Old South into the present by compressing the story poetically and powerfully into five words, "I have rape-colored skin." She offers that her "light-brown-blackness is a living testament to the rules, the practices, the causes of the Old South." Her body and her skin are "a monument."[23]

In another kind of monument, Kentucky historian Emily Bingham speaks of the "sonic monument" that is "My Old Kentucky Home," composed by Stephen Collins Foster (in 1852) and made into the state song in 1928. Many admirers of this nostalgic, sentimental tune fail to recognize that it is composed from the perspective of an elderly enslaved man, sold "downriver," pining for the supposedly better environs of his old home (a slave cabin) in Kentucky. Bingham contends that America "erected" this sonic monument to "white feeling and white forgetting," as it misremembered the lyrics' meaning.[24]

When the integration era began, the Bluegrass State had 301 Black elementary and fifty-eight high schools. Six were stand-alone high schools, while fifty-two combined grades 1 to 12.[25] Western Kentucky had a string of all-Black high schools from the Mississippi to Bowling Green until integration. These included Beaver Dam Bruce High (where Mittie K. Render taught after graduating from Kentucky State College). Next, Bowling Green had High Street High (formed in 1883), where Black Butler Countians commuted unless they lived in the western part of the county and traveled to Drakesboro Community. This latter school in Muhlenberg opened in 1930 and closed in May 1964. In 1902, Bowling Green opened a private school for students of color—the Bowling Green Academy on State Street. This school became State Street Junior and Senior High. Next, Henderson set up Frederick Douglass High School, Hickman had Riverview, and Hopkinsville had Attucks, where bell hooks graduated.

Other Black high schools included Madisonville Rosenwald, Mayfield Dunbar, Morganfield Dunbar, Murray Douglass, Owensboro

Western, Princeton Dotson, Simpson County Lincoln, Todd County Training, and Paducah Lincoln, opening in 1908. Paducah also had the West Kentucky Industrial College (beginning in 1909), a high school and junior college for trades and teacher training that drew students further away (including Mittie K. Render). Finally, Russellville had Knob City School, grades 1 to 10, where national journalist Alice Allison Dunnigan (1906-1983) graduated. Dunnigan recalled that this two-year high school had no science lab or classes.[26]

Before official school integration came in the 1950s-1960s, the quality of Black school education in the Commonwealth was mixed but sometimes comparable to white schools. However, educators have many ways to evaluate schools and education. Unfortunately, historical analysis is problematic due to a severe lack of data; for example, which schools had science labs and classes? Nevertheless, historians could award relatively high marks to the state's Black education if evaluating the quality of instruction by assessing the respective teacher corps' formal training. For example, in 1888, the *Muhlenberg Echo* thought it newsworthy to report that "Miss Nattie Hamilton (col.)" achieved the second highest score among all Black and white teachers on the county teachers' examination.[27]

Almost seven decades later, in 1956, among all Black teachers statewide, 23.1 percent held a master's degree, compared to the 15.2 percent of white teachers statewide who had this same degree. Regarding those teaching with fewer than 129 college semester hours, 42.9 percent of white teachers were at this level of training, while only

14.6 percent of Black teachers worked with fewer than 129 semester hours.[28]

These data show similar formal teacher professionalism when disaggregated into elementary and high school levels. For instance, 13.8 percent of Black elementary teachers held a master's. In comparison, just 6.3 percent of the white teachers had trained at this level. Among white elementary teachers, 59.7 percent taught with fewer than 129 semester hours, which was the case for only 22.6 percent of Black teachers.[29]

In 1954, the Supreme Court ruled its earlier "separate-but-equal" doctrine from the 1896 *Plessy v. Ferguson* case as inherently unequal in theory and application. Nonetheless, in the years before integration, the overall education quality for Black Kentuckians appeared on par with that offered by white schools, as judged, that is, by the separate teacher corps' respective training. However, some—perhaps most—Black school buildings, facilities, and materials, such as lab equipment and textbooks, tell a story of government-sanctioned inferiority. For example, in its accreditation report for 1962-1963, the state rated Black Lincoln High School in Franklin as merely "provisional" partly due to its "inadequate" science equipment.[30]

To conclude, historian Adam Fairclough writes about Black teachers in the segregated South: "For about a hundred years, black teachers helped black southerners adapt to emancipation, the loss of political rights, and the imposition of Jim Crow laws. But they did much more than that. They shaped and guided communities. They inspired and empowered individuals." These teachers accomplished this by espousing "Christian values, middle-class virtues, and American ideals." They also "inculcated ambition, confidence, self-respect, and racial pride," and they "insisted upon dignity and decorum." Much of this study has focused on the Jim Crow system of racial subordination. Fortunately for the United States, the 100 years of Southern Black teachers after the Civil War "helped to discredit and undermine Jim Crow" by their application of the American ideal and principle of human equality.[31] As we now understand, their student body encompassed the entire nation.

Chapter 12

SCHOOL INTEGRATION, 'AS CONDITIONS WARRANT'

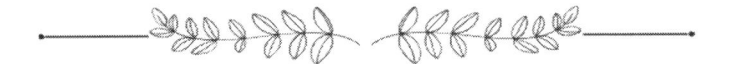

*How we remember our history
is also a part of our history.*[1]

A year before the Supreme Court's 1954 *Brown* decision, a lengthy feature article by political reporter Allan Trout (1903-1972) in the *Courier-Journal* reached what historian George Wright labeled an "absurd conclusion" about the state's public schools.[2] The Louisville journalist concluded that the existing dual school system adequately served students of color. Trout believed the Bluegrass State had "toted fair with the Negro." Like the Supreme Court, Wright concluded, to the contrary, that "separate" regarding education materialized as decidedly unequal. The Louisville chapter of the NAACP, led by Everette Ray and Lyman Johnson, joined the fray with a letter to the editor. They pointed out that many counties had no Black schools and shirked their legal responsibilities for providing funds and transportation to schools elsewhere. They concluded that segregation caused the problems.[3]

However, from this temporal distance, the researcher cannot readily assess the state's quality of instruction for either Black or white students, although, in the 1950s, it ranked at the nation's bottom.

Nonetheless, the 1896 "separate but equal" ruling in *Plessy* undoubtedly instigated upgrades of Black schools due to increased funding and attention. Much of the credit for these improvements goes to the state office of the NAACP and its "equalization strategy," which pushed for equal funding for Black schools, even though a widely ignored 1882 law required equalization. The NAACP strategized that school segregation would collapse since districts (and taxpayers) could not afford or want to maintain two matching sets of schools.

As noted above, in the early 1950s, many Kentucky counties established no school facilities for students of color, primarily in eastern Kentucky. Moreover, they offered only token funds for school attendance outside their respective counties, as mandated by state law.[4] Before desegregation began in 1956, fewer than half (fifty-five) of the state's 120 counties supported a local high school for Black students.[5] Butler County had no Black school, so it transported its students to Bowling Green. Others traveled to Drakesboro Community if they lived in the Rochester area.

Out-of-county transportation was not the case in Muhlenberg, however. Instead, the Central City School District built a school building for students of color, ready for school in the fall of 1921, near the present Ebenezer Baptist Church on North First Street, within the informal boundaries of Colored Town. Led by long-time physician Robert T. Bailey, local citizens of color raised more than 40 percent of the building funds.[6] Later, in 1938, the federal WPA constructed a new five-room brick school and gymnasium on North First Street. School officials set up this separate school (grades 1 to 12) for Black Central Citians and neighboring communities, including South Carrollton.

Before integration, Daviess County and Owensboro had Paul Lawrence Dunbar Elementary (usually shortened to Dunbar School) and Western High. In 1955, the all-white Owensboro High partially desegregated in a transition period. The school integrated with a few purposefully selected 12th-grade students from Western, taking single classes of their choice at white Owensboro High but restricted to courses not offered at Western. For example, Daisy James chose Latin, while some males joined the ROTC classes.

Black school administrators carefully selected these few students of color for their higher academic abilities—students who "would adjust better." James also thought that school officials considered her an appropriate candidate. Since age 12, she had worked for a high-profile Jewish family, the Levis, watching after their children. For this reason, she explains that she "had had exposure to the white race." James offered the historical irony that her father had helped construct the segregated white school, which she later helped integrate.[7]

Records are inadequate, but school integration in Central City must have generated some dissent from the white public. A controversy began with Central City schools superintendent George T. Taylor's statement to a *Courier-Journal* reporter, published on May 18, 1954. His remarks came the day after the *Brown v. Board of Education* Supreme Court decision that ended school segregation and *Plessy*'s "separate-but-equal" doctrine. Part of Supt. Taylor's comment, as printed in the *Courier-Journal* (which included the mysterious ellipsis):

"We will not encounter the problems that face other cities. Central City has lost much of its Negro population in recent years. ... *I don't anticipate any sentiment against the end of segregation here.*"[8] Inexplicably, the *Courier-Journal* had mistakenly attached the pro-integration final sentence to the end of Taylor's pronouncement—so claimed the *Central City Messenger*.

The latter paper dealt with this supposed erroneous quote when it printed the superintendent's complete statement but with a corrected final sentence. In this local follow-up article, Supt. Taylor seemed eager to clarify what he claimed was the earlier misquote by the *Courier-Journal*. According to the *Central City Messenger* (whose staff seems to have been coordinating a message with Supt. Taylor): "The final sentence [about not anticipating any public sentiment against integration] was not in Supt. Taylor's statement" to the *Courier-Journal* reporter. On the contrary, the *Messenger* continues: "This should have been his [Taylor's] closing sentence: 'The Central City Board of Education is *opposed to the end of segregation* but will abide by the law.'"[9] In other words, the Board opposed integration in this official clarification but would follow the court's ruling. Nonetheless, as presented in the *Messenger* article, Taylor does not deny the final sentence that the *Courier-Journal* had included (or added as its interpretation) that the School Board anticipated no problems with integration.

We can speculate that the original statement's pro-integration last sentence might have been a personal belief voiced by Supt. Taylor to the reporter, but not intended as an official Board position. Furthermore, some anti-integrationist white Central Citians must have pressured the Board. In his later clarification, the superintendent felt he had to announce the revision that he was "opposed to the end of segregation." Against integration but holding up the law as paramount became a typical school board stance across the Commonwealth.

Another scenario is possible. The final sentence about the Board's opposition to integration—but that it nonetheless would abide by the law—may have been a clarifying addendum given to the Central City newspaper solely for the local pro-segregationist public's consumption. The Board's anti-integration words may have been a temporary strategy to mollify some oppositional and vocal white Central Citians. In this case, the added clarification performed as "code language" directed to the public, indicating that the Board remained in no hurry to integrate. It would await further developments and probable pressures from other local stakeholders, neighboring counties, and elsewhere in the state and the Kentucky Department of Education (KDOE). In other words, the Board signaled that it did not want to integrate the schools and that outside interests would force it to act. This stance had the advantage of removing pressure and responsibility from the Board.

None of this should be surprising. The Central City Board of Education's sentiment, no doubt, aligned with the thinking of most of the local white community at that time. Namely, in 1954, most of the public set itself against school integration. Still, it would reluctantly comply with "the law of the land." In other words, they would follow the court ruling whether or not they agreed with it since it constituted a judicial fait accompli. This racially conservative attitude proved congruent with most of the Bluegrass State. As a result, white school boards throughout the Commonwealth declared they would abide by the *Brown* decision.[10] Nonetheless, many school districts took steps—or, in many instances, refrained from proactive actions—that caused a considerable intentional delay in the integration process.

The year 1955 proved to be a tense time in the Commonwealth. In states farther south, the continuing anti-Black brutality claimed numerous lives in the freedom struggle. Among several high-profile events, on August 28, Roy Bryant and J. W. Milam tortured and murdered 14-year-old Emmett Till in Money, Mississippi, for allegedly accosting Bryant's wife. In Mississippi and the other former slaveholding states, ruthless anti-Blackness was rampant.

In his tour through the South in 1955, Kentucky writer Robert Penn Warren (soon to win the second Pulitzer of his three) interviewed an array of Southerners about school integration. He recorded an unnamed school superintendent in an unspecified county in southern Kentucky. "When this thing [Court-mandated school integration] first came up," explained the superintendent, "the whole school board said they'd walk out."[11] Additionally, the Central City Colored School's empty classrooms seem irrelevant. Moreover, it contrasts with the reason given by some school districts that white schools were overcrowded.[12] For this reason, integration would cause insufficient space, they claimed. For example, according to the Madisonville Schools superintendent: "Because of the merger of the City and County school systems [Madisonville and Hopkins County], our physical properties will not be adequate to meet the challenge [of integration]."[13]

Kentucky school districts, including the three in Muhlenberg—Central City, Greenville, and the county district—awaited further guidance and instructions from KDOE. State guidance came a year later, in May 1955, after the Supreme Court's *Brown II* decision, admonishing that desegregation should proceed "with all deliberate speed" but offering no further stipulations. The KDOE then issued a directive for all school districts to follow suit (in some fashion). However, since the court's language appeared vague about the timetable for implementing integration (how to define "deliberate?"), the KDOE directed all school districts to, at minimum, begin studying ways of carrying out the court's rulings, including working with community leaders.[14] Therefore, for many school districts, "with all deliberate speed" began with prolonged desultory, indeliberate "study."

The KDOE advisory was probably why the Greenville Board of Education voted unanimously (on September 8, 1955) to send Superintendent O. L. Adams to the desegregation workshop for school officials in Louisville on September 11-12. The next move of the Greenville School Board, also on September 8, recommended to itself that

> the Greenville City Board of Education comply with the [U.S.] Supreme Court's decision handed down May 17, 1954 and the Supreme Court's directive May 31, 1955 and in keeping with the State Board of Education Resolution of June 23, 1955 that local authorities proceed as rapidly *as conditions warrant*. Therefore, the Greenville City Board of Education approves the following plan to implement the program of integration.[15]

This official Greenville "plan to implement the program" entailed only one or two actions. First, it "request[ed] the [Greenville] Superintendent to begin a study of the Supreme Court decision on integration." Second, the Greenville School Board moved to

> authorize the [Greenville] Superintendent to cooperate with the Superintendent of Central City and the Muhlenberg County Superintendent in the appointment of an educational committee or committees to assist in making a study of local conditions and making recommendations as to the best procedure to conform to the [U.S.] Supreme Court's decision on integrating *as soon as local conditions permit*.[16]

Unfortunately, local records are rare to nonexistent for these three local school districts, with no information about the respective school committees (noted above), including whether they ever met. For instance, Muhlenberger native Jo McCown Ferguson, the state attorney general (1956-1961), pointed out that the Webster County School Board's integration planning committee never reported.[17] This lack of a committee planning report in Webster suggests that the three districts in Muhlenberg also had no "report," no "study," and no actual plans to implement school integration.

The Supreme Court's ambiguous wording of "all deliberate speed," with the state's guide to "begin studying" local circumstances, and the degree of probable local white opinion against integration favored a drawn-out timetable for dismantling school segregation in Muhlenberg. Accordingly, the Greenville School Board, as did the boards of the county and Central City, "studied" and stalled until "as conditions warrant[ed]" and "as soon as local conditions permit[ted]" (see above).

To use a sports analogy: The three Muhlenberg school districts awarded themselves a "bye" to the unscheduled integration finals. Regardless, the local boards remained on a go-slow or inactive status, like most of the state. As a result, it would take eight more years to integrate the three local school systems.

In the meantime, in some parts of the Bluegrass State, the rapidly developing era of school integration began immediately after the vague imperative of *Brown II*. Perhaps the first student to integrate into a white Kentucky high school was Lexington Douglass High School student Helen Carey Caise, who enrolled in a summer class at Lafayette High in 1955.[18] That fall, the first district to integrate was Wayne County (county seat: Monticello), in south-central Kentucky, which opened without incident. Simultaneously, the Lexington and Fayette County schools implemented an integration plan for students to choose schools to attend.[19] Across the Commonwealth, eighty-five schools integrated in 1955 without any reported problems.[20] Yet Muhlenberg and others delayed.

The NAACP devised a broad strategy. This civil-rights organization considered Kentucky key in the movement toward school integration that could influence other states—so thought Roy Wilkins of the NAACP's national office.[21] The state office carefully studied the situation and filed suit in federal court on September 1, 1955, against the Columbia School District in Adair County, based on its failure to plan for integration. Madisonville, Paducah, and Shelbyville also were considered for litigation due to their lack of plans. These districts objected to integration because they contended that their facilities were overcrowded, as had others.[22]

Many smaller districts in 1955, such as the three in Muhlenberg, remained on self-imposed standby status. However, the county must have felt the pressure since the Logan County schools in Adairville, Auburn, Lewisburg, Olmstead, and Russellville had integrated the following year. The integration of these Logan schools meant that by the fall of 1956, Lewisburg High, located just over the southern border with Muhlenberg, had integrated seven years before the process began seriously in Muhlenberg.

In that same year, out of 160 school districts in the state, 92 (58%) reported "mixed enrollments"; in other words, they had at least partially integrated. In eastern Kentucky, the schools in Prestonsburg opened with plans for partial integration. Western Kentucky, however, lagged the other state regions, as some communities developed "stout resistance."[23]

Nonetheless, several school districts in western Kentucky had some form of integration by the fall of 1956. These integrated county districts included Calloway, Daviess, Henderson, Logan, and McLean. The independent (city) districts that had integrated (usually partially) were Henderson, Marion, Mayfield, Murray, Owensboro, Paducah, and Russellville.[24] Additionally, Western Kentucky University integrated its 1956 summer school. However, as of March 1961, only twenty-two Black students were in its student body of 3,513.

After the *Brown II* ruling, the 1956-1957 school year developed as another strained time in western Kentucky. Several school districts suffered racial strife. In the fall of 1956, Louise Gordon listened apprehensively to her courageous ten-year-old son James ask about enrolling at Clay, the local all-white school in Webster County. "If you got the guts to go," she responded, "I got the guts to take ye."[25] Gordon twice attempted to register her two elementary children. Hostile crowds of a hundred locals, including the town mayor on the second occasion, turned her away. As a result, only the two Gordon children and a single white child attended school on the second day. The other students and about half the teachers absented themselves in protest of the two Black children's presence. A teacher, a Baptist preacher, resigned from his position, presumably to not have to instruct Black students.

That same year, ten students of color attempted to enroll at nearby Sturgis High in Union County. Angry crowds greeted them on the second day. White protesters burned a cross in a local town park a few days later. Governor Happy Chandler called out the State Police and mobilized the National Guard (with an Army tank) to Clay and Sturgis (about 11 miles from Clay) to protect the Black students enrolled in the two schools.[26]

Jo M. Ferguson espoused a different (and official) view as the state attorney general. Ferguson later admitted he was a "gradualist" regarding integration and preferred to delay further.[27] Ferguson argued that he presented a "solid legal opinion" and a "framework of legal reasoning" in 1956. He based it on this fundamental position: "The Supreme Court put primary responsibility of desegregation upon local boards of education."[28]

On this legality, Attorney General Ferguson ruled that those wanting to integrate their schools had no legal standing without an official plan devised by their local school boards. Therefore, since the school boards of Clay and Sturgis had no officially designed plans, these schools could legally deny admission to Black students. This ruling by the state attorney general put citizen efforts to integrate their schools in a Catch-22 bind. Citizen-led school integration could not occur without local school board plans. For this, many local school boards were not actively planning.

These two attempts at integration in Webster and Union counties were unsuccessful in that first year, 1956. The remedy for the students and parents? Attorney General Ferguson produced this official opinion: "The remedy at law, then, is for a parent or group of parents to petition a State or federal court to compel the [local] Board of Education to integrate."[29] This "remedy" is precisely the strategy subsequently pursued by these same parents and students, with the legal assistance of the Louisville NAACP. They filed suits against the boards of education of Webster and Union counties. Regarding this, Ferguson and probably many white Kentuckians were critical of the NAACP for inadvisably rushing, in their view, the statewide integration process.[30]

In December, in the next move, the U.S. District Court directed the Clay and Sturgis boards to submit integration strategies by early February 1957. Both school systems complied by providing plans. That fall, in 1957, Union and Webster integrated.[31] Additionally, a federal court ordered Adair, Hopkins, McCracken, and Scott counties to desegregate.[32] Muhlenberg and many other school districts were under no such court orders.

For some school districts, interscholastic sports yielded the first crack in the wall of school segregation. Muhlenberg citizens and school officials did not foresee the rapidly approaching state and local changes in the hallowed institution of hometown sports, which overcame the considerable inertia toward integration. This advent performed as the *deus ex machina* for which some were waiting. For the tardy local school officials, interscholastic sports supplied the initial outside force that descended onto the public stage. A 1959 study foretold this first fissure in Muhlenberg's school segregation wall. That study found that cross-racial sports had already blazed a successful path to racial integration nationwide.[33] Even so, from the 1874 opening of the first Black public school in Muhlenberg, eight decades of public school segregation had to be overcome in the 1960s.

The above points to the reinforced structures of American and Muhlenbergian culture that had to undergo a fundamental transformation. "Frankly speaking, for generations of Americans," historian Ibram X. Kendi remarks, "racist ideas have been their common sense."[34] Cultural inertia and racialized "common sense" had shored up the wall of segregation. Nevertheless, as it played out, the cultural institution of sports—professional, collegiate, and interscholastic—fractured its ancient edifice.

For the first time in late winter 1958, the Drakesboro Community High School Buffaloes boys' basketball team played a local white squad. Their opponent was the Graham Nighthawks. The venue was the district boys' basketball tournament.[35] The timing came after the Kentucky High School Athletics Association (KHSAA) allowed accredited Black high schools to join the association and participate in tournaments at the state level for the first time. If permitted to participate at the state level, logic dictated (and the KHSAA demanded) that Black teams compete in local tournaments.

From 1930 to the end of World War II, Drakesboro Community graduated only one to five male students in most years.[36] However, as early as 1948, this Black school had varsity boys basketball teams with a coach and student managers.[37] Thus, from 1948 (or earlier) until spring 1958, officials did not permit Drakesboro Community to play ball in the gymnasiums of the white schools. Consequently, the local newspapers kept them off their sports pages, thus rendering them partially invisible to the public.

After 37 years in existence—located just six miles from Greenville, seven miles down U.S. 431 from Central City, and in the same town as the all-white Drakesboro High—county officials finally allowed Drakesboro Community to play ball against white local sports teams. Tangible to a basketball-loving populace, the 1958 district tournament developed as the first official step of Muhlenberg's postwar civil rights era. However, metaphorically, this era began as a jump ball. The outcome at that moment was contested and in some doubt.

The first public pronouncement of this crack in the masonry of school segregation appeared in the *Central City Messenger* in early 1958. The headline announced simply: "Graham to Play Negroes in District." The article explained that the Graham Nighthawks would become the first white Muhlenberg school "to meet an all-Negro team."[38] It was the opening round of the 1958 district tournament. But it was also the opening round of school integration. Still, it would take another six years after the 1958 tournament before Muhlenberg partially integrated its schools.

Nineteen fifty-eight became a watershed time, giving more public presence to the previously partially invisible. In the same edition as the sports headline and announcement above, the Central City newspaper ran a story and photo, uncharacteristically, of a non-sports event at Drakesboro Community. This article pictured and captioned the crowning of the homecoming queen and her escort.[39] Some weeks later, on January 20, the same paper began covering the basketball games of the Black school. (In its regular-season schedule, DCHS competed only with other Black teams in western Kentucky.) The following week, the Central City newspaper published a photo of the Drakesboro Community boys' basketball team.

In its sports and student events, this more significant local press coverage of Drakesboro Community mirrored a broader shift in public visibility and societal changes throughout the nation. Although the local schools had not yet integrated, minor signals showed that the wider society had changed in a few racial matters. For example, in 1958, the Chicago Cubs' Ernie Banks became the National League's home-run champion and Most Valuable Player. Concert singer Paul Robeson sang in a sold-out, one-person recital at Carnegie Hall with a newly reinstated passport. On the other hand, it was also when Arkansas Democratic governor Orval Faubus, under pressure from militant segregationists, closed the four Little Rock high schools for the 1958-1959 school year for all students. That same year, Virginia Democratic senator Harry F. Byrd, Sr., announced his "massive resistance" strategy against school integration, culminating in many school closings, including an entire school district.

As with many other school districts, Muhlenberg did not integrate until the fall of 1963. Even then, it came at the pressuring directive of the state Board of Education. The timing was critical. The *Central City Messenger* broke the news to the public on August 8, 1963. This article disclosed that the KDOE had sent letters to the boards of the three districts in the county. These letters strongly hinted that state funding might not be forthcoming if they did not immediately implement integration.

After receiving the KDOE letter two days earlier, the Central City School Board voted to integrate grades seven through twelve. Its official release claimed that its decision resulted from pressure from the KDOE. Although six Black students had already enrolled, the Greenville Board had not met. Moreover, according to the letter, the county district had never submitted the required plan for eventual integration. (Greenville and Central City had plans on file.) However, the state classified these three districts as "emergency" since they had procrastinated until the last moment.[40] With school scheduled to open on the 26th—nine years after *Brown I*—the three districts had just two weeks to plan and implement school integration.[41]

Like Owensboro High, in the fall of 1963, local school officials selected students to transfer from Drakesboro Community to Greenville

High (GHS) for their academic or athletic abilities.[42] The same pattern prevailed in Louisville, where officials "carefully selected" the Black students to attend the white schools. Many of these pioneering students possessed outstanding athletic abilities, a feature "all too common in Louisville." Nonetheless, academics also counted. The students of color attending Male High were academically sound. And they scored high on intelligence tests—"a surprise to many whites."[43]

On the other hand, unlike the restrictive selection procedure used by Greenville, Owensboro, and Louisville schools, the small influx of students of color transferring from Drakesboro Community to CCHS included only those living within the district boundary. In 1963, Black students in CCHS's seven grades numbered thirty-eight.[44]

Several regional and nearby districts had already integrated. So, why did the three in Muhlenberg (and other locales) dawdle until the 11th hour to integrate? Local teacher Leslie Shively Smith remarked that officials had made "plans" in 1955 to "slowly desegregate" the county's three school districts.[45] She might be mistaken about these "plans" unless she meant that the county officials intended to integrate only at some vague, unstipulated future time.

With numerous school districts integrating across the Commonwealth beginning in 1955, including a few near Muhlenberg (e.g., Butler County in the fall of 1959), was something unusual in the generalized Muhlenberger mental makeup involving racial issues? Where were the church pastors and other civic leaders, Black and white, who could have called for the county to keep pace with much of the Bluegrass State in the inexorable march toward integration? Did the county continue along the same course of Reconstruction's dashed hopes, sentimental Southernization, and segregationist Jim Crowism into the 1950s and 1960s?

The investigator must consider two possibilities besides the underlying commitment to racial apartheid. Jo M. Ferguson learned through a local informant that the "leader of the black educators" in Muhlenberg—Mittie Keown Render—"deliberately delayed desegregation" in the early 1960s. Why? Ferguson surmised that Render wanted a delay "to make it possible for the [Black and white] kids to get along" when integration finally came. However, officials in Muhlenberg and other locales—except for the glaring events at Clay and Sturgis—could see school integration proceeding across the state with "surprising ease."[46] Second, Ferguson thought Render wanted to "make it possible for Negro teachers to hold their jobs awhile."[47]

We have only Ferguson's testimony, relying on his single local informant, that Mittie K. Render's views were correctly transmitted and understood. Render (1895-1999) became a respected Black educator and a member of the Muhlenberg Community Hospital Board, with a street named for her in Central City.[48] Due to her elevated status, Ferguson assumed Render controlled local integration, at least among her fellow Black teachers. Alternatively, perhaps Render accurately reflected the worries of Black teachers losing their teaching positions in a future integrated arrangement. That Render had much say in the official decision-making seems improbable. However, on the other hand, Ferguson may have spoken of her as a figure representative of all

Black teachers in the county, most of whom, we can presume, wanted to retain their teaching jobs.

Even if accurate, the question hinges on whether the white public school officials took Black teachers' views and livelihoods seriously. Because statewide, they mostly did not. However, another local Black teacher acknowledged they fretted over losing their jobs. Nonetheless, she maintains that most Black Muhlenberger teachers transferred into the now-integrated schools.[49] Leslie Shively Smith confirms that ten Black teachers were absorbed into the three county districts by the beginning of the 1965-1966 school year.[50] If so, perhaps the Muhlenberg district administrators proved more progressive than others. Nevertheless, these questions remain unresolved since investigators cannot adequately assess the forces arrayed against integration in Muhlenberg with so few primary sources.

Nonetheless, the Kentucky Commission on Human Rights points out that Black teachers "became the real losers" in desegregation. When schools integrated, the Black teachers "took [i.e., were assigned] a back seat."[51] Many left the teaching profession, and others moved out of state. From 1956 to 1970, the number of Black teachers in the Commonwealth increased by only 120 (from 1,439 to 1,559, an increase of 7.7%). However, Black students increased by 24,429 (40,000 to 64,429), 61 percent. In this same period, the teacher ratio of Black teachers to Black students dropped substantially from 1:28 to 1:41.[52]

About Muhlenberg, Jo M. Ferguson asserted, "I was proud of my own county" for its gradualist, non-confrontational approach.[53] Other local stakeholders felt similarly. After a month of school integration, the *Greenville Leader* editorialized its evaluation. "[T]he superb manner in which we have resolved, at least partially, the question of school integration is to be commended," the editorial reads. "There is, perhaps, no area in the nation which has gone about the process with more cool-headedness, moral precision, or common good sense" than Muhlenberg.[54]

However, with the delay of almost a decade, even though most school districts in the state had already integrated, including several surrounding ones, the "superb manner" and "common good sense" evidently required a long time to formulate. Moreover, one questions the "moral precision" applied to the failure to rehire any experienced Black teachers. With resonant precedents, this neglect was a statewide policy failure and a personal misfortune for many.

As already explained, the limited hiring of the existing Black teachers in the state was a policy failure in the face of their generally higher qualifications as a teaching corps. For example, more Black teachers held advanced college degrees in 1955-1956 than white teachers.[55] However, besides losing their jobs, the more significant failure was the future loss of the positive role modeling that those teachers of color historically furnished to the Black students and, not to be lost in the analysis, would have provided to white students, too. "Black teachers became the epitome of respectability," observes a historian, "the embodiment of the anti-[Black]-menace."[56] Their absence from schools after integration reverberated as a cultural loss for all Black and white stakeholders.

In 1961-1962, seven years after the *Brown I* ruling, only 119 Black teachers in seventeen districts had found employment in integrated schools.[57] For years after integration in Muhlenberg, students went through 12 years of schooling without ever experiencing a Black teacher in their classrooms.[58] This development points to how the once-honored Black professional teaching corps, which enveloped the Black community in its social embrace, "died with *Brown*."[59] Perhaps this is what Mittie K. Render and the other Black teachers in Muhlenberg and western Kentucky foresaw as they delayed the onset of integration (if they did). They sensed the coming erosion of Black culture and community.

The discussion above presented three possible reasons (albeit with sparse evidence) for local Black citizens' desire to delay school integration if they indeed did. To summarize the reasons for the delay: So Black teachers could retain their teaching positions, to allow more time for Black and white school children to "get along," and to preserve for a while longer a cultural institution—Drakesboro Community—that functioned as the social glue for the countywide Black populace.

However, a corollary fourth reason is possible. Render and the other Black teachers and community stakeholders believed Drakesboro Community was not a learning institution inferior to white schools. Additionally, Black schools supplied advantages not found in white schools. If this was their thinking, it contradicted the very basis of the 1954 *Brown I* Supreme Court ruling. The court decreed that separate Black schools were unequal and thus unconstitutional; they were also presumed deficient. Indeed, this "deficiency view" of Black schools was valid in many states and districts in the Deep South and northern cities due to their sharply inequitable funding. To be sure, the 1896 *Plessy* ruling raised white supremacy to the level of a Supreme Court decree. (The lone dissenter was Justice John Marshall Harlan of Kentucky.[60]) Moreover, "separate but equal" never intended to achieve equity in schools, public transportation, or anywhere else.

Nonetheless, one could make the case that Drakesboro Community's buildings were generally comparable to the white schools. Moreover, the Black teacher staff may have been superior in some ways. Render and the other Black stakeholders may have understood this. They were not alone. Doris Wilkinson, a University of Kentucky sociology professor who attended all-Black schools pre-*Brown* in Lexington, was similarly skeptical. She speculated: "Was the dismantling of the Black segregated school a 'necessary and sufficient' condition for structural [racial] integration?" She concluded that the "demolition of the black school has had a devastating impact on African American children."[61] One way to look at their loss—like the Black Dunham High School students in Jenkins (Letcher County): They "lost a space of their own." [62]

With the prospect of disbanding Drakesboro Community and the likely fraying of the Black community's fabric, integration might not have been a welcome prospect to local Black leaders. Moreover, officials gave no thought to the rich heritage of Drakesboro Community as a cultural institution of Black identity and pride or the importance of its positive adult role modeling. As a Black student in the county's only Black high school during the early 1960s observed: "The education at

Drakesboro Community was good." Why? "The teachers were caring and helpful. I just don't think we could have had any better teachers. They did well with the means that they had [which were] not as much as the [white] other schools."[63] Her view matches the evidence that, across the Commonwealth, Black teachers were, on average, better educated than white teachers.[64] They may also have been more nurturing, as required by a segregated society.

Today, education observers would retrospectively apply a term developed by American pedagogical theorist Gloria Ladson-Billings that Drakesboro Community provided a "culturally relevant pedagogy" to its students.[65] Furthermore, no review looked at the social psychology of Black students moving from a nurturing environment to a scenario where they were minorities, often ignored, sometimes unwelcomed, with little nurturance from the white administrations and faculty.[66] In other words, "the way integration always worked," as Barack Obama wrote before becoming president, was a "one-way street. The minority assimilated into the dominant culture, not the other way around."[67]

Historians have other ways to examine the theory justifying school integration as presented (but disregarded) by the Supreme Court in the *Brown* ruling. Sherrilyn Ifill, legal theorist and head of the NAACP Legal Defense and Educational Fund (LDF), writes that the Warren Court ignored the expert testimony in LDF's 1954 legal brief. Instead, the nine justices united around recognizing segregation as a form of racial subordination and an "affront to black citizenship."[68] "Segregation of White and colored children," the unanimous Court wrote, "has a detrimental effect upon the colored children." Ifill asks her listeners (at a 2015 lecture) to pause momentarily on that powerful legal and social stance that she says is "so glaringly asymmetrical." Ifill explains: "There's a missing part to the equation, more important than the narrative about how segregation harms black children." What might this be? "The missing narrative," she reasons, "is about the way in which segregation harmed and harms white children." In 1954, the LDF presented to the Supreme Court the conclusions, signed by thirty social scientists, of segregation's psychic harm to white children—how it distorts their self-conceptualization, ideas of personal status, and views on authority, justice, and fair play. The scholars warned the Court: "Some individuals may attempt to resolve this conflict [between moral, religious, and democratic ideals, on the one hand, and social reality, on the other] by intensifying their hostility toward the minority group."[69]

The Warren Court justices ignored this expert testimony. Ifill thinks their oversight was "monumental." She concludes: "The result is that the entire project of desegregation and of integration is described, understood, and internalized as a project to help black people, to help little black children with their self-esteem, to restore the dignity of black people."[70] Indeed, it does this, but the justices flubbed the opportunity to prepare "white children for citizenship in a pluralistic society."[71] With this, the nation headed down a path less united than if the desegregation equation had been more symmetrical regarding the benefits for Black and white children. Later generations have suffered from it.

Chapter 13

RESISTANCE AND CHANGE

For there is reciprocal relationship between truth about the past and justice in the present.[1]

Local newspapers, as cultural artifacts—in this case, the *Greenville Leader* and the *Central City Messenger* and *Times-Argus*—serve as rhetorical platforms that provide insight into complex social histories. For example, when the local editorial discussed in the previous chapter lauds the "cool-headedness" of the white citizenry for not obstructing integration, it references the previously widely publicized school problems in Clay and Dixon (and possibly to the events five years before in Arkansas and Virginia where schools were closed for everyone). An observer could conclude that many, if not most, white Muhlenbergers were pleased with the "superb" process of school integration in the three county districts. However, in this complicated social history of the nine years from *Brown I* to the Muhlenberg school integration in the fall of 1963, we do not have any contemporary primary accounts about the thoughts and attitudes of Black countians. No rhetorical platform, such as a local newspaper, was there to capture their views.

White fury was rampant across much of the South. On that ground, the *Greenville Leader* editorial welcomed the nonconfrontational orderliness of the local school integration. However, on the same day as the editorial in that paper (Sept. 5, 1963), George Corley Wallace (1919-1998), the governor of Alabama, in a *New York Times* interview, contended that "society is coming apart at the seams." To counter integration and his notion of social disintegration, he advised: "What this country needs is a few first-class funerals."[2]

Ten days after Gov. Wallace's ominous utterance and the Greenville editorial, Klan vigilantes killed four Black schoolgirls in the Birmingham bombing at the 16th Street Baptist Church before their Sunday morning worship service. In light of these shocking events, and without knowledge of personal microaggressions in some schools, it is little wonder that local leaders welcomed what appeared to be the positive uneventfulness of Muhlenberg's school integration.[3]

During the intense struggles in the twentieth century, organized civic activism occurred in some areas of western Kentucky, particularly Hopkinsville. An Owensboro Human Rights Commission member thinks that no local citizens or financial support went to the Montgomery Bus Boycott (Dec. 5, 1955, to Dec. 20, 1956). "Owensboro was always laid-back," he recalled, "subdued, kind of disconnected from the [civil rights] movement."[4] However, on March 5, 1964, a delegation from Owensboro joined 10,000 others in the March on Frankfort. Also attending were Baseball Hall of Famer Jackie Robinson, folk singers Peter, Paul and Mary, Dr. M. L. King, Jr., and Georgia Davis Powers, who became the first person of color elected to the Kentucky state senate, serving from 1968 to 1989. This march called attention to the public accommodations law the General Assembly was considering. (It did not pass.)[5]

No Black Butler Countians took part directly in the civil rights movement.[6] However, at least one Central Citian, Dorothy Mae (Alexander) Woods (1923-2011), a granddaughter of enslaved ancestors and niece of the publicly executed Harrison Alexander, joined the March on Washington for Jobs and Freedom on August 28, 1963. Woods proudly recollects: "My most memorable civic duty was the day we marched on Washington, D.C., on Aug. 18 [*sic*], 1963. We were standing near the Lincoln Memorial reflecting pool when the Rev. Dr. Martin Luther King, Jr., delivered his 'I Have a Dream' speech. That day, I shall never forget."[7] Alexander may not have been close enough to hear singer Mahalia Jackson, standing close to Rev. King, say to him, when his address was struggling to move his audience, "Tell 'em about the dream, Martin." At that moment, he rose above his text to speak soaring "words of American scripture." Indeed, as historian Jon Meacham marveled, King "lift[ed] his speech from the ordinary to the historic, from the mundane to the sacred."[8] King drew a straight line from Thomas Jefferson's momentous first sentence of the second paragraph of the Declaration of Independence—"We hold these truths to be self-evident, that all men are created equal"—to Lincoln's oratory at Gettysburg.

In the 1960s, besides the few peaceful protests in Hopkinsville, only a few efforts for school integration appeared in the western region.[9] Still, the lack of local direct action did not mean unawareness of events in other parts of the country. To be sure, "activism" must have arisen in the minds of every Black citizen who kept informed of national affairs. They watched closely while most agitation and public advocacy occurred in the more populous southern cities of Atlanta, Birmingham, Montgomery, Memphis, and Louisville. Indeed, national events prompted much notice and discussion within Black homes, churches, and organizations.

Reason dictates that there was intense emotional involvement, even from a distance. After all, the struggle for Black inclusion captured the nation's attention and directly touched many lives—and indirectly affected everyone—as this and the previous chapter have shown. Whether people of color in western Kentucky directly participated in political activities or only followed closely through local and national channels of communication, the success of the movement, in time, engendered within them the "psychological triumph" so often heralded by Rev. King.[10]

The local "triumph" was still in the making in August 1963. At this point, the Central City weekly newspaper interjected itself as a factor in the public discourse. Perhaps it was the last gasp of resistance to integration or only a yellow journalistic move for sensationalized attention. Regardless, after the first week of local school integration, the front page of the next issue blared these intentionally provocative headlines in oversized type, four columns wide: "Greenville Negro Dances With Greenville White Girls at Dance Saturday." These incendiary headlines occupied more page space than the text, which read:

When Central City [schools] integrated last week, it didn't take long to *go full circle* and integrate socially as well as scholastically.

Less than one week to be exact.

For the first time in history Central City schools were integrated when school opened on Monday, Aug. 26 [1963].

The first school dance, held on Friday night was also integrated. Then on Saturday night, with the assistance of several Greenville High School students, the Central City Youth Center was totally integrated.

Although students of both races were present at the high school dance [the previous night], they remained segregated while dancing.

But on Saturday night at the Youth Center dance, one Greenville High School negro boy and several Greenville High School white girls completed the social integration by dancing together. The Greenville students, of both races, were visitors at the Central City Youth Center.

Although the Youth Center is located in the City Building, and is operated by Councilman Joe Oates, it is financed primarily by donations from private individuals and businesses.

Although the Youth Center has no particular policy on integration, the situation never having come up before, Mayor Robert Wheeldon said that he guessed that if the negroes wanted to attend that they would have to be permitted to do so.[11]

Tellingly, the racially conservative Central City newspaper's house-style printed "Negro" with lower-case *n*, reflecting an editorial decision stemming from its social views. By 1930, the *New York Times* had changed its house style to capitalize "Negro" after intense lobbying by the NAACP. The paper clarified its position: "In our Style Book,

Negro is now added to the list of words to be capitalized. It is not merely a typographical change, it is an act in recognition of racial self-respect for those who have been for generations in the 'lower case.'"[12]

Thirty-three years after the influential *New York Times* style guide changed its spelling "in recognition of racial self-respect," the Central City newspaper still "lower-cased" countians of color. In capitalization and lower-casing, these two publications registered their respective and opposing journalistic social policies and social constructionist views of the racial issue. In this matter, the cultural landscape of the color line materialized in newspaper spelling.

In its September 12 follow-up story, the Central City paper interviewed a "delegation" of six white male Greenville youths who had attended the Youth Center dance two weeks before.[13] This group felt compelled to visit the newspaper's office to present its case about the now-sensationalized cross-racial dancing. Their main points were that white youths from Central City asked the Black Greenvillian to leave the venue, but he ignored the request. Second, he had twice "butted in" on their group dancing, and each time, the white youths sat down in response. Their explanation deflected the responsibility onto the Black teen. Also, the delegation probably intended this as a central angle to their story: "At no time did any Greenville white girl dance alone with the negro boy from Greenville." [14]

The editors attached an astonishing comment to this second article that also performed as an editorial. First, the newspaper declared that the cross-racial dance incident "has caused a lot of commotion" in the county. (More accurate is that the news article itself created much of the "commotion.") Next, this editor's note explained that the newspaper's policy was to "present all the news as it happens" in the county. This comment hides that the editors selected what constituted "news." Furthermore, if the article offended any Greenville residents, the newspaper was "sorry," it said (perhaps disingenuously). However, the editorial quickly added that the Black youth did, without question, "dance with Greenville white girls—even if it were only for a short time."[15]

This newspaper suggested that the white Greenville parents "should be proud of their children" because "they did sit down and refuse to dance" with the Black youth. Moreover, they should have been pleased that the delegation of six "so ably" and maturely presented its case. Finally, in this long comment, the editors announced their segregationist stance. "We believe that social integration [of Black and white youth] should be nipped in the bud at the very beginning and not wait until it has gotten out of hand. The people of Muhlenberg County are dead set against the mixing of races socially and no Supreme Court highhanded order can change this."[16]

The *Central City Messenger*'s comment about private donations providing the Youth Center's operating expenses looks to have been a strategy to encourage citizens to pressure the Youth Center management. To do what? To change its racial inclusion policy (which had remained untested until two weeks earlier). If nothing else, the newspaper mirrored racially conservative views in the community—perhaps only a segment but possibly more widely held.

On the other hand, the Greenville newspaper took a different tack, as its editorial noted above shows. Its published opinion appeared the same day as the initial inflammatory article in the *Central City Messenger*. The Greenville paper spoke of "cool-headedness," "moral precision," and "common good sense" exhibited by the community in implementing a relatively smooth process of school integration.[17] These opposing editorial positions point to at least two sides and some citizens' contention over the local advent of racial integration in schools and elsewhere.

In truth, the Central City newspaper's dissenting, racially conservative views were more widely held locally and across the Commonwealth. Two months before the Youth Center integration, Democratic governor Bert T. Combs issued his highly controversial executive order of June 26, 1963. This order ended racial discrimination in all professions and public establishments requiring state licensing. However, local and statewide political forces mobilized against it.

The Muhlenberg County Republican Campaign Committee ran a large, quarter-page advertisement in the *Central City Messenger* that attacked the governor's executive order. The political ad emblazoned these headlines: "EXECUTIVE ORDER…a Danger to YOUR Freedom." It pointed out: "Rule by executive decree, if permitted to stand, sounds the death knell to the Freedoms of all Kentuckyians" [*sic*]. The advertisement warned: "The Department of Economic Security this week filed regulations, effective September 1, banning discrimination in personal-care homes for the aged." [And] "Enforcement has already begun—on those too old and feeble to vote in large numbers." Quoting

U.S. News and World Report, the ad also proclaimed: "The [Combs executive] Order is described as one of the most sweeping rules of its kind. Persons denied service for racial reasons could complain to the licensing agency. Action to suspend or revoke the license could follow."[18] The specific scare that the ad promoted was multiracial nursing homes.

Muhlenberg's Republican campaign committee's paid political advertisement invoked a national connection by claiming that Combs and Democratic gubernatorial candidate Ned Breathitt (Hopkinsville) had traveled to Washington to confer with the Kennedy brothers—Robert, the attorney general, and John, the president. Supposedly, they strategized about the executive order and approaching state elections. Additionally, the ad pointed to Attorney General Kennedy's praise (on July 1, before the U.S. Senate Commerce Committee) of Governor Combs's efforts to protect and promote Black Kentuckians' civil rights.

Concerning state politics, a national journal labeled Republican Louie B. Nunn's 1963 campaign against Breathitt "the first outright segregationist campaign in Kentucky."[19] In an imaginative ploy to win votes, candidate Nunn appeared on television with a Bible and American flag. He declared, "My first act will be to abolish this," pointing to the Combs civil rights executive order. The local political ad in the Central City newspaper was part of the Nunn anti-civil rights campaign tactic targeting the western region.[20]

Nonetheless, Nunn lost statewide by 13,055 votes but won Butler and Ohio counties and Muhlenberg, 4,672 to 3,867. Every county to the west went for Breathitt except Crittenden. The local Republican candidates mentioned in the political ad—for sheriff, circuit court clerk, and state representative—won their respective elections.[21]

However, contra the statement above, this statewide campaign was not the first to use racially alarmist rhetoric. It mirrored the local Democratic politicking during the Negro Equality Panic of temporally distant 1865-1870. Even though they were almost a century apart, significant public segments used the same rhetoric of white grievance in both eras. In 1870, the Democrats ran on a "White Man's Ticket."[22] The 1963 Republicans, without outright acknowledgment, also constructed a white citizen's party platform. In its two articles above, the Central City newspaper bellowed its twentieth-century version of "dark forebodings of a fearful future"—the words used to describe the events of 1870.[23]

Furthermore, the Central City newspaper's 1963 editorial rhetoric paralleled some of the political stump speeches of 1870. For example, at an 1870 political debate at the county courthouse lawn, Col. S. P. Love, the Democratic candidate for a second term as county judge, asked the crowd: "Do you want to see your sons making love to negro wenches and taking them for wives?"[24] Similarly, almost a century later, the 1963 Central City paper drew attention to integrated dancing to pressure its readers to "nip ['the social integration'] in the bud at the very beginning and not wait until it has gotten out of hand."[25] The same white psychosexual racial fears in Muhlenberg were at play almost a century apart.

The two eras of the 1870s and the 1960s demonstrate how political attitudes persist over time. People maintain attitudes and beliefs across generations through what scholars label as *behavioral path dependence*—the direct, generation-to-generation, downstream socialization of community norms and traditions.[26] When a social form develops as a fundamental part of a culture, it regenerates in successive generations. The account above of the two eras demonstrates the same discourse that echoes similar racial attitudes and beliefs that come down to today through pathways of historical persistence. To this historical continuity, we can add the enduring influences of the six-decade-long institution of human bondage. These antecedent conditions of racial enslavement leading to the postwar Jim Crow social order set the stage for the long-continuing racial hierarchy of dominator culture that continued into the twentieth century.[27]

Did the local and statewide 1870 Democratic and 1963 Republican campaigns show similarities in racial rhetoric? Yes. Were they successful? Democratic Col. Love won his 1870 run for a second judgeship term. In his October 17, 1963, "Mulebergers" column, the Central City paper's co-editor pointed to a seismic political shift at the local Republican county meeting a few weeks earlier. "When [Republican County] Chairman W. D. Bratcher of Greenville asked all the Democrats to stand at the dinner," reported the columnist, "at least a third of the total attendance stood up."[28]

These numbers—112 out of 344—illustrate that local white Democrats were streaming to the Republican Party, presaging the changes in political identification throughout the South that would be completed in western Kentucky, according to Muhlenberger historian George Humphreys, in the 1994 election cycle.[29] A few weeks before the Republican county meeting, Rev. M. L. King, Jr., gave his "I Have a Dream" speech to a national audience and a quarter-million attendees in front of the Lincoln Memorial. His speech, perhaps, was an influencing factor locally in that defining year of the struggle for racial equality and democracy.

After most Congressional Republicans voted for the Civil Rights Act of 1964 (and Southern Democrats mostly against it), on July 15, the Republican Party nominated Sen. Barry Goldwater for president. The Arizona senator had voted against this landmark legislation based on states' rights. The Goldwater campaign opened the door for segregationist Democrats to shift en masse to the Republicans, culminating in 1968 with the Republican Richard Nixon's "Solid South" campaign. Consequently, the Southern Democrats' defection heralded a racial realignment, with the two parties switching positions on Black civil rights.[30] Nevertheless, Democrats Lyndon Johnson and Hubert Humphrey carried Muhlenberg (65.9% to Goldwater's 33.9%) in 1964. The two Democrats won in ninety-nine of the 120 Kentucky counties and forty-four states, except five in the Deep South and Goldwater's home state of Arizona.

We can construe 1865-1870 and 1954-1963 as bookends for the intervening geohistorical setting. This long span of years included the white panic and rage during Reconstruction. It also entailed the reassertion of white "redeemer" politics that led to the racial terror during Jim Crowism, the anti-Black brutality in the Tobacco Wars

(1906-1915), and the racial persecution by the Possum Hunters (1914-1916). The economic hardships after World War I and during the Great Depression appeared next on the horizon. Finally, after World War II, the resistance to freedom struggles merely continued the racial marginalization that was always a cultural undercurrent if not fully displayed.

Although the 1964 Kentucky civil rights bill did not pass, Congress passed the federal civil rights bill a few months later. President Lyndon Johnson signed it into law. The two Kentucky senators (Republicans) voted for it, as did one (a Democrat) of the five Kentucky members of Congress. This national legislation set the stage for a more robust Kentucky bill in 1966. This time, it readily passed the General Assembly with Democratic Gov. Ned Breathitt's enthusiastic support. The governor signed this bill into law in the Capitol rotunda under the visage of the statue of Abraham Lincoln.[31]

For the 1966 local elections, the Muhlenberg Republican Party printed a pamphlet delineating its 14-point political platform. Contrary to its 1963 scaremongering advertisement, this one dealt with administrative efficiency and pledges of effective local governance. This circular did not address racial issues, school integration, or nondiscrimination requirements for licensing the professions (both *faits accomplis*).[32] In racial matters, the Commonwealth had moved on. As already noted, in 1963, Louie Nunn lost his campaign for the governorship. However, four years later, he won that office, the first Republican since 1947.

In 1967, more local political changes appeared when Earl Frazier joined the Drakesboro City Council as Muhlenberg's first elected Black official. Drakesborans voted in Councilman Frazier for the four following terms. The second Black official was Edgar T. "Trib" Reynolds, elected unopposed to the Greenville City Council from 1968 to 1974.[32] Reynolds operated a barbershop in downtown Greenville.

In 1974, in that time of growing political openness, the county sheriff appointed Willie Parker, Jr., deputy sheriff. The following year, local electorates voted two more Black countians into office: Bobby McCoy to the Drakesboro city council and Bernes L. Bibbs to the Greenville city council.[34] In the 1970s, Drakesborans elected Rev. Dan Washington (1906-1994) to the Drakesboro city council. He also served as one of its police commissioners.[35] In 1982, when they elected him mayor, Washington was one of only three Black mayoral Kentuckians.[36]

Even though political equality was then in its opening stages, historical continuity exerted social inertia behind the scenes. For instance, in 1969, a special correspondent for the *New York Times* visited the Reynolds barbershop and pointed out his election as the first citizen of color on the city council. However, according to that correspondent, his election victory occurred in "a community where race relations, while essentially of the Old South variety characterized by the frequent use of 'colored folk' and '[N-word]' and similar verbalisms, are nonetheless cordial."[37] Polite racial relations seemed well on the surface, but some continuing racial animus lurked beneath the surface.

That same year, the Greenville post of the Veterans of Foreign Wars (VFW) called off a membership drive, not wanting to attract veterans of color returning from the Vietnam War. Nonetheless, the local post festooned downtown with American flags for Veterans Day.[38] Again, this act illustrates that racial attitudes lagged even as political rights progressed.

Three seemingly unrelated events described below shared a commonality. They reflected the nation's social changes in the twentieth century, especially in the decades after World War II. Notwithstanding the fearmongering in the Central City newspaper about cross-racial dancing, each instance hints that the Muhlenbergian sociopolitical structure incorporated some acceptance of Black equality. As the Central City news article accurately portrayed, albeit in a direful tone of warning: Social integration was now coming "full circle."

First, former Central City mayor Hugh Sweatt relates a positive cross-racial occurrence that transcended the unwritten racial rules in the 1950s:

> I (like many of you) remember the old State Theater [in Central City]. I never saw a lot of Blacks in there because most were so dirt poor they couldn't afford to go. I remember Blacks (they were called 'Coloreds' in those days [the 1950s]) had to sit up in the balcony. Even then, it seemed strange to me that I could go and sit up there with Elwood [Pendleton] but he couldn't come downstairs and sit with me. I'm not sure whether they could purchase 'goodies' from the concession stand but I doubt they could.

None of them I knew had money to 'squander' on luxuries like that. Usually, I'd get a box of Milk Duds and we'd share them.[39]

In the second circumstance, school library services continued to improve for students of color throughout the twentieth century. By 1935, and presumably after that, Drakesboro Community designated someone as a librarian or a teacher-librarian. The Black Greenville Training School had a librarian or teacher-librarian by 1941. For the Black public, the Central City public library in 1953 and the Muhlenberg branch library in Greenville in 1956 belatedly began unrestricted services to Black patrons.[40] Consider the timeline: For over five decades of the twentieth century, Muhlenberg's citizens of color could not borrow a book from the local libraries.

Finally, the year before both the integration of local schools and the erection of the historical marker dedicated to Confederate General Nathan Bedford Forrest on the lawn of the county courthouse, a professional Black baseball team, the famous Indianapolis Clowns, rolled into Central City, on June 30, 1962, for a night game at the city ballpark.[41] For some decades, the Clowns had been barnstorming across the country. By 1962, they played a full schedule against other teams in the Negro American League and a combination of local semi-pro and amateur teams and their co-traveling team, the New York Stars.

On that day, the interim business manager (son of the long-time owner Syd Pollock) spoke with an unnamed, eighty-plus-year-old, lifelong Black resident of Central City. The latter walked the short distance from Colored Town. The two talked for over an hour, exchanging stories about their lives and families. The elderly Central Citian became tearful when Pollock shook hands with him. "What's wrong?" Pollock asked. "First time in my whole life a white man done shook my hand," the Black man declared. "Your skin don't feel no different than mine, only just younger."[42]

In this vignette, the response of the Black Central Citian demonstrates that the short walking distance on the physical landscape from Colored Town belied the vast social space long established in the cultural landscape. However, the Black/white handshake also illustrates that broad geographic and social distances could be overcome, at least in personal interactions. This handshake bridged the social and spatial divides across the color line at that moment.[43]

This unnamed elderly Black man knew separation and social distance. However, with profound social and legal changes peering just over the horizon, he also experienced a moment when he became more than mere second-class color. He witnessed the hierarchical apartheid society overcoming some of its socio-spatial divisions. The Black resident became, for that one moment, a Muhlenberger, a man in full standing. Moreover, it was a sign that, in Muhlenberg and elsewhere, social and political changes were rapidly approaching.

However, this incident showed two-way meaning-making, not only because the Black man supposedly needed validation from a white man. But because Pollock, the white man, was just as validated as the elderly Black man by their egalitarian communication. Assuredly, the lifeworlds of the two were immensely different. Nonetheless, this episode "humanized" Pollack as much as the elderly person of color when they conversed on equal terms. On both sides, the event revealed itself as a psychic triumph. However, positional differences remained in their respective lifeworlds, as they did for society generally. Black novelist and essayist Ralph Ellison (1913-1994) spoke about how these positionings entered the individual psychologies of all Americans when he referred to the Black and white victims of "the American hierarchical psychosis."[44]

This vignette of the serendipitous encounter between the white, out-of-state businessman and the local Black man helps us gaze into a historical secret place of race relations. The known facts are few: A white out-of-towner meets a local person of color, and ordinary conversation ensues. They make a human connection, with the Black man touched by the encounter's uncanniness. The secret place of that event is its racialized uniqueness, as expressed by the unnamed Black man and exemplified by the handshake. For a moment in time, in the summer of 1962, two people transcended the borders of racial apartheid and hierarchy with the proxemics of a human handshake, communicating across the color line in the perennial but slowly changing cultural landscapes of western Kentucky.

EPILOGUE

History is always **now,** *even as it is also* **then.**[1]

As we uneasily traversed the Bluegrass State's unsanitized geohistorical landscape in this study, we saw that it appeared only vaguely familiar and, in some instances, as an outlandish place far away. Nonetheless, Kentucky it is—or was—even though perceptibly displaced in timespace.

The historical Black experience examined here suggested a worldview that psychiatrist and Nazi concentration camp survivor Viktor Frankl labeled *tragic optimism*. Frankl described it as "optimism in the face of tragedy." The personal will to create meaning requires courage and tenacity, particularly in the face of the massive adversity and tragic experiences this study has illuminated. Frankl learned that even in the environment of routine horror in Nazi concentration camps, maintaining affirmations of purpose led to a positive outlook on life. He understood that creating goals despite hopeless situations—a will-to-meaning—engendered transformative growth. Frankl realized life is—or can be—meaningful regardless of the circumstances. We can conclude that tragic optimism must have permeated the Black experience in America. How else could Du Bois write this at the end of his *The Souls of Black Folk* masterwork?—"My children, my little children, are singing to the sunshine."[2]

Individuals corral actual and imagined events from past and present lifeworlds to create meanings for their current frames of reference. For example, the General Nathan Bedford Forrest historical marker on Greenville's courthouse lawn is a material reality that promotes the racialization of that local landscape. This sign/symbol of a Confederate hero (earlier in his life, a prominent slave trader; postwar, a leader of the first Klan) presents an example of the racialized nature of local space. With the 1963 endeavor to erect the sign in his honor, authorities demonstrated the inherent cultural power of the "absent presence of whiteness."[3] The decision to create this marker in a public space came, perhaps not coincidentally, in the same year Muhlenberg schools integrated.

The Black/white handshake discussed above was also a documented historical event. However, that episode represents more than two individuals merely transcending the traditional geosocial divide of the color line. Why? Because the "making history" of cross-racial encounters, like the ballpark handshake, can serve as a plotline to narrativize present positive meanings, like "that fuller story" of America intoned by former First Lady Michelle Obama at the September 7, 2022, White House official portrait unveiling.

The cultural meanings and the racialized facets of the Muhlenbergian cultural landscape's autobiography have a long and arcing chronology. The story begins with the firstcomers' initial *cultural impress* on the landscape imported into the area from Virginia in 1795-1820. This cultural impress—the initial cultural lifeways that influenced later arrivals—included and depended on the institution of hereditary chattel bondage.[4]

Also existing as historical events were Muhlenberg's 1870 Negro Equality Panic, the Reconstruction lynchings in 1870 and 1874, the Possum Hunters' racial violence, the 1948 Confederate reenactment in Greenville, the blackface entertainment of the first half of the twentieth century, and the postwar segregationist, neo-Dixiecrat Central City newspaper.[5] The facticity and meanings of place events like these can revivify personal and communal worldviews if people use them as authentic building blocks of their historical comprehension. After all, as Abraham Lincoln admonished his "Fellow citizens": "[W]e cannot escape history."[6] In our era, journalist Michelle Norris expressed it like this: The "effort to sweep away an uncomfortable history is like trying to step out from under the sky. Go ahead and try. In the end, you can't escape."[7]

We must remind ourselves that the Black experience *is* American history under a single, shared sky. This reminder also applies to the local: Black Kentucky's past is an integral and necessary part of the state's history *in toto*. This study has illustrated that the historiography could not separate Black and white folks' integrated stories without injustice to the whole account's integrity. Robert Penn Warren described the web of these inseverable narratives: "History trails its meanings like old cobwebs caught in a cellar broom."[8]

A comprehensive reconstruction of the historical narrative "invites re-assessment from the standpoint of those [people] previously overlooked or viewed through a distorting lens," historian Beverly Southgate proposes. We might sweep the cellar, but the historically meaningful cobwebs cling to the effort. Moreover, a perspective that opens possibilities for new formulations of the past "offers the possibility of re-definition."[9]

What else? Southgate argues this: "An opportunity is provided for retrieving from their traditional obscurity these 'others,' whether slaves, workers, or women or 'colonials' or any other minority, who have previously been relegated to the status of *'people without history.'*"[10] British playwright Oscar Wilde asserted that we in the present must understand our duty to rewrite history. Of course, historical comprehension is never final, and Wilde, or any historian, does not suggest revisionism merely for its own sake. Instead, "historyings" reframe narratives using new facts, sources, knowledge, and perspectives. As historian-journalist Jelani Cobb puts it: "Revising history is the whole point of having historians."[11] Especially if it is about a people who "generation after generation, in an overlooked but vital role," have been "perfecters of this country's history."[12] The goals of reading history are to understand and assess the revisions.

Finally, if a written and remembered historical narrative pursues a purpose, it influences the present. Otherwise, it merely constructs a chronological ordering of sterile disconnected events on a meaningless timeline. As people investigate past human activities and interactions, they reassign these facts to today's living perceptions. However, present people must use caution since "[h]istory is not the end," historian Matthew Karp insists. "[I]t is only one more battleground where we must meet the vast demands of the ever-living now."[13] In other words, historical continuities do not necessarily determine the present, even though they are with us today, suffusing our lifeworlds.

With this struggle, Kentucky and the entire nation can accomplish an autobiographical rewriting and "re-righting" of the past, present, and future of the cultural landscape. The goal of this book has been to resurrect some silenced narratives to fold into the *idea of Kentucky*. A democratized historical narrative would benefit everyone by embedding the newly remembered Green River Country story into the national historical drama. Then, any group without a comprehensively recognized history could see the erasures exposed, re-righted, and merged into humanity's progressing present. Only then, at last, can the contours of the Promised Land of new beginnings be seen from the mountaintop.

NOTES

Prologue

1. This epigraph comes from Liliana Maggione, Bruce VanSledright, and Patricia A. Alexander, "Walking on the Borders: A Measure of Epistemic Cognition in History," *Journal of Experimental Psychology* 77, no. 3 (2009): 210.

2. In capitalizing "Black" but not "white," I follow the style guidelines of a growing number of authors, news organizations (e.g., the *Chicago Tribune*, *Los Angeles Times*, *New York Times*, *Wall Street Journal*, Associated Press [AP], and the *USA Today* network), professional organizations, and scholarly journals (e.g., the *Columbia Journalism Review* [CJR]). For example, the CJR explains that it follows this style when referring to racial, ethnic, or cultural groups.

   However, much history and sociology lie behind this usage. The CJR continues: "For many people, *Black* reflects a shared sense of identity and community. White carries a different set of meanings; capitalizing the word in this context risks following the lead of white supremacists." This practice carries the recognition that "it is a kind of orthographic injustice to lowercase the *B*: to do so is to perpetuate the iniquity of an institution that uprooted people from the most ethnically diverse place on the planet, systematically obliterating any and all distinctions regarding ethnicity and culture." The CJR also points out that standard practice already capitalizes "African American," "Asian," "Hispanic," "Indigenous," "Native American," and "South Asian," and that "Black" avoids a hyphenated designation as in "African American." (See Mike Laws, "Why We Capitalize 'Black' (but Not 'White')," *Columbia Journalism Review* [June 16, 2020]). (https://www.cjr.org/analysis/capital-b-black-styleguide.php). The AP explains that it follows this capitalization style because "white people in general have much less shared history and culture, and don't have the experience of being discriminated against because of skin color." (David Bauder, "AP Says It Will Capitalize Black But Not White," the Associated Press [July 20, 2020]). (https://www.ap.org/ap-in-the-news/2020/ap-says-it-will-capitalize-black-but-not-white) The *New York Times* (July 5, 2020) backed its style change with this: "White doesn't represent a shared culture and history in the way Black does." (Cited in the AP article above.)

Nevertheless, this style is contentious and still under discussion, as history and sociology point others in the opposite direction. For example, Eve Ewing, a sociologist of race and education at the University of Chicago, prefers the capitalization of "White" because "Whiteness remains invisible, and as is the case with all power structures, its invisibility does crucial work to maintain its power." (Cited in the AP article above.)

3. I thank Margaret Ann Williams of Central City, my classmate and fellow participant-observer, for reminding me of this event on that memorable movie day (personal communication, 2015). However, the interpretation is entirely mine.

   Bill Hicks was also present that day at the State Theater. However, one year older, his cohort class sat upstairs in the balcony section. He recalls that the Black children sat in a walled-off area, to one side and farther back at the very top of the balcony in the worst seats in the house. Hicks must have been struggling with the "informal, hidden curriculum" of *othering* since he did not comprehend, as he says to his credit, the segregated situation (personal communication, 2015).

4. Adolph L. Reed, Jr., *The South: Jim Crow and Its Afterlives* (London and New York: Verso, 2022), 4-5. Drew Gilpin Faust is the author of a memoir that delineates her upbringing in a white Virginia family of privilege and her surmounting its strictures of race and gender. See her *Necessary Trouble: Growing Up at Midcentury* (New York: Farrar, Straus and Giroux, 2023).

5. Ted Poston, *The Dark Side of Hopkinsville: Stories by Ted Poston*, ed. Kathleen A. Hauke (Athens and London: University of Georgia Press, 1991), 72; Maya Angelou, "Interview: Maya Angelou, Poet and Historian," Academy of Achievement (Jan. 22, 1997). https://achievement.org/achiever/maya-angelou/#interview; Maggie Dulin, "Maggie Dulin," in *Remembering Jim Crow: African Americans Tell about Life in the Segregated South*, ed. William H. Chafe, Raymond Gavins, and Robert Korstad (New York: New Press, 2001), 100. Dulin grew up on a farm near Depoy and later lived in Browder and Drakesboro.

6. Zora Neale Hurston, "How It Feels to Be Colored," *The World Tomorrow* (May 1928), para 2.

https://lhsenglishdepartment.wikispaces.com/file/view/How+It+Feels+to+be+Colored+Me+by+Zora+Neale+Hurston.pdf.

Hurston was one of those independent thinkers who did not always agree with the Black intellectuals of the Harlem Renaissance. To this, she declares in her essay that she would not conform to expectations of Blackness.

7. Perhaps the first use of the term "color line" was by Frederick Douglass in his article, "The Color Line," *North American Review* 132 (June 1, 1881): 567-577. https://archive.org/details/jstor-25100970/mode/2up. W. E. B. Du Bois borrowed the term and famously used it metaphorically in this phrase: "The problem of the twentieth century is the problem of the color line." However, he did not intend this to be a comment about only a unidimensional Black-white social practice. Instead, the rest of the phrase indicates he understood colonialism and multiple and international color lines: "the relation of the darker to the lighter races of men." (W. E. B. Du Bois, *The Souls of Black Folk* [New York: Simon & Schuster Paperbacks, 2009 (1903)]). Today, immigration, intermarriage, and multiraciality have expanded the color lines even more. (See Katrina Quisumbing King, "Recentering U.S. Empire: A Structural Perspective of the Color Line," *Sociology of Race and Ethnicity* 5, no. 1 [2019]: 11-12.) However, in the western Kentucky context, the color line was nearly uniformly biracial.

8. Katherine Du Pre Lumpkin, *The Making of a Southerner* (Athens and London: University of Georgia Press, 1991 [1946]), 133.

9. W. E. B. Du Bois claims that *Sorrow Songs*—or Negro spirituals—are the best expression of the "black soul." (See Du Bois, *The Souls of Black Folk*.) Moreover, in "[t]he power of the song in the struggle for black survival," Black theologian James Cone explains, "[T]hat is what the spiritual and the blues are about." Furthermore, Cone generalizes that Black music is theological, social, political, and a "living reality." He also shows that Black music, especially Sorrow Songs, exhibits a *social transactionalism* circulating between the individual and the community as informed by its history. (James H. Cone, *The Spirituals and the Blues: An Interpretation* [Maryknoll, NY: Orbis Books, 1972], 1).

10. Martin Luther King, Jr., "I Have a Dream Speech," delivered at the Lincoln Memorial, in the March on Washington (August 28, 1963), para. 4, 5. https://www.americanrhetoric.com/speeches/mlkihaveadream.htm.

11. Philip W. Jackson, *Life in Classrooms* (New York: Teachers College Press, 1990).

Chapter 1: Introduction: Place, Memory, and Historiography

1. This epigraph comes from Edward Connery Latham, ed., *Interviews with Robert Frost* (Guilford, CT: Jeffrey Norton Publishers, 1997), 17.

2. Gordon S. Wood, *The Radicalism of the American Revolution* (New York: Vintage Books, 1993), 6.

3. The seven contiguous counties to Muhlenberg (clockwise beginning at the north) are McLean, Ohio, Butler, Logan, Todd, Christian, and Hopkins. In 2019, these eight counties contained 231,245 inhabitants. (My summation from "Annual Estimates of the Resident Population for Kentucky, ADDs, and Counties: April 1, 2010, to July 1, 2019," Kentucky State Data Center [University of Louisville, College of Arts and Sciences]). http://ksdc.louisville.edu/data-downloads/estimates/.

    I use George Humphreys' regionalization scheme for western Kentucky. This geographical delimitation encompasses the 11,130 square miles of territory in 28 counties from the Mississippi River to the eastern boundaries of Hancock, Butler, Warren, and Simpson counties. (George G. Humphreys, "Western Kentucky in the Twentieth Century: From the End of Isolation to the 'Gibraltar of Democracy,'" *Register of the Kentucky Historical Society* 113, no. 2/3 [Spring/Summer 2015]: 360-361)

    In 2019, these twenty-eight counties contained 814,869 inhabitants. (My summation of county data from the Kentucky State Data Center [see above].)

4. W. E. B. Du Bois, *The Souls of Black Folk*, 17.

5. Philosopher of place Edward Casey posits the *place-world* as "not only perceived or conceived but actively lived." It portrays more than just the spatial world that humans inhabit. It is also constitutive of the self since place insinuates into personal identity. (Edward Casey, "Body, Self, and Landscape: A Geophilosophical Inquiry into the Place-World," in *Textures of Place: Exploring Humanist Geographies*, ed. Paul C. Adams, Steven Hoelscher, and Karen E. Till [Minneapolis and London: University of Minnesota Press, 2001], 403-425.) Therefore, people live in a culturally structured "somewhere" and a temporally deep "somewhen" that gathers up the past and corrals it into their present. My study attempts to gather

and assemble a narrative of some of the somewhere and "somewhen" of the lived places called Muhlenberg, western Kentucky, and Kentucky.

6. Joseph A. Amato, *Rethinking Home: A Case for Writing Local History* (Berkeley: University of California Press, 2012), 10.

7. Jack Glazier, *Been Coming Through Some Hard Times: Race, History, and Memory in Western Kentucky* (Knoxville: University of Tennessee Press, 2012), 4.

8. Mona Domosh, Roderick P. Neuman, and Patricia L. Price, *The Human Mosaic: A Cultural Approach to Human Geography*, 13th ed. (New York: W.H. Freeman and Co., 2013), 24.

9. Don Mitchell, "Landscape," in *Cultural Geography: A Critical Dictionary of Key Concepts*, ed. David Atkinson, Peter Jackson, David Sibley, and Neil Washbourne (London and New York: I.B. Tauris, 2005), 53 (emphasis in the original).

10. Racialization is "the process by which whiteness operates possessively to define and construct itself as the pinnacle of its own hierarchy." (Aileen Moreton-Robinson, *The White Possessive: Property, Power, and Indigenous Sovereignty* [Minneapolis: University of Minnesota Press, 2015], xx) My social sciences background tells me that race manifests in minds, social structures, and spacings.

11. "Dominator culture" is in bell hooks, *Belonging: A Culture of Place* (New York and London: Routledge, 2009). Hooks (1952-2021) also uses this concept to include patriarchy. I am predisposed to use it because hooks (Gloria Watkins) grew up in the hills of Christian County and graduated from Hopkinsville Attucks High. Social scientists regard hooks as a leading light in cultural criticism and theory. Her forty books and numerous papers focus on the intersectionality of race, class, gender, and capitalism. She returned to Kentucky, in ca. 2004, to take a position as Distinguished Professor in Residence at Berea College.

My study appears to present anti-Blackness as a transhistorical phenomenon performing as a primary engine of history. However, a discussion of race and color prejudice as historical, sociological, and political phenomena—and how to alleviate their adverse effects—is beyond the scope of this survey. So, I take no side. Moreover, the discussion is far from settled. Nevertheless, interested readers might consult the thought-provoking accounts by Touré F. Reed (and others, including his father, Adolph Reed, Jr.). They critique "race reductionism" and reinsert racial disparities into a framework of class analysis and political economy. (See To Reed, *Toward Freedom: The Case Against Race Reductionism* [London and New York: Verso, 2020]; and "Between Obama and Coates," *Catalyst* 1, no. 4 [winter 2018].) https://catalyst-journal.com/vol1/no4/between-obama-and-coates.

12. Sam Wineburg, Susan Mosborg, Dan Porat, and Ariel Duncan, "Common Belief and Cultural Curriculum: An Intergenerational Study of Historical Consciousness," *American Educational Research Journal* 44, no. 1 (March 2007): 66.

13. Martha S. Jones, "Tackling a Century-Old Mystery: Did My Grandmother Vote?" *New York Times* (Aug. 14, 2020). https://www.nytimes.com/2020/08/14/us/suffrage-segregation-voting-black-women-19th-amendment.html.

14. Salamishah Tillet, *Sites of Slavery: Citizenship and Racial Democracy in the Post-Civil Rights Imagination* (Durham, NC: Duke University Press, 2012), 152.

15. Paul Ricoeur, *Memory, History, Forgetting* (Chicago and London: University of Chicago Press, 2006), 106.

16. Alun Munslow uses "historying" as an action verb to highlight the authorial act of narrative creation. (See Alun Munslow, "Genre and History/Historying," *Rethinking History* 19, no. 2: 158-176.) I agree with Munslow that history is always about interpretation (160). I also recognize that "history" must not be confused with the "past" (167). However, unlike Munslow, I contend that *historying* is about discovery, even as it is "an authored and fictive construal" (172). Hence, I believe the fictive act of historying should be diminished or framed within an acknowledged reference field. My frame for this volume is the documented Black experience, especially relating to white-instigated traumatic events.

17. Richard White, *Remembering Ahanagran: Storytelling in a Family's Past* (New York: Hill & Wang, 1998), 13; quoted in Sam Wineburg, *Historical Thinking and Other Unnatural Acts: Charting the Future of Teaching the Past* (Philadelphia: Temple University Press, 2001), 11.

18. Emily Bingham, *My Old Kentucky Home: The Astonishing Life and Reckoning of an Iconic American Song* (New York: Alfred A. Knopf, 2022), 229.

19. James A. W. Heffernan, "Why We Need the Humanities; The Word Itself Contains the Answer," *American Scholar* (Oct. 30, 2021). https://theamericanscholar.org/why-we-need-the-humanities/.

20. Carlo Ginzburg, quoted in Jonathan Kandell, "Was the World Made Out of Cheese? Carlo Ginzburg Is Fascinated by Questions that Others Ignore," *New York Times Magazine* (Nov. 17, 1991): 47.

21. Winthrop D. Jordan, *White Over Black: American Attitudes Toward the Negro, 1550-1812*, 2nd ed. (Chapel Hill: University of North Carolina Press, 2012), xxix (emphasis in the original).

22. James Baldwin, "The White Man's Guilt," *Ebony* (Aug. 1965): 47.

23. Mark Gismondi, "Tragedy, Realism, and Postmodernity: *Kulturpessimismus* in the Theories of Max Weber, E. H. Carr, Hans J. Morgenthau, and Henry Kissinger," *Diplomacy and Statecraft* 15, no. 3 (Sept. 2004): 437 (emphasis in the original).

24. E. H. Carr, *What Is History?* (New York: Random House, 1961), 9.

25. For the adjective modifying the toponym Muhlenberg, I coined the neologism *Muhlenbergian* for abstract phenomena, for example, the Muhlenbergian social structure. Otto Rothert (1913; see citation below) uses the term *Muhlenberger* at least twice, including a nineteenth-century newspaper's name. Here, I use it as the demonym and adjective referring to the denizens of Muhlenberg. This descriptor is reminiscent of Larry L. Stone, Sr.'s decades-long local-colorist newspaper column in the *Central City Messenger* and *Times-Argus*, titled "Mulebergers."

26. Oscar Wilde, quoted in Conal Furay and Michael J. Salevouris, *The Methods and Skills of History: A Practical Guide*, 3rd ed. (Wheeling, IL: Harlan Davidson, 2010), 107.

27. James McPherson, "Revisionist Historians," *Perspectives on History* (Sept. 1, 2003). https://www.historians.org/publications-and-directories/perspectives-on-history/september-2003/revisionist-historians. McPherson also provides the more everyday use of "revisionist history": "consciously falsified or distorted interpretation of the past to serve partisan or ideological purposes in the present."

28. Nell Irvin Painter, "Black and Blue," review of Leon F. Litwack, *Trouble in Mind: Black Southerners in the Age of Jim Crow* (New York: Knopf, 1998), in *The Nation* (May 11, 1998): 38.

29. David W. Blight, *Race and Reunion: The Civil War in American Memory* (Cambridge, MA, and London: Belknap Press of Harvard University Press, 2001), 109, 418n23.

30. Trudier Harris, *Exorcising Blackness: Historical and Literary Lynching and Burning Rituals* (Bloomington: Indiana University Press, 1984), 70; quoted in David W. Blight, *Race and Reunion*, 109.

31. Jill Lepore, "The Lingering of Loss," *The New Yorker* (July 1, 2019).

32. Claudia Tate, *Psychoanalysis and Black Novels: Desire and the Protocols of Race* (Oxford and New York: Oxford University Press, 1998).

33. Anastasia C. Curwood, *Stormy Weather: Middle-Class African American Marriages between the Two World Wars* (Chapel Hill: University of North Carolina Press, 2010), 7.

34. Andrew Hartman, *A War for the Soul of America: A History of the Culture Wars*, 2nd ed. (Chicago and London: University of Chicago Press, 2019), 2.

35. Nikole Hannah-Jones, "Our Democracy's Founding Ideals Were False When They Were Written. Black Americans Have Fought to Make Them True," *New York Times Magazine* (Aug. 14, 2019), para. 10. https://www.nytimes.com/interactive/2019/08/14/magazine/black-history-american-democracy.html.

36. Rudine Sims Bishop, "Mirrors, Windows, and Sliding Glass Doors," *Perspectives: Choosing and Using Books for the Classroom* 6, no. 3 (Summer 1990): ix (emphasis added).

Chapter 2: Jim Crow and the Lost Cause

1. Stuart McConnell, "Epilogue: The Geography of Memory," in *The Memory of the Civil War in American Culture*, ed. Alice Fahs and Joan Waugh (Chapel Hill and London: University of North Carolina Press, 2004), 259.

2. A common regionalization for the South is the eleven states of the Confederacy plus Kentucky.

3. Tony Horwitz, *Spying on the South: An Odyssey Across the American Divide* (New York: Penguin Press, 2019), 63.

4. Andrew Delbanco, "Endowed by Slavery," *New York Review of Books* (June 23, 2022): 59.

5. Christopher Phillips, *The Rivers Ran Backward: The Civil War and the Remaking of the American Middle Border* (New York: Oxford University Press, 2016), 322.

   An 1866 law applying to impaired Civil War veterans prohibited homestead sales for debt in Kentucky. Another exempted the men from state and local taxation. Unfortunately, neither law applied to Black veterans (Marion B. Lucas, *A History of Blacks in Kentucky: From Slavery to Segregation, 1760-1891* (Frankfort: Kentucky Historical Society, 1992), 292).

6. Leon Litwack, "Jim Crow Blues," *Magazine of History* 18, no. 2 (2004): 7.

7. Michelle Alexander, *The New Jim Crow: Mass Incarceration in the Age of Colorblindness*, rev. ed. (New York: The New Press, 2011), 197.

8. Henry Louis Gates, Jr., *Life Upon These Shores: Looking at African American History, 1513-2008* (New York: Alfred A. Knopf, 2011), 240.

9. Edward Ayers, *The Promise of the New South: Life after Reconstruction* (Oxford and New York: Oxford University Press, 2007 [1992]), 24.

10. Richard Wright, *Black Boy (American Hunger): A Record of Childhood and Youth* (New York: Perennial Classics, 1998 [1944]), 263.

11. Thomas Curwen, "Theodore Roosevelt Whipped Up a Frenzy of Populism in 1912; We're Still Living with the Consequences," Book Reviews, *Los Angeles Times* (July 15, 2016). http://www.latimes.com/books/reviews/la-ca-jc-cowan-people-rule-20160706-snap-story.html?track=lat-email-bookshelf.

12. Clement Eaton, *The Waning of the Old South Civilization, 1860-1880's*, Mercer University Lamar Memorial Lectures, No. 10 (Athens: University of Georgia Press, 1968), 171.

13. W. J. Cash, *The Mind of the South* (New York: Vintage Books, 1991 [1941]), 167-68 (emphasis added).

14. C. Vann Woodward, *Origins of the New South, 1877-1913* (Baton Rouge: Louisiana State University Press, 1951), 3.

    Various scholars use the term "redemption" to encapsulate this political moment. Even so, many still debate its appropriateness for naming this era.

15. Michael Perman, "Redemption," in *The New Encyclopedia of Southern Culture; Volume 10: Law & Politics*, vol. ed. James W. Ely, Jr., and

Bradley G. Bond (Chapel Hill: University of North Carolina Press, 2008), 273.

16. Douglas R. Egerton, *The Wars of Reconstruction: The Brief, Violent History of America's Most Progressive Era* (New York: Bloomsbury Press, 2014), 19.

17. Luke E. Harlow, *Religion, Race, and the Making of Confederate Kentucky, 1830-1880* (Knoxville: University of Tennessee Press, 2014), 189.

18. Henry Louis Gates, Jr., "The 'Lost Cause' that Built Jim Crow," *New York Times* (Nov. 8, 2019). https://www.nytimes.com/2019/11/08/opinion/sunday/jim-crow-laws.html?smid=url-share.

19. Bill Cunningham, *Castle: The Story of a Kentucky Prison* (Kuttawa, KY: McClanahan Publishing, 1995), 9.

20. Luke E. Harlow, *Religion, Race, and the Making of Confederate Kentucky*, 189.

21. Gaines M. Foster, *Ghosts of the Confederacy: Defeat, the Lost Cause, and the Emergence of the New South* (New York and Oxford: Oxford University Press, 1987), 5.

22. Charles Reagan Wilson, *Baptized in Blood: The Religion of the Lost Cause, 1865-1920* (Athens: University of Georgia Press, 2009 [1980]), xiv.

23. *Louisville Courier-Journal*, "Unveiling of Shaft to Confederate Dead" (May 29, 1909), 1.

24. *Madisonville Hustler*, "Ex-Confederates Welcomed to Madisonville in Eloquent Manner" (June 1, 1909), 1.

25. Anne Sarah Rubin uses this phrase in her *A Shattered Nation: The Rise and Fall of the Confederacy, 1861-1868* (Chapel Hill: University of North Carolina Press, 2005), 2.

26. The content of this paragraph, including the two quotes, comes from David W. Blight, *Race and Reunion*, 198.

27. Kenneth S. Lynn, "The Torment of D. W. Griffith," *American Scholar* 59, no. 2 (1990): 259.

28. Nikki Brown, "Lillian Horace and the Respectable Black Woman: Black Women's Activism in Combatting Jim Crow," in *Recovering* Five Generations Hence*: The Life and Writings of Lillian Jones Horace*, ed.

Karen Kossie-Chernyshev (College Station: Texas A&M University Press, 2013), 245.

According to historian Nell Irvin Painter, a common assumption was that only white women could be victims of rape. (Nell Irvin Painter, *Southern History Across the Color Line* [Chapel Hill and London: University of North Carolina Press, 2002], 121)

29. Henry Louis Gates, Jr., "The 'Lost Cause' that Built Jim Crow."

30. Woodrow Wilson, *A History of the American People* (New York: Harper & Brothers, 1902), vol. 5: 58.

31. Otto A. Rothert, *A History of Muhlenberg* County (Louisville: John P. Morton & Co., 1913), 339.

Conducting his research before publishing in 1913, Rothert must have interviewed the formerly enslaved "Uncle" John Oates. In its caption, he dates a photo of Oates as 1912. Further, Rothert uses at least one present-tense construction in relating particulars about Oates, revealing that he knew him.

In Jim Crow racial etiquette, white folk frequently used the quasi-polite "uncle" as the title for older Black men. This title avoided awarding the higher status title of "mister," reserved for white men and was a Jim Crow labeling that helped maintain the social order. The custom required the denigrating generic name "boy" for younger adult males and "uncle" for older men. In both cases, the intent was to emasculate Black men regardless of age.

Rothert's mostly sanitized story of bondage fits within the reigning historical interpretation (known as the Dunning School) of enslavery in the late nineteenth and early twentieth centuries. His treatment is understandable for this reason. Regrettably, his composition's brevity on this subject amounts to just over six pages. Moreover, Greenville and Muhlenberg had dozens of former bondservants still living in the first decade of the twentieth century when he was researching and writing.

32. Anne E. Marshall, *Creating a Confederate Kentucky: The Lost Cause and Civil War Memory in a Border State* (Chapel Hill: University of North Carolina Press, 2010), 56.

33. Marshall, 56.

34. George C. Wright, *A History of Blacks in Kentucky; Volume 2: In Pursuit of Equality, 1890-1980* (Frankfort: Kentucky Historical Society, 1992), 59.

35. Rayford W. Logan, *The Betrayal of the Negro: From Rutherford B. Hayes to Woodrow Wilson* (New York: Collier Books, 1965); originally published as *The Negro in American Life and Thought: The Nadir, 1877-1901* (New York: Dial Press, 1954); Eric Foner, "Introduction," in Rayford W. Logan, *The Betrayal of the Negro*, xiii.

36. Charles Reagan Wilson, *Baptized in Blood*, 1.

Chapter 3: Out of the 'Silent Archives'

1. This epigraph, an African proverb, comes from Martin H. Manser, *The Facts on File Dictionary of Proverbs*, 2nd rev. ed. (New York: Facts on File, Inc., 2007).

2. Mike Fannin, "The Truth in Black and White: An Apology from the Kansas City Star," *Kansas City Star* (Dec. 20, 2020). https://www.kansascity.com/news/local/article247928045.html; Timothy Bella, "Kansas City Star Apologizes for Decades of Racist Coverage of Black People: 'It is Time that We Own Our History,'" *Washington Post* (Dec. 21, 2020).
https://www.washingtonpost.com/nation/2020/12/21/kansas-city-apology-black-people/

3. *The Railroad Gazette* (July 22, 1892, 547) incorrectly dates the collision to June 25.
http://lhldigital.lindahall.org/utils/getfile/collection/rrjournal/id/622/filename/665.pdf

   It is instructive that June 1892—a typical month—had 75 train collisions across the U.S. and 88 derailments, totaling 165 accidents. These accidents killed 70 people and injured 299 (ibid.). These figures evidence the scale of train travel and its real dangers for just a month.

4. Paul Camplin, *A New History of Muhlenberg* (Greenville, KY: Caney Station Books, 1984), 114; *Earlington Bee*, "The O&N Wreck" (June 9, 1892), 3; *Louisville Courier-Journal*, "A Fatal Mistake; Time Card Wrongfully Read Causes a Deadly Wreck" (June 6, 1892), 1.

   (See the note about a Black Owensboran, a veteran of the Civil War injured in this 1892 South Carrollton train collision, at the History of Owensboro website:
http://wiki.historyofowensboro.com/index.php?title=Amos_Smedly

5. West Kentucky College, "Railroad Material. South Carrollton, a Review of Her Business Men and Institutions," in *The Reunion* (June 1897),

Joanna Fox collection, in possession of Barry Duvall, Greenville. Someone posted the clippings on the Muhlenberg County Kentucky History Group (Facebook) (April 24, 2016).

6. Leslie Shively Smith, *Around Muhlenberg*, 61-62.

7. M. S. Kimley in "South Carrollton," *Owensboro Kentucky Reporter* (March 22, 1903), 4, Library of Congress, Chronicling America. https://chroniclingamerica.loc.gov/lccn/sn86069325/1902-03-22/ed-1/; Ves Lindley in West Kentucky College, *The Reunion* (June 1897).

8. *New York Times*, "Two Colored Men Deputies" (July 8, 1897), 1.

9. *Owensboro Daily Messenger*, "Scoring Roosevelt; The President Condemned for Inviting a Negro to Dinner" (Oct. 20, 1901), 1.

10. *Greenville Record* (May 19, 1910).

11. Otto Rothert republished the report by an anonymous eyewitness reporter that appeared in the *Greenville Kentucky Republican* (May 18, 1870) of the lynching of Bob Gray (Otto A. Rothert, *A History of Muhlenberg County*, 362-364.

12. The news story in the *Central City Muhlenberg Argus* (Aug. 20, 1909) using the label "burr-head" appeared in the *Greenville Record* (Oct. 21, 1909, 2) as criticism of the *Muhlenberg Argus*. (No copies of the *Muhlenberg Argus* are known to exist.)

13. William J. Campbell, born in 1863, grew up near Huntsville, Alabama. He was "hired out" (after enslavement ended) at an early age to a white man (I presume) who allowed Campbell to attend school in Huntsville. In the same school, he later became a teacher. Moving to Birmingham in 1880, Campbell worked as a barber for a brief time before moving on to Pratt City and a job in the coal mines. At Pratt City, he began his long, distinguished career as a civil rights advocate and labor organizer that propelled him to national responsibilities. In 1881, Campbell became the local secretary of the new, nationally organized Knights of Labor. He managed the first Knights' locals in Montgomery and Birmingham the following year. In Chattanooga, Tennessee, Campbell formed the locals of the Federation of Mine Laborers and the United Mine Workers.

At this point, Campbell began his involvement in local, state, and national politics. In 1882, Republicans elected him secretary of the Republican Committee of Jefferson County, Alabama, and as a delegate to the state convention of Alabama Republicans. In 1892, Republicans chose Campbell as a National Republican Convention delegate. Campbell and his wife moved to Muhlenberg in 1894. He continued his involvement in civil rights, labor organizing, and interracial unionism. (See Notable Kentucky African Americans Database, University of Kentucky Libraries, "Campbell, William Joseph.") http://nkaa.uky.edu/record.php?note_id=2563. Campbell died in 1912. His wife, Sallie L. Campbell, continued her career as a public school teacher in Muhlenberg for many more years. (Leslie Shively Smith, *Around Muhlenberg, passim*)

14. Notable Kentucky African Americans Database, "Campbell, William Joseph."

    The 1898 Miners' Pay legislation, formulated, or at least proposed by Campbell, is found in the section titled "Mines and Mining" (Chapter 88), in *Annotated Supplement to the Kentucky Statutes, Edition 1894* (Louisville: John P. Morton & Co., 1895), 69.

15. W. E. B. Du Bois, *Black Reconstruction in America, 1860-1880* (New York and London: The Free Press, 1998 [1935]), 700.

16. Notable Kentucky African Americans Database, "Campbell, William Joseph."

17. Leslie Shively Smith, *Around Muhlenberg*, 46, 76, 78; 263; Sallie Campbell's photo on 82.

18. William J. Campbell had a highly accomplished life. Muhlenbergers would do well to honor him, including as a candidate for a historical marker.

19. W. E. B. Du Bois, *The Souls of Black Folk* (emphasis added), 7.

20. William Stuart Nelson, "William Stuart Nelson," in *Robert Penn Warren's 'Who Speaks for the Negro': An Archival Collection* (transcript of taped conversations) (Robert Penn Warren Center for the Humanities, Vanderbilt University, 1964).
    http://whospeaks.library.vanderbilt.edu/interview/william-stuart-nelson

21. Ibram X. Kendi, *How to Be an Antiracist* (New York: One World, 2019), 29 (emphasis in the original).

22. Note on language: I vacillated over using the N-word in these two instances. Initially, I wrote this:

I follow the lead of historian Douglas Blackmon (in his Pulitzer Prize-winning work, *Slavery by Another Name: The Re-Enslavement of Black Americans from the Civil War to World War II*) vis-à-vis his use of historical quotations containing offensive racial labels. He explains: "I chose not to sanitize these historical statements but to present the authentic language of the period" (xi). I concur with the use of this historically authentic language. However, I also regret (as does Blackmon) any discomfort the unacceptable, crude idioms may elicit from readers. Consequently, this text [i.e., this book] includes two unsanitized phenomena: the racialized events in the cultural landscape and the (intentionally sparing) use of authentic language.

Nevertheless, more recently, I read Black philosopher George Yancy's conversation with Black historian Elizabeth Pryor, author of a study and a much-watched TED Talk on the N-word. As a result, I have decided that I am not qualified to use this "authentic language," even though I claim to be a historian. The blood-stained cultural landscape in this book, though, obviously remains unsanitized. See George Yancy, "White Journalists' Use of the N-Word Is an Intolerable Assault on Black Freedom," *Truthout* (Feb. 27, 2021). https://truthout.org/articles/white-journalists-use-of-the-n-word-is-an-intolerable-assault-on-black-freedom/

23. James W. Loewen, *Lies My Teacher Told Me: Everything Your American History Textbook Got Wrong* (New York: Touchstone Book, 2007), 389n8.

24. Rita Dove, "Bellringer," *Playlist for the Apocalypse* (New York: W. W. Norton, 2021), 6.

25. John R. Burch, Jr., "Minstrelsy," in *The Kentucky African American Encyclopedia*, ed. Gerald L. Smith, Karen Cotton McDaniel, and John A. Hardin (Lexington: University Press of Kentucky, 2015), 365.

26. *Greenville Record* (May 19, 1910, and shorter notices on Jan. 6 and Jan. 20, 1910).

Laura Stateler Kincheloe (1884-1973) was the same entertainer who performed at the gala event on May 28, 1909, the night before the unveiling of the Madisonville Confederate statue. One of Kincheloe's musical talents was whistling patriotic songs. At the Confederate celebration, the attendees applauded her "so vigorously" that she "was compelled" to reappear for an encore. Kincheloe responded by whistling "Dixie," which "carried the house by storm." She was the wife of Madisonville attorney David Hayes Kincheloe (1877-1950), whom Second District voters elected for the first of eight terms to Congress in 1915. (*Madisonville Hustler*, "Ex-Confederates Welcomed to Madisonville," 1).

27. Anne E. Marshall, *Creating a Confederate Kentucky*, 170.

28. Christopher Phillips, *The Rivers Ran Backward: The Civil War and the Remaking of the American Middle Border* (New York: Oxford University Press, 2016), 330.

29. Melvin Patrick Ely, *The Adventures of Amos 'n' Andy: A Social History of an American Phenomenon* (Charlottesville: University Press of Virginia, 2001).

30. These details about the Lions Club vaudeville-minstrel show come from a photograph in the John Brizendine photographic collection in possession of Jack Simpson. At the bottom, someone labeled it: "Lion's Club Minstrel—Central City 1965." This date is incorrect; the event happened ca. 1952. An informant confirms that the Lions Club performed its vaudeville-minstrel shows for several years in the early 1950s. No playbill has turned up. Unfortunately, the club discarded its archives a few years ago.

    At least as late as February 1928, Central City High School staged a minstrel show. The 1928 CCHS "Oriole" (the school yearbook) includes the program and photo of the ensemble of student performers, fourteen of whom wear blackface (64-65). Thistle Cottage, Greenville Public Library, archives this yearbook and others from county high schools.

31. Emily Bingham, *My Old Kentucky Home*, 229, xx.

32. Thomas D. Clark, "My Old Kentucky Home in Retrospect," *Filson Club History Quarterly* 22 (April 1948): 110.

33. For Hattie McDaniel, see Carlton Jackson, *Hattie: The Life of Hattie McDaniel* [Lanham, MD: Madison Books, 1990]). For the poem, see Rita Dove, "Hattie McDaniel Arrives at the Coconut Grove." https://poets.org/poem/hattie-mcdaniel-arrives-coconut-grove?page=3

34. In 1923, the U.S. Senate passed a bill proposed by the United Daughters of the Confederacy to build a "monument to the faithful colored mammies" in Washington, DC. The House declined to pass it due to the

pressure applied by Black women. (Alison M. Parker, "When White Women Wanted a Monument to Black 'Mammies,'" *New York Times* [Feb. 6, 2020])
https://www.nytimes.com/2020/02/06/opinion/sunday/confederate-monuments-mammy.html?fbclid=IwAR2k-BblMtfgZqby9h4GrTorWWzxtauzz-V6n3QLS0IukM48S3Sn_zyou4U

35. Salamishah Tillet, *Sites of Slavery: Citizenship and Racial Democracy in the Post-Civil Rights Imagination* (Durham, NC: Duke University Press, 2012), 152.

36. The "Uncle" Winton Robinson obituary is in the *Central City Messenger* (Sept. 29, 1932).
(See https://www.findagrave.com/memorial/83028678/winton-robinson.)

37. *Central City Messenger* (Sept. 29, 1932).

38. George C. Wright, *Life Behind a Veil: Blacks in Louisville, Kentucky, 1865-1930* (Baton Rouge and London: Louisiana State University Press), 2.

39. "Colored Town" was the white designation of the neighborhood in north Central City that contained almost the entire segregated Black population of Central City. (The designator "colored" had changed from earlier more racist usage.) I use this historically relevant toponym for more than convenience—white residents used it, so it is historically accurate. At the same time, I recognize how the name must sound derogatorily to Black readers. However, his eminence W. E. B. Du Bois used the term "'colored' town" for a section of Hopkinsville when he visited Hopkinsville in 1921 (via the L&N from Cincinnati. (W. E. B. Du Bois, "Hopkinsville, Chicago and Idlewild," *The Crisis* [Aug. 1921]: 158-160) Hopkinsville had predominantly Black Eastside and Westside (and more recently D. A., the area around Durrett Avenue).

40. Crawford Cemetery, Central City, is an unused and unattended burial ground for African Americans and possibly Black and white paupers. It contains between one hundred and two hundred gravesites. The last burials, perhaps, were in 1940. Crawford is located 200 feet off U.S. 62, south of its intersection with Center Street. No one maintains the site, and there is no public access. Marian Hammers does not list Crawford or West End, Greenville, in her compilation of Muhlenberg's cemeteries. Also, the Find-A-Grave online database does not include Crawford (in 2018), but it is included, with 20 names, on this website:

http://www.kykinfolk.com/muhlenberg/cemeteries/cemeteriesC/crawford.htm

41. Frederick Douglass, public address, "Colored People's Day at the World Columbian Exposition," August 25, 1893, *Chicago Tribune* (Aug. 26, 1893).

42. David W. Blight, *Race and Reunion*, 9.

43. *Louisville Courier-Journal*, editorial, "Gettysburg (1863-1913)" (July 4, 1913), 6 (emphasis added).

44. David W. Blight, *Race and Reunion*, 9.

45. W. E. B. Du Bois, referenced in Ibram X. Kendi, *Stamped from the Beginning: The Definitive History of Racist Ideas in America* (New York: Nation Books, 2016), 507.

Chapter 4: Working the 'Steamboat Sublime,' Main Street, and 'Caverns of Night'

1. This epigraph comes from Joseph A. Amato, *Rethinking Home: A Case for Writing Local History* (Berkeley: University of California Press, 2002), 10.

2. Agnes S. Harralson, *Steamboats on the Green, and the Colorful Men Who Operated Them* (Berea, KY: Kentucke Imprints, 1981), 43. Despite stereotyping the "natural penchant" of the Black rousters on the steamer packets, her text provides valuable information.

3. Photo in Harralson, 68.

4. Harralson, 42-44.

5. Historian Walter Johnson describes the era of the culturally significant steamboat as the "grand steamboat sublime." (Walter Johnson, *River of Dark Dreams: Slavery and Empire in the Cotton Kingdom* [Cambridge, MA, and London: Belknap Press of Harvard University Press, 2013], 73) The historian Douglas Burgess writes: "Into this wild landscape the steamboat was the floating embodiment of expanding civilization. Wherever it touched, whoever crossed its threshold and witnessed the wonders therein, was instantly drawn into the 'civilized' world it represented." (Douglas R. Burgess, Jr., *Engines of Empire: Steamships and the Victorian Imagination* [Stanford, CA: Stanford University Press, 2016], 132)

In the late 1830s, navigation improvements on the Green River made connections to the Ohio-Mississippi river network much more efficient. With these developments and the steamboat—sometimes called "floating palaces"—Green River Country integrated into the national interior of the Ohio Valley and the Mississippian Empire. These national connections and global trade structures generated cultural amenities and expansive commercial and cultural worldviews.

6. Arnold Shultz was born in Ohio County in 1886, the son of formerly enslaved people. Shultz traveled around a small area as an itinerant laborer and miner as a young man. Meanwhile, he learned to play the fiddle and guitar from a relative. Musicologists credit him with, if not its development, at least considerable influence on and dissemination of the "thumb-style" or (Merle) "Travis-style" of guitar playing. The four-county "Shultz-Travis region" of McLean, Ohio, Butler, and Muhlenberg refers to the source area of this guitar-picking method. Shultz died in Butler in 1931. Someone buried him in an unmarked grave in Morgantown. However, in 1994, Butler County erected a monument at the gravesite. (See William E. Lightfoot, "A Regional Musical Style: The Legacy of Arnold Shultz," in *Sense of Place: American Regional Cultures*, ed. Barbara Allen and Thomas J. Schlereth [Lexington: University Press of Kentucky, 1990], 120-137; Erika Brady, "Contested Origins: Arnold Shultz and the Music of Western Kentucky," in *Hidden in the Mix: The African American Presence in Country Music*, ed. Diane Pecknold [Durham and London: Duke University Press, 2013], 100-118.)

7. Leslie Souther and Bee Hines, interview by John Knoepfle, "Leslie Souther Memoir," *Steamboats and Inland Rivers*, Archives/Special Collections (Illinois Digital Archives, University of Illinois at Springfield, 1957).
http://www.idaillinois.org/cdm/ref/collection/uis/id/1450

8. Gayle Carver, "Interview with Gayle Carver Regarding His Life (FA 154)," Manuscripts & Folklife Archives Project, TopSCHOLAR Western Kentucky University, 1989.
http://digitalcommons.wku.edu/cgi/viewcontent.cgi?article=1045&context=dlsc_fa_oral_hist

There are discrepancies between the two accounts of the James Gang affair in Muhlenberg: Otto A. Rothert (*A History of Muhlenberg County*, 387-388) and a contemporary news article. (*St. Joseph* [MO] *Weekly Herald*, "Conscience Stricken; Jesse James' Widow Returning the Valuables

Stolen by Her Husband" [Aug. 3, 1882], 1). The news article reports that the robbery happened in June 1880; Rothert fixed the theft in the summer of 1881. The article claims there were four men; Rothert has it as three. The news in the article was that after Jesse died on April 3, 1882, his wife returned a gold watch purloined in the Dovey robbery. The timepiece first went to those Dovey sons remaining in Muhlenberg and then forwarded to Philadelphia to another brother. However, the article names the Dovey in Philadelphia as Charles; Rothert has it as George B. Of these two accounts, Rothert is most likely accurate.

9. Leslie Shively Smith, *Around Muhlenberg*, 186.

10. Smith, 186.

11. Smith, 185-188.

12. Smith, 129-130.

13. For information on the roller-skating rink, the Kentucky Digital Library (part of the Kentucky Virtual Library) has Sanborn Maps of Greenville for 1886 (two sheets), 1893 (two sheets), 1898 (two sheets), 1898 (two sheets), 1903 (three sheets), and 1910 (six sheets); at kdl.kyvl.org/catalog?q=greenville&search_field=all_fields&commit=search. This KYVL section begins with several Works Progress Administration (WPA) photographs of Greenville, including the new WPA-built hospital.

    KYVL also has Sanborn Maps of Central City for 1901 (two sheets), 1907 (four sheets), and 1912 (seven sheets). kdl.kyvl.org/?commit=search&page=1&q=central+city&search_field=all_fields. This KYVL section begins with a photograph of the new WPA-built "Central City Negro School."

    Sanborn Maps devoted seven map sheets to Central City in 1912, whereas Greenville had six in 1910, demonstrating the relative sizes of the two towns. The four map sheets for Central City in 1907 and the seven in 1912 show how rapidly Central City grew in only a half-decade.

14. Leslie Shively Smith, *Around Muhlenberg*, 189-195.

15. *Greenville Leader*, "Jack Mathis, 82, Dies Thursday in Nashville" (May 29, 1952), 4.

16. Leslie Shively Smith, *Around Muhlenberg*, 189-195.

17. Paul Camplin, *A New History of Muhlenberg*, 63.

The 1910 U.S. Census for Muhlenberg lists a Mathis as "black," age 41, in Greenville, and as "B. Mathis," just as Camplin says. The same name, "B. Mathis," is carved on his gravestone in Greenville's West End Cemetery. Confusingly, there is a four-year discrepancy between the Census and the tombstone. The latter shows his birth on September 11, 1865, and death on May 6, 1941. Since Kentucky was the last state to end enforced Black servitude, postponing until the passage of the Thirteenth Amendment, Mathis was probably born a bondservant.

18. Leslie Shively Smith, *Around Muhlenberg*, 129-130.

19. Alice Dunnigan notes Dr. Ulysses Simpson Porter in her *Alone at the Top: The Autobiography of Alice Dunnigan, Pioneer of the National Black Press*, ed. Carol McCabe Booker (Athens and London: University of Georgia Press, 2015), 28.

20. Leslie Shively Smith, 129-130.

21. A ca. 1914 photo of the main production room in the S. E. Rice Tobacco Co. factory shows six or seven Black men and women workers. Photo in Paul Camplin, *A New History of Muhlenberg*, 160.

22. Death certificate of A. J. Robinson found at kykinfolk.com/Muhlenberg/death-certificates/imagesR/robinson-aj24960.pdf. Robinson's burial took place in the Old Greenville Cemetery.

23. An untitled news item in the *Owensboro Twice-A-Week* (Jan. 14, 1892).

24. George C. Wright, *A History of Blacks in Kentucky; Volume 2: In Pursuit of Equality, 1890-1980* (Frankfort: Kentucky Historical Society, 1992), 16. The overrepresentation of Black workers in low-wage occupations (especially Black women) and their underrepresentation in higher-wage fields has a long genealogy.

25. Herbert G. Gutman, *The Black Family in Slavery and Freedom, 1750-1925* (New York: Random House, 1976), 442-450, 624-642.

26. Imani Perry, "What Black Women Hear When They're Called 'Auntie': Thoughts on a Word that Provokes a Wide Range of Feelings," *The Atlantic* (April 6, 2022), para. 18.

27. John C. Espie, quoted in Business and Professional Women's Club of Central City, *The History of Central City* (n.p.: Centennial Book Committee, n.d. [1973]), n.p.

28. Daisy James, "Oral History Interview with Daisy James" (transcript), in *Civil Rights Movement in Kentucky*, Catalog no. 1999OH01.19 (Oral History Project, Kentucky Historical Society, 1999). Oral History Interview with Daisy James (kyoralhistory.com)

29. Langston Hughes, "On Leaping and Shouting," "Here to Yonder" column, *Chicago Defender* (July 3, 1943), in *Langston Hughes and the Chicago Defender: Essays on Race, Politics, and Culture*, ed. Christopher C. De Santis (Urbana and Chicago: University of Illinois Press, 1995), 200.

30. Adolph L. Reed, Jr., *The South: Jim Crow and Its Afterlives* (London and New York: Verso, 2022), 8.

31. I hesitate to label this high point of Black culture, with thriving Black businesses, a "golden era" since it materialized amid oppressive Jim Crowism.

32. For Lexington, see "Deweese Street" in *The Kentucky African American Encyclopedia*, 141-142; for Louisville, see "Walnut Street" in the *Encyclopedia of Louisville*.

33. Catherine Fosl and Tracy E. K'Meyer, "Economic Opportunity," in *Freedom on the Border: An Oral History of the Civil Rights Movement in Kentucky*, ed. Catherine Fosl and Tracy E. K'Meyer (Lexington: University Press of Kentucky, 2009), 150.

34. Ronald L. Lewis, *Black Coal Miners in America: Race, Class, and Community Conflict, 1780-1980* (Lexington: University Press of Kentucky, 1987).

35. Otto A. Rothert, *A History of Muhlenberg County*, 398, table.

36. *U.S. Census of Agriculture, 1930: Vol. II, Part 2, The Southern States: Kentucky*, 612, 613, table. http://lib-usda-05.serverfarm.cornell.edu/usda/AgCensusImages/1910/06/01/1833/41033898v6ch5.pdf

37. George C. Wright, *A History of Blacks in Kentucky*, 25.

38. Otto A. Rothert, *A History of Muhlenberg County*, 387.

39. Rothert, 387; Barry Duvall, *My Last Day in Browder: Explosion 1910* (Olaton, KY: Sandefur Printing, 2015). That same year, 1910, Congress established the U.S. Bureau of Mines due to the large number of mining accidents in the American coalfields over the previous few years.

40. Rothert, 387.

41. *Louisville Courier-Journal,* "7 Killed,3 Dying in Kentucky Mine Blast" (Feb. 17, 1926), 1.

42. *Cincinnati Enquirer*, "Six Are Imprisoned in Kentucky Coal Pit" (Dec. 20, 1928), Kentucky Edition.

43. Garret Mathews, "40th Anniversary of Mine Explosion Stirs Memories," *Evansville Courier-Press* (Journal Media Group) (Aug. 3, 2008), 14. http://www.courierpress.com/news/local/40th-anniversary-of-mine-explosion-stirs-memories-ep-448296404-327007401.html

    In 1968, among the nine miners killed at the River Queen Underground Mine were four from Muhlenberg: Paul Creekmore, age 44, Central City; Bobby English, 34, Beech Creek; Frank Epley, 45, Greenville; and Ernest Miller, 45, Central City. Five miners from other counties: James Bryant, 25, Cromwell; William Fridinger, 36, Madisonville; James Harris, 33, Sacramento; William Rice, 31, McHenry; and Denny Salig, 58, Echols. GenDisasters.com (n.d.), "Greenville, KY fiery coal mine explosion, Aug 1968." www3.gendisasterss.com/Kentucky/19774/Greenville-ky-fiery-coal-mine-explosion-aug-1968

44. The death certificate (no. 26796) of Willie Render, South Carrollton, shows that a slate fall killed him in Crescent Mines on October 27, 1914. www.kykinfolk.com/muhlenberg/death-certificate/imagesR/render-willie26796.pdf

45. Henry C. Mayer, "Miners' Safety and Health," in *The Kentucky Encyclopedia*, ed.-in-chief John E. Kleber (Lexington: University Press of Kentucky, 1992), 640.

46. Henry C. Mayer, "Coal Mining," in *The Kentucky Encyclopedia*, 209-211.

Table 2: Muhlenberg Mining Fatalities, 1964-1980

Year	Underground Deaths	Strip-Mine Deaths
1964	6	0
1965	2	0
1966	3	0
1967	11	0

1968	11	0
1969	1	0
1970	1	2
1971	0	0
1972	0	2
1973	2	0
1974	0	1
1975	4	0
1976	0	0
1977	1	0
1978	0	0
1979	1	0
1980	1	0
Totals	**44**	**5**

Source: Adapted from Paul Camplin, *A New History of Muhlenberg*, 222, table. Note: Camplin supplies no citations for his data sources.

47. This count of mining deaths is in an untitled item in the *Greenville Record* (Feb. 24, 1910), 2.

48. Ronald L. Mitchelson and Richard Ulack, with Yu Luo, "Mineral, Energy, and Timber Resources," in *Atlas of Kentucky*, ed.-in-chief Richard Ulack, co-ed. Karl Raitz, and cart. ed. Gyula Pauer (Lexington: University Press of Kentucky, 1998), 143.

49. How many mining deaths happened in Muhlenberg through its long history with coal? First, start with a crucial (albeit somewhat arbitrary) assumption of an average of three mining fatalities per year from 1872 through 1968. (Mining in Muhlenberg entered its intensive phase in 1872 when the Central Coal & Iron Co. opened two mines near Central City.) With this assumption, these 96 years add up to an estimated 288 deaths. Adding the sixteen documented casualties in Muhlenberg from 1969 to 1980, the estimated total for the 108 years—1872 to 1980—comes to 304 mortalities due to mining accidents. The estimate of Paul McRee of at least three hundred accidental mining deaths through all the years of mining in

the county seems reasonable. I know of no other reliable estimates. His estimate appeared in an online article, no longer available since SurfKy News Group permanently deleted all items before 2014 (personal communication, 2016). The citation for the deleted article is Paul McRee, "Muhlenberg Coal Miners Memorial Receives Check from TVA," *SurfkyNews* (Aug. 26, 2013). However, these two figures (304 and at least 300) do not include mortalities due to black lung disease. Therefore, I estimate that an additional thousand Muhlenberger miners suffered an early death due to the complications of black lung and other lung ailments.

50. Harry M. Caudill, "Betrayal in the Mines," *The New York Review of Books* (Dec. 2, 1971).
https://www.nybooks.com/articles/1971/12/02/betrayal-in-the-mines/

51. Business and Professional Women's Club of Central City, *The History of Central City*.

52. *Cincinnati Enquirer*, "Six Are Imprisoned in Kentucky Coal Pit." (Dec. 20, 1928).

53. Quoted in Ronald L. Lewis, *Black Coal Miners in America*, 93.

54. Otto A. Rothert, "Coal Mining in Muhlenberg County, Ky.," *Coal Age* 5, no. 1 (1914): 10-11.

55. It is abundantly evident from social media posts dedicated to Muhlenbergian history that natives massively violated these child-labor law restrictions. The mines often added an underage son's work—and sometimes that of daughters and other relatives—to the father's work "ticket" to hide the illegality of using underaged workers.

56. Ronald L. Lewis, *Black Coal Miners in America*, 171.

57. Lewis, 180.

58. *Louisville Courier-Journal*, "Four Killed in Mine Disaster" (Jan. 18, 1912), 1.

59. William B. Thesing, ed., *Caverns of Night: Coal Mining in Art, Literature, and Film* (Columbia: University of South Carolina Press, 2000).

60. The Carter Family released a song titled "Coal Miner's Blues" (A. P. Carter composer and lyricist [Peer International Corporation, 1938]). Its lines indicate one of the underground dangers: "These blues are so blue, they are coal black blues/ For my place will cave in and my life I lose."

61. Merle Travis, "Dark as a Dungeon, on *Folk Songs of the Hills* (Capitol Records, 1947).

    The "demons of death-fall of the slate" couplet is half a stanza in the U.S. Copyright Office version when American Music, Inc. belatedly registered the album in 1956. Nevertheless, it has a distinctive Travis lyrical signature. He sometimes sang this couplet instead of the more common one: "Like a fiend with his dope and a drunkard his wine/ A man will have lust for the lure of the mine." (See Archie Green, *Only a Miner: Studies in Recorded Coal-Mining Songs* [Urbana: University of Illinois Press, 1972], 290-291.)

62. Paul Camplin, *A New History of Muhlenberg*, 223.

63. Ronald L. Lewis, interview, in *The Mine Wars*, program transcript, ed. Mark Dugas, in *The American Experience* (multi-segment television/video program), 2016. http://www.pbs.org/wgbh/americanexperience/features/transcript/minewars-transcript

64. Merle Travis, "Nine Pound Hammer," on *Folk Songs of the Hills* (Capitol Records, 1947).

Chapter 5: Trial and Execution of Harrison Alexander

1. This epigraph comes from Jack Glazier, *Been Coming Through Some Hard Times: Race, History, and Memory in Western Kentucky* (Knoxville: University of Tennessee Press, 2021), 4.

2. Most of this documentation comes from the self-published booklet by Mike Moore (*The Hanging of Harrison Alexander*, Central City, KY: Moore Publications, 2005). Moore conducted much of his research at the State Archives in Frankfort. The State Archives house the trial transcripts, more court documents, and various source materials among Gov. J. C. W. Beckham's papers. Besides Moore's work and the incorrect single-sentence footnote in Otto A. Rothert, no other Muhlenberg histories (including Camplin's and Smith's) have dealt with this affair. For this reason, Moore deserves credit for compiling the primary source materials, including letters, trial transcripts, and other legal proceedings, and self-publishing his volume. Why the credit? Because, from 1907 until 2005, no one had plucked this trial and execution from the silent archives. Rothert did not.

3. Mari N. Crabtree, "Black Resistance and Lynching Memory: An Interview with Mari N. Crabtree, Part 1," *Black Perspectives* (May 2, 2023). Black Resistance and Lynching Memory: An Interview with Mari N. Crabtree Part I | AAIHS

4. The reasons that the Central Citians wrote the "Petition of Seventy-Six" (the label is mine) are unknown, so scholars must interpret from only a few facts. However, the most reasonable answer is that they wanted justice.

5. *Louisville Courier-Journal*, "No Interference; Harrison Alexander Dies on the Gallows" (Aug. 10, 1907), 3.

6. Mike Moore, *The Hanging of Harrison Alexander*, 152.

7. *Hartford* [KY] *Republican*, "Died Thirty Minutes After the Trap Sprung; Legal Execution of Harrison Alexander Took Place Last Friday" (Aug. 16, 1907), 1.

Rather than the rope a few inches too long, the authorities built the platform as many as three feet too short. An efficient hanging calculates the "drop energy" using weight and distance. Alexander was 16 years old and probably lightweight. Therefore, sufficient drop energy would have required a fall of as much as more than nine feet. Arguably, hanging is the least cruel form of execution if done correctly. As it happened, one must wonder: Was this tragically administered public hanging an accident?

8. Unnamed Roark funeral home director, quoted in Mike Moore, *The Hanging of Harrison Alexander*, 154.

In an unrelated event, 78 days later, on October 26, 1907, the house near Paradise of the former Union General Don Carlos Buell burned to the ground (Otto A. Rothert, *A History of Muhlenberg County*, 237). Though demonstrative of his interests, it is puzzling that Rothert mentions the isolated house fire (Buell died nine years before) but not the public execution that garnered so much attention across the Commonwealth.

9. See the complete list of petitioners in Moore, 141-143.

These physicians included Milton P. Creel, W. R. McDowell, J. E. Woodburn, and the young J. P. Walton. (The latter did not sign with his M.D. title since he obtained his medical degree the following year.) The other signers included Albin C. Drake, a dentist; Benjamin F. Creel, a jeweler; Squire F. Howey, the Central Coal & Iron General Store manager; and Columbus W. Jones, a general store owner. Other petitioners for leniency for the accused included William E. Fowler, a former Central City postmaster; John M. Vick, owner of a "marble works" and the then-current postmaster; and Jess K. Freeman, Jr., a future postmaster (these three in Camplin, *A New History of Muhlenberg*, 32). The signers included James D. Wood, editor of the *Central City Farmers' and Miners' Advocate* (Otto A. Rothert, *A History of Muhlenberg County*, 352). Five biographies of these distinguished men appeared in *Battle's Kentucky: A History of the State* (Battle, Perrin, and Kniffin, 1885; Rothert, 405). These men were doctors Creel and McDowell, George Gordon, Columbus W. Jones, and William E. Robinson. Finally, two future police judges signed the petition: Hugh E. Coche and John T. May (Camplin, 33). (The state abolished the office of police judge when it re-patterned local government.) A directory lists these last four men in R. L. Polk & Co., *R. L. Polk & Co.'s Kentucky State Gazetteer and Business Directory for 1895-96* (Detroit: R. L. Polk & Co., 1896),40; rpt. 1984; and Utica, KY: McDowell Publications, rpt. 2015; also, in *Kentucky Explorer* (Feb. 2015), 53. (See Muhlenberg County Kentucky, "Local History, Central City 1895 Business Directory" at kykinfolk.com/muhlenberg/history/central-city1895.htm. The entire state directory at https://dcms.lds.org/delivery/DeliveryManagerServlet?dps_pid=IE45279 34.)

10. In Paul Camplin, *A New History of Muhlenberg*, 33; Rothert, *A History of Muhlenberg County*, 416, 396n2.

11. In Mike Moore, *The Hanging of Harrison Alexander*, 141.

12. Rebekah Smith, "Comment; Protecting the Victim: Rape and Sexual Harassment Shields Under Maine and Federal Law," *Maine Legal Review* 49: 450-451 (1997).

13. Mike Moore, *The Hanging of Harrison Alexander*, 59-60.

14. Defense attorney John Feland, quoted in Moore, 147-148 (emphasis added).

15. Victor B. Howard, "The Breckinridge Family and the Negro Testimony Controversy in Kentucky, 1866-1872," *Filson Club History Quarterly* 49 (Jan. 1975): 56. The Kentucky General Assembly passed this law allowing Black testimony when the federal government threatened to prosecute state judges in federal court.

16. *Louisville Courier-Journal*, "No Interference," 3.

17. *Hopkinsville Kentuckian*, "Attracts Big Crowd; Troops Guard Negro Accused of Criminal Assault" (Aug. 21, 1906), 5.

18. Mike Moore, *The Hanging of Harrison Alexander*, 122.

19. Moore, 122.

20. Moore, 135-137, 149.

21. *Hopkinsville Kentuckian*, "Alexander Was Hanged Friday at Greenville" (Aug. 10, 1907), 1; *Louisville Courier-Journal*, "No Interference," 3.

22. Kentucky Educational Television (KET), "The Eighth of August," Kentucky Educational Television (Aug. 5, 2016). https://www.ket.org/promos/kentucky/the-eighth-of-august/

23. Darrel E. Bigham, *Towns and Villages of the Lower Ohio* (Lexington: University Press of Kentucky, 1998); George C. Wright, *A History of Blacks in Kentucky*, 30.

24. Anonymous reporter, (n.t.), *Greenville Kentucky Republican* (May 18, 1870), repr. in *A History of Muhlenberg County*, by Otto A. Rothert, 362-65. (This article is no longer available anywhere other than in Rothert.)

25. See the biography of R. Y. Thomas, Jr., in Paul Camplin, *A New History of Muhlenberg*, 171-175.

26. Otto A. Rothert, *A History of Muhlenberg County*, 351.

27. Paul Camplin, *A New History of Muhlenberg*, 171. Will E. Eaves, the editor-owner of the *Muhlenberg Echo* and political adversary of R. Y. Thomas within the Democratic Party, described Thomas "in all his fiery and untamed eloquence." This description fits Thomas throughout his life, including his long years in the U.S. Congress. (Will E. Eaves, untitled editorial, *Muhlenberg Echo* [Feb. 17, 1887], 2)

28. Camplin, 171.

29. Otto A. Rothert, *A History of Muhlenberg County*, front matter.

30. Rothert, 184n3.

31. Ernest J. Gaines, *A Lesson Before Dying* (New York: Vintage Contemporaries, 1993).

Chapter 6: Endemic Violence

1. This epigraph comes from the first stanza of "Riders in the Night," by prolific Kentucky poet Madison Julius Cawein, in *New Poems* (London: Grant Richards, 1909), 191-195.

    In the complete first stanza, Cawein portrays vigilantism as macabre:

    > *Death rides black-masked to-night; and through the land*
    > *Madness beside him brandishes a torch.*
    > *The peaceful farmhouse with its vine-wreathed porch*
    > *Lies in their way. Death lifts a bony hand*
    > *And knocks, and Madness makes a wild demand*

    Otto Rothert wrote a biography of Cawein. (Otto A. Rothert, *The Story of a Poet, Madison Cawein* [Louisville: John P. Morton & Co., 1921]). Born in Louisville in 1865, Cawein died in the same city in 1914. He was a poet of nature, landscape, and, in this one, the cultural landscape.

2. Richard Maxwell Brown, *Strain of Violence: Historical Studies of American Violence and Vigilantism* (New York: Oxford University Press, 1975), viii.

3. Richard Maxwell Brown, "The American Vigilante Tradition," Appendix, "The American Vigilante Movements," in *The History of Violence in America: Historical and Comparative Perspectives*, ed. Hugh Davis Graham and Ted Robert Gurr (New York: Frederick A. Praeger, 1969), 222.

4. James A. Tyner, Joshua F. J. Inwood, and Derek H. Alderman, "Theorizing Violence and the Dialectics of Landscape Memorialization: A Case Study of Greensboro, North Carolina," *Environment and Planning D: Society and Space* 32, no. 5 (Oct. 2014): 903.

5. Suzanne Marshall, *Violence in the Black Patch and Tennessee* (Columbia and London: University of Missouri Press, 1994).

6. William Lynnwood Montell, *Killings: Folk Justice in the Upper South* (Lexington: University Press of Kentucky, 1986).

7. Mid-eighteenth-century Regulator violence occurred in 1850 when citizens formed a "regulating party" to combat a "gang of villains" who roamed southern Muhlenberg. The Regulators whipped one man, forcing his flight from the county. The authorities charged another man with house arson in county court but acquitted him. Subsequently, Regulators

convened an extrajudicial citizen's court to hear this case. This time, a local "minister of the gospel" presided, with a second minister as recorder. With a vote of 50 to 10 or 12, the citizen's council found the accused guilty and ordered him to vacate the county. (*Hopkinsville Whig*, n.d., reprinted in the *Louisville Morning Courier*, "Doings in Muhlenburg" [June 3, 1850], 3).

8. Diane Miller Sommerville, *Aberration of Mind: Suicide and Suffering in the Civil War-Era South* (Chapel Hill: University of North Carolina Press, 2018), 153.

9. Diane Miller Sommerville, interview, "Time of Despair," *Civil War Times* (April 2020), 25.

10. Drew Gilpin Faust, *This Republic of Suffering: Death and the American Civil War* (Vintage Books: New York, 2008), 267.

11. David Lowenthal, "The Place of the Past in the American Landscape," in *Geographies of the Mind: Essays in Historical Geography in Honor of John Kirtland Wright*, ed. David Lowenthal and Martyn J. Bowman (New York: Oxford University Press), 106.

12. Charles Reagan Wilson, *Baptized in Blood*, 1.

13. Jelani Cobb, "Charlottesville and the Trouble with the Civil War Hypotheticals," *New Yorker* (Aug. 16, 2017). https://www.newyorker.com/news/daily-comment/charlottesville-and-the-trouble-with-civil-war-hypotheticals

14. Robert Penn Warren, *The Legacy of the Civil War*, 15.

15. Jelani Cobb, "Charlottesville and the Trouble."

16. Allen C. Guelzo, "Lecture 12: The Agony of Reunion," The American Civil War, course lecture transcript (Pace University, Dec. 8, 2021).

17. Anne E. Marshall, *Creating a Confederate Kentucky*, 56.

18. Booker T. Washington, "The Educational Outlook in the South," "Address Delivered to the National Education Association at Madison, Wisconsin, July 16, 1884," in *African-American Social and Political Thought, 1850-1920*, ed. Howard Brotz (New Brunswick, NJ: Transaction Publishers, 1992 [1966]), 354 (emphasis added).

19. Alexis de Tocqueville, *Democracy in America*, vol. 1, trans. Henry Reeve (London: Saunders and Otley, 1838), 355.

20. Suzanne Marshall, *Violence in the Black Patch*, 87.

21. Lowell H. Harrison and James C. Klotter, *A New History of Kentucky*, 216.

22. Lowell H. Harrison, *The Civil War in Kentucky*, 103.

23. Otto A. Rothert, *A History of Unity Baptist Church, Muhlenberg County, Kentucky* (Louisville: John P. Morton & Co., 1914), 37. https://archive.org/details/historyofunityba00roth

24. David W. Blight, *Race and Reunion*, 2.

25. W. E. B. Du Bois, *Black Reconstruction in America*.

26. Vincent Harding, *There Is a River: The Black Struggle for Freedom in America* (New York and London: Harcourt Brace Jovanovich, Publishers, 1981).

27. David W. Blight, *Race and Reunion*, 2.

28. Suzanne Marshall, *Violence in the Black Patch*, 24.

29. James C. Klotter, *Kentucky: Portrait in Paradox, 1900-1950* (Frankfort: Kentucky Historical Society, 1996), 63; Marshall, *Violence in the Black Patch*, 23-24, and passim: "guerilas of the tobacco war" in an untitled news item in the *Hopkinsville Kentuckian* (Aug. 10, 1907), 5.

30. *Greenville Record*, "Night Riders Make Their First Visit to Muhlenberg County Monday Night" (Dec. 17, 1908).

31. Federal Writers' Project of the Works Projects Administration for the State of Kentucky, *Military History of Kentucky, Chronologically Arranged* (Frankfort: Printed by the State Journal, 1939), 321. http://kynghistory.ky.gov/Media/Publications/DMA/MilitaryHistoryKY1939AnlRpt.pdf

32. Planters' Protective Association, "Tobacco Matters Adjusted," and advertisement, *Greenville Record* (Jan. 7, 1909), 2, 3.

33. Cameron Knight, "History: 'Possum Hunters' Terrorized, Killed," *Cincinnati Enquirer* (Mar. 13, 2016). http://www.cincinnati.com/story/news/history/2016/03/07/history-possum-hunters-terrorized-killed-dark/80706386/

34. George C. Wright (*Racial Violence in Kentucky*, 280) and several newspaper articles correctly give Browder's first name as Rufus. Despite this, the Federal Writers Project has Russell as his name. (Federal Writers

Project, *Military History*, 320). Tom Noe informed me that James S. Cunningham may have been the local Possum Hunter leader (personal communication, 2023).

35. C. B. Moore, in the *Louisville Courier-Journal*, "Protest Against Pardon of Rufus Browder" (Nov. 23, 1911), 3.

36. George C. Wright, *A History of Blacks in Kentucky*, 3.

37. *Louisville Courier-Journal*, "Four Negroes on Cedar Tree" (Aug. 2, 1908), 1, 3; George C. Wright, *Racial Violence in Kentucky*, 124-125. A WKU PBS film is the most detailed source: Western Kentucky University Public Broadcasting Service, *By Parties Unknown* (June 28, 2023), YouTube. https://www.youtube.com/watch?v=oeFn3fiMqSM&list=LL&index=20&ab_channel=WKUPBS. Tom Rhea was the Logan County sheriff. This multiple-victim lynching was photographed and made into grisly postcards that locals sent around the country.

38. Livermore is the largest city (but not the county seat) in McLean County, with 1,400 townspeople.

39. *Louisville Courier-Journal*, "Lynched Before the Footlights; Bloody Drama Is Staged in Livermore, Ky." (April 21, 1911), 1.

40. *Louisville Courier-Journal*, "Murder Is the Charge Made; Alleged Members of the Livermore Mob Arrested" (May 13, 1911), 1.

41. John E. Kleber, "Livermore Lynching," in *The Kentucky Encyclopedia*, ed.-in-chief John E. Kleber, 563.

42. *Louisville Courier-Journal*, "Murder Is the Charge Made," 1.

43. John E. Kleber, "Livermore Lynching," 563.

44. In George C. Wright, *Racial Violence in Kentucky*; a depiction with caption after 163.

Chapter 7: Possum Hunter Reign of Terror

1. This epigraph comes from Ben Okri, *A Way of Being There* (London: Head of Zeus, 2014), 43.

2. Confusingly, some news organizations, after 1909, continued to use the name Night Riders for these violent gangs. Additionally, some rings of the earlier Night Riders were self-named "Possum Hunters."

3. Paul Camplin, *A New History of Muhlenberg*, 101.
4. Cameron Knight, "History: 'Possum Hunters' Terrorized, Killed."
5. Claud W. Perry, "'Possum Hunters' Bring Terror to Muhlenberg," *Louisville Courier-Journal* (April 5, 1914), 1, 6.
6. *York Daily* (Pennsylvania), "'Possum Hunters' Outlaws; Kentucky Band Directs Outrages Against Negroes" (Dec. 17, 1914), 9.
7. *York Daily*, 9.
8. *Louisville Courier-Journal,* "Judge Pace's Garage Burned; Trouble in Muhlenberg" (June 8, 1914), 1.
9. *Louisville Courier-Journal*, "Denies Being Possum Hunter" (April 14, 1915), 1.
10. *Louisville Courier-Journal*, "Judge Pace's Garage Burned," 1.
11. Sallie Carr Drake Isaac, *The Story of Drakesboro and Its Founder* (Drakesboro, KY: self-published by Sallie Carr Drake Isaac, n.d. [1952]), 67; available at Muhlenberg County Libraries, and the Muhlenberg County shelf at the Martin F. Schmidt Research Library, Kentucky Historical Society, Frankfort.
12. Judge James F. Gordon, Madisonville, interviews by Ethel White, June 22-Aug. 14, 1987, in *Freedom on the Border*, 33.
13. *York Daily*, "'Possum Hunters' Outlaws," 9.
14. *Hartford Herald* (Kentucky), "Oath Taken by Possum Hunters at Altar of Guns, Halter and Strap" (Jan. 19, 1916).
15. *Coal Age*, untitled news items, vol. 6/7 (1914): 290, 845. Two informants think that the Black Galilee neighborhood of Central City was a section on the north end of what became known to white Central Citians as Colored Town.
16. *Coal Age*, 290, 845.
17. Suzanne Marshall, *Violence in the Black Patch*, xi.
18. Thomas Jefferson, *Notes on the State of Virginia* (New York: Penguin Books, 1999 [1787]), 146.
19. *York Daily*, "'Possum Hunters' Outlaws," 9.

20. *Lewisburg Leader*, "Negro Colony Is Raided by Mob" (April 30, 1915), 1.

21. *Owensboro Messenger*, "Negro Dies; Who Was Victim of Ohio County Possum Hunters" (May 2, 1915).

22. *York Daily*, 9.

23. Sallie Carr Drake Isaac, *The Story of Drakesboro*, 67-68.

24. *York Daily*, "'Possum Hunters' Outlaws," 9.

25. *Owensboro Twice-A-Week Messenger*, "Reward of $200 for 'Possum Hunters' Arrest" (Jan. 16, 1915), 3.

26. *Danville Advocate-Messenger* (Nov. 30, 1915), 4.

27. Suzanne Marshall, *Violence in the Black Patch*, 133.

28. Pearl Perguson (of Horse Branch, Ohio County), in Cameron Knight, "History: 'Possum Hunters' Terrorized, Killed." This Pearl Perguson quote comes from her interview with Kevin Eans, archived at the Western Kentucky University Folklife Archives Project, WKU Special Collections Library.

29. Nancy Richey, quoted in Knight.

30. Claud W. Perry, "'Possum Hunters' Bring Terror to Muhlenberg," 1.

31. Perry, 6.

32. Perry, 6.

33. Jackson Lears, *Rebirth of a Nation: The Making of Modern America, 1877-1920* (New York: HarperCollins, 2009), 79.

34. When the Great Depression subjected the capitalist system to potent strains, various labor and political interests formed around the country, attempting to unite workers. In 1938, organizers of the Workers Alliance of America (WAA) called for a meeting on July 15 at the Central City Colored School (completed that year by the federal Works Progress Administration [WPA]). The announced speakers included Russell O'Neill, county attorney, and W. H. Hunt, Muhlenberg state representative. (*Central City Times-Argus*, "Workers Alliance Calls for Meeting for Night of July 15" [July 8, 1938], 1)

    In 1935, the Socialist Party of America formed the WAA as a trade union for WPA workers. The WAA soon became an umbrella organization uniting three distinct political entities—the socialists, communists (the Communist Party USA), and the American Workers Party—for joint efforts against unemployment. By the time of the Central City meeting in 1938, the communists dominated the group. The WAA functioned more like a typical political pressure group for the WPA's Congressional budgetary and employment interests.

No more documentation has surfaced on the WAA meeting's organizational activities. Nevertheless, a researcher would find more details about its efforts if the group had been successful. In any case, the national WAA had disintegrated by the following year.

But why Muhlenberg? The reason was probably due to the county's lengthy list of WPA projects, hence the substantial number of WPA workers.

The following lists Muhlenberg WPA projects completed in 1936-1939: Bremen school gymnasium; Cleaton School; Drakesboro High School gymnasium; Greenville City Hall and Fire Station; Greenville Hospital; Greenville High School gymnasium and auditorium; Greenville U.S. Post Office; and Hughes-Kirkpatrick School. In Central City: the City Ballpark grandstand and athletic field; Central City swimming pool, bathhouses, and tennis courts; a Training Work Center sewing room for women upstairs in the City Building; and noted above, the Central City Colored School (the name on the building above the front entrance). The WPA also constructed roads: Graham Road, Greenville-Madisonville Road, Harpers [*sic*] Hill Road, and Penrod Road.

This list of WPA projects comes from the Goodman-Paxton Photographic Collection, Special Collections, University of Kentucky Libraries. From the photos in this collection, many laborers were Black Americans, as they were throughout the country. Some of these included those who worked on the Central City Swimming Pool. Paradoxically, however, they and their families were barred from swimming there.

35. *Louisville Courier-Journal*, "Denies Being Possum Hunter" (April 14, 1915), 1.

36. *Owensboro Messenger*, "A Strike at the Tobacco Manufactory" (July 26, 1887).

37. Paul Camplin, *A New History of Muhlenberg*, 99-100.

38. Michael Barga, "Terrence V. Powderly (1849-1924): Union Leader, Politician, Machinist, Lawyer," *Social Welfare History Project* (Virginia Commonwealth University Libraries, 2012). http://socialwelfare.library.vcu.edu/people/powderly-terrence/

39. Peter M. Bergman, *The Chronological History of the Negro in America* (New York: Harper & Row, 1969), 299.

40. *Cincinnati Enquirer*, "Oath Taken by 'Possum Hunters' at Altar of Guns, Rope Halter and Strap, Jenkins Says" (Jan. 12, 1916); the same article reprinted in *Hartford Herald*, "Oath Taken by Possum Hunters at Altar of Guns, Halter and Strap" (Jan. 19, 1916).

41. *Cincinnati Enquirer*; *Hartford Herald*.

42. Berry Craig, "What Do You Get When You Mix Christian Socialists with Deep Red Kentucky?" *Louisville Courier-Journal*, Opinion (July 26, 2021). https://www.courier-journal.com/story/opinion/2021/07/26/when-christian-socialists-came-to-deep-red-graves-county-kentucky/7976222002/

43. *Owensboro Inquirer*, "Socialists Organizing" (Dec. 2, 1915), 3; *Owensboro Messenger*, "Meeting Is Held in Owensboro by Socialists" (Dec. 2. 1915), 6.

44. Suzanne Marshall, *Violence in the Black Patch*, 19.

45. Marshall, xi.

46. Bobby Anderson, *Hazel Creek Missionary Baptist Church Organized December 3, 1797: A 200 Year History* (Hazel Creek Church History Committee, n.d. [1997?]).

47. Christopher Waldrep, "'So Much Sin': The Decline of Religious Discipline and the 'Tidal Wave' of Crime," *Journal of Social History* 23, no. 3 (Spring 1990): 536.

48. George C. Wright, *Racial Violence in Kentucky*, 143.

49. Otto A. Rothert, *A History of Muhlenberg County*, 343.

50. *Hartford Herald*, "Convictions of Possum Hunters Is Sought" (Dec. 23, 1914), 1.

51. Agnes S. Harralson, and Elmer Cornette, "Vigilantes Hanged Possum Hunters' Leader in 1914," *Central City Times-Argus* (Jan. 25, 1962), 4. In this article, Harralson includes Elmer Cornette's short 1,600-word

remembrance of the Possum Hunters. In addition, she recorded that he signed it. Harralson also announced she sent a copy of Cornette's account to the Kentucky Building, Western Kentucky University archives.

52. *Hartford Republican*, "Possum Hunter Is Strung Up; Muhlenberg County Scene of Lynching" (Nov. 20, 1914), 3. Hillside is near Powderly.

53. Joyce Walker, "Possum Hunters: A Vigilance Committee" (Manuscripts & Folklore Archives, Library Special Collections, Western Kentucky University, 1970), 6.

54. Elmer Cornette, in Harralson and Cornette, "Vigilantes Hanged Possum Hunters' Leader," 4.

55. Robert M. Ireland, *Little Kingdoms: The Counties of Kentucky, 1850-1891* (Lexington: University Press of Kentucky, 1977), 38.

56. Ireland, 71.

57. *Hartford Republican*, "Possum Hunter Is Strung Up," 3 (emphasis added).

58. Elmer Cornette, in Harralson and Cornette, "Vigilantes Hanged Possum Hunters' Leader," 4.

59. Paul Camplin, *A New History of Muhlenberg*, 101.

60. Elmer Cornette, in Haralson and Cornette, "Vigilantes Hanged Possum Hunters' Leader," 4.

61. Cornette, 4.

62. See the biography of Arthur Iler in Paul Camplin, *A New History of Muhlenberg*, 135-138.

63. Arthur Iler, quoted in Joyce Walker, "Possum Hunters: A Vigilance Committee."

It is astonishing that Iler—a former county judge, assistant Kentucky attorney general, and law partner of Hubert Meredith (himself a highly regarded attorney and Kentucky attorney general)—would implicate Meredith in a homicide conspiracy and coverup. However, Judge Iler may have been forthcoming in his comments because he thought his interview would never reach beyond a college student's class paper (now available to anyone; see note 53 above). Alternatively, he may have felt compelled to get the true story out in the interest of justice and the historical record.

64. See Hubert Meredith's biography in Paul Camplin, *A New History of Muhlenberg*, 151-154.

65. Arthur Iler, quoted in Joyce Walker, "Possum Hunters: A Vigilance Committee," 25 (emphasis added).

66. Elmer Cornette, in Harralson and Cornette, "Vigilantes Hanged Possum Hunters' Leader," 4.

67. An untitled news item in "The Labor Situation" section of *Coal Age* (Nov. 21, 1914), 823.

68. *Hartford Herald*, "Called Out and Strung Up; Henry Allen's Death Is Mysterious" (Nov. 18, 1914), 1.

69. *Earlington Bee*, editorial, "Savagery and Ignorance" (Nov. 17, 1914), 1; rpt. from *Louisville Courier-Journal*.

70. J. D. Langley, the Central City police chief—one of the co-conspirators identified by Judge Iler—moved to Kansas City in late 1916 and died there in early 1917. He resigned his office after the Allen murder after suffering an emotional crisis. Langley's poor mental health was due to "his activities during the 'possum hunter' disorder in this county [Muhlenberg]," according to this news article, "[which] are believed to have been responsible for a nervous breakdown." The 60-year-old Langley went missing for several months in Kansas City before someone found his body washed into a storm drain. (*Hartford Herald*, "Kentuckian's Body Is Found in Sewer" [Mar. 21, 1917])

71. Elliot Jaspin, *Buried in the Bitter Waters: The Hidden History of Racial Cleansing in America* (New York: Basic Books, 2007), 166-183.

72. Lannie Jackson, letter to the editor, "The Klan at Central City," *Louisville Courier-Journal* (Aug. 19, 1923), 5:4 (44); International Labor News Service, "Ku Klux Klan Menace to Union Labor, Says Mayor of Kentucky City," *The Garment Worker* 22, no. 45 (Aug. 31, 1923): 3. https://babel.hathitrust.org/cgi/pt?id=coo.31924054440924&view=1up&seq=349&skin=2021

Another Klan group formed in Powderly in 1999. (*Louisville Courier-Journal*, "Klan Leader Says FBI Raiders Asked about Bomb, Assassination Plot [April 16, 1999], A1, A10). After a time, its "wizard" moved to another county.

73. Hambleton Tapp and James C. Klotter, *Kentucky: Decades of Discord, 1865-1900* (Frankfort: Kentucky Historical Society, 1977), 408.

74. James Baldwin, "Here Be Dragons," in *The Price of the Ticket: Collected Nonfiction, 1948-1985*, by James Baldwin (Boston: Beacon Press, 2021 [1985]), 686.

Chapter 8: The Strange Case of Dr. R. T. Bailey

1. This epigraph comes from Michel-Rolph Trouillot, *Silencing the Past: Power and the Production of History* (Boston: Beacon Press, 1995), xxiii.

2. Kenneth Mills, "Widths Within and Without," *Perspectives on History*. Online ed. (Summer 2013), para. 9.
www.historians.org/Perspectives/issues/2013/1306/small-world-forum-mills.cfm

3. Leslie Shively Smith, *Around Muhlenberg*, 57. Thanks to J. P. Johnson and Dorann O'Neal Lam for their aid in finding information on Dr. R. T. and Ora Lee Bailey (personal communications, 2016).

4. Most of these details come from the news article in the *Central City Messenger* ("Colored Doctor Commits Suicide" [(April 19, 1934]).

    The legal charge against R. T. Baily appears in Muhlenberg County Kentucky Circuit Court, Criminal Order Book 10, 1933-1936; case title: *Commonwealth of Kentucky v. Dr. R. T. Bailey* (Muhlenberg County Kentucky, Circuit Court Records).
www.kykinfolk.com/muhlenberg/court-records/circuit/commonwealth-bailey.htm

5. *Hartford Herald*, "Rewards Offered to Convict Bootleggers; The Law and Order League Will Pay the Bill" (June 7, 1916), 3. The difference in the reward tells of the racial value assigned to each group.

6. Details about the residency of the Baileys come from the 1930 U.S. Census.

7. Leslie Shively Smith, *Around Muhlenberg*, 57, 59, 76, 263.

    Smith, a long-serving local teacher, must have known the Baileys. She noted Dr. Bailey twice and Ora Lee several times as a teacher. However, Smith does not broach Bailey's suicide. This approach suits her historiographic standpoint of African American *contributionism*, with no negativity allowed.

8. A resident of Central City believes his older sister died from malnutrition during the Great Depression in Muhlenberg (personal communication, 2018; name withheld).

9. The entire article, verbatim, from the *Central City Messenger* (April 19, 1934) with the sub-headline: "Dr. R. T. Bailey Takes His Own Life Before Going on Trial in Circuit Court":

   > Dr. Robert T. Bailey, colored physician of Central City, Kentucky, 52 years of age, committed suicide in Greenville, Ky, Tuesday morning, where he was about to go on trial on a charge of illegal operation on a white woman. It is understood he took the poison in a colored restaurant. He then walked to the court room where he collapsed in his seat. Greenville doctors pumped out his stomach and sent him on to his own sanitarium in Central City, where he died almost as soon as he arrived. Dr. Bailey is survived by his widow. He had practiced medicine for many years in this city. Funeral services will be conducted at the Central City Baptist church tomorrow (Friday), and interment will occur in the afternoon in the colored cemetery in Greenville. (*Central City Messenger*, "Colored Doctor Commits Suicide" [April 19, 1934])

   A discrepancy appears between the news account in the *Central City Messenger* and the death certificate concerning Bailey's age. The former has 52 years; the latter is probably the accurate version with 55. A further mystery is that I have found no other news accounts of Bailey's suicide in the *Courier-Journal* or regional newspapers. This news void is highly unusual and inexplicable.

10. Leslie J. Reagan, *When Abortion Was a Crime: Women, Medicine, and Law in the United States, 1867-1973* (Berkeley: University of California Press, 1997), 132, 138-139.

    The Kentucky General Assembly enacted the Kentucky law relating to abortions in 1910; the same one existed in 1934. (The relevant statute is in K.S. Section 1219a-2.)

11. William Faulkner, *Requiem for a Nun* (New York: Vintage International, 2011 [1950]), 28.

12. Roger Frazier, Drakesboro, provided details about the separate restrooms and drinking fountains at the Muhlenberg County Courthouse. He, three others, and I met in a group interview session at Ebenezer Baptist Church, Central City, on April 8, 2017.

13. Richard Wright, *Black Boy*.

14. Ralph Ellison, "Richard Wright's Blues," in *Richard Wright's* Black Boy (American Hunger): *A Casebook*, ed. William L. Andrews and Douglas Taylor (Oxford: Oxford University Press, 2003), 60; quoted and discussed in Tom Fielder, "Psychoanalysis and Anti-Racism in Mid-20th-Century America: An Alternative Angle of Vision," *History of the Human Sciences* 35, no. 3/4: 208.

Chapter 9: Black Soldiers in the World Wars

1. This epigraph comes from John H. Arnold, *History: A Very Short Introduction* (Oxford: Oxford University Press, 2000), 16.

2. Aaron Astor, *Rebels on the Border: Civil War, Emancipation, and the Reconstruction of Kentucky and Missouri* (Baton Rouge: Louisiana State University Press, 2012), 126; Ira Berlin, Joseph P. Reidy, and Leslie S. Rowland, eds., *Freedom's Soldiers: The Black Military Experience in the Civil War* (Cambridge: Cambridge University Press, 1998), 16, Table I.

3. Jefferson Davis Monument souvenir pamphlet (1928), quoted in Anne E. Marshall, *Creating a Confederate Kentucky*, 181.

4. R. Y. Thomas, Jr., "Letter to President Woodrow Wilson" (Feb. 20, 1918), file #3735, ser. 4, Woodrow Wilson Papers, Library of Congress.

5. Leslie Shively Smith, *Around Muhlenberg*, 97, 119. By my count, Leslie Shively Smith identifies at least eighty-three Black Muhlenberger WW I soldiers.

6. Leslie Shively Smith, *Around Muhlenberg*, 109.

7. In recognition of their World War I bravery and outstanding service, President Joe Biden signed into law (on Aug. 25, 2021) H.R. 3642—the "Harlem Hellfighters Congressional Gold Medal Act," awarding a Congressional Gold Medal to the Harlem Hellfighters.

8. Tom Eblen, "Who Knew? World War I's Famous 'Harlem Hellfighters' Included Many Kentuckians," *Lexington Herald-Leader* (April 7, 2017). www.kentucky.com/news/local/news-columns-blogs/tom-eblen/article143388064.html

9. Winona L. Fletcher, sr. ed., et al., *Community Memories: A Glimpse of African American Life in Frankfort, Kentucky* (Frankfort: Kentucky Historical Society, 2003), 70.

10. Donald L. Grant, *The Way It Was in the South: The Black Experience in Georgia*, ed. Jonathan Grant (Athens: University of Georgia Press, 1993), 307-308.

11. Michael S. Neiberg, *The Path to War: How the First World War Created Modern America* (New York: Oxford University Press, 2016), 200.

12. Donald L. Grant, *The Way It Was in the South*, 307.

13. Matthew F. Delmont, *Half American: The Epic Story of African Americans Fighting World War II at Home and Abroad* (New York: Viking, 2022). This chapter on the wartime experiences of Black Americans is a barebones treatment—indeed, inadequate—especially for World War II. The reader might consult the excellent, award-winning text by Dartmouth College historian Delmont, who looks at the war, including the home experience, from the perspective of African Americans.

14. This section about Black Muhlenbergers in WW II comes almost entirely from Leslie Shively Smith, *Around Muhlenberg*, 145-149, 155. Smith confides that her list of those serving in WW II is incomplete. Her sources were locals she interviewed (she called it "remembered history"), Veteran's Discharge Records (formerly archived at the Muhlenberg County Court Clerk's Office), and Agnes Harralson's files.

    While Graham's postmaster, Agnes Simpson Harralson (author of *Steamboats on the Green*) began a letter-writing project to Muhlenberger soldiers in WW I, continuing beyond WW II. In 1951, when Harralson became the society page editor of the *Central City Messenger* and *Times-Argus*, she mailed her "Service Star" page about county soldiers to each serviceperson (see Smith, 159-160). (At that time, the editors/owners published the two papers with the same content with a mid-run masthead change.)

15. Daina Ramey Berry and Kali Nicole Gross, *A Black Women's History of the United States* (Boston: Beacon Press, 2020), 147

16. Smith provides no further details on Central Citian Charles Baker, the WW II sailor, about his injuries or life after the war.

17. A steward's mate is a cook and personal assistant to a naval officer and a step up from a mess cook.

18. Smith provides no further details on the death of PFC Blasengane, whether accidental or by some other cause. Nevertheless, like the white Muhlenbergers in Army units fighting in the Italian Campaign,

Blasengane must have been involved in military action on the peninsula. This action was a high-casualty slog through mud and blood.

19. Robert F. Jefferson, *Fighting for Hope: African American Troops of the 93rd Infantry Division in World War II and Postwar America* (Baltimore: Johns Hopkins Press, 2008).

20. Le'Trice D. Donaldson, *Duty Beyond the Battlefield: African American Soldiers Fight for Racial Uplift, Citizenship, and Manhood, 1870-1920* (Carbondale: Southern Illinois University Press, 2020).

21. James G. Thompson, letter to the editor, "Should I Sacrifice to Live 'Half-American?'" *Pittsburgh Courier* (Jan. 31, 1942), 3.

22. Langston Hughes, "Beaumont to Detroit: 1943," in *The Collected Poems of Langston Hughes*, ed. Arnold Rampersad, assoc. ed. David Roessel (New York: Vintage, 1995), 281 (capitalization in the original). I have included stanzas 3, 6, 7, and 8. Hughes's title refers to the "race riots" in Beaumont and Detroit during WW II.

23. Horace R. Cayton, "An Awakening: The Negro Now Fights for Democratic Rights of All the World's Peoples," *Pittsburgh Courier* (Feb. 27, 1943), 13.

24. Edward J. K. Gitre, ed., *The American Soldier in World War II; Race & Ethnicity* (Blacksburg: Virginia Tech University, 2021). https://americansoldierww2.org/topics/race-and-ethnicity

Chapter 10: Complexity, Continuity, and Racialized Spaces

1. This epigraph comes from Katherine McKittrick, *Demonic Grounds: Black Women and the Cartographies of Struggle* (Minneapolis and London: University of Minnesota Press, 2006), xii.

2. Rosalyn Terborg-Penn, *African American Women in the Struggle for the Vote, 1850-1920* (Bloomington and Indianapolis: University of Indiana Press, 1998), 7.

3. Bettiola Heloise Fortson, untitled poem, in *Mental Pearls: Original Poems and Essays* (n.p.: Julius F. Taylor [pub.], 1915). See Randolph Hollingsworth, "Bettiola Heloise Fortson, Poet and Suffragist from Hopkinsville," *H-Net: Humanities & Social Sciences Online, H-Kentucky* (April 8, 2017). https://networks.h-net.org/node/2289/discussions/174933/bettiola-heloise-fortson-poet-and-suffragist-hopkinsville

4. Annie Simms Banks, quoted in Rosalyn Terborg-Penn, *African American Women*, 150.

5. Merle Travis, interview by Ed Kahn, "Merle Travis Interview July 10th, 1961 RARE." YouTube.com. (beginning at 6:00) (my transcription of the video).

6. Carter G. Woodson, *The Mis-Education of the Negro* (Mineola, NY: Dover Publications, 2005 [1933]), 55.

7. James W. Loewen, *Sundown Towns: A Hidden Dimension of Racism* (New York: Touchstone, 2005), 141.

   Marshall County is still overwhelmingly white. The 2020 U.S. Census lists Marshall County as 96.0 percent "White alone, not Hispanic or Latino," 1.9 percent as "Hispanic or Latino," 1.0 percent as "two or more races," 0.5 percent as "Asian alone," 0.5 percent "Black or African American alone," and 0.3 percent "American Indian." For comparison, Trigg County, contiguous to Marshall, has more than fourteen times the percentage of Blacks at 7.1 percent.
   https://www.census.gov/quickfacts/marshallcountykentucky;
   https://www.census.gov/quickfacts/triggcountykentucky

8. Curtis G. Brasfield, *The Ancestry of Harold Washington* (Berwyn Heights, MD: Heritage Books, 2014),11; Isabel Wilkerson briefly notes this in her *The Warmth of Other Suns: The Epic Story of America's Great Migration* (New York: Vintage Books, 2010), 509.

9. Christopher Phillips, *The Rivers Ran Backward*, 332.

10. C. Vann Woodward, *The Strange Career of Jim Crow* (Oxford and New York: Oxford University Press, 2002 [1955]), 10.

11. Langston Hughes, "Here to Yonder" column, *Chicago Defender* (March 29, 1947), in Chitown Kev, commentary, "Here to Yonder: The Chicago Defender Columns of Langston Hughes," *Daily Kos* (Nov. 9, 2021).
    https://www.dailykos.com/stories/2021/11/9/2062683/-Black-Kos-Tuesday-s-Chile-Here-to-Yonder-The-Chicago-Defender-columns-of-Langston-Hughes

12. Description of General Buckner's visit is in Otto A. Rothert, *A History of Muhlenberg County*, 257; re-enactment photo with caption in Cleo Roberson and Jan Anderson, *Muhlenberg County*, Images of America series (Charleston, SC: Arcadia Publishing, 2008), 14. Unfortunately, we do not know whether the reenactment included representations of Wing's

eight bondservants, whom he enslaved in 1860. (1860 U.S. Census Slave Schedules, Kentucky, District No. One, Muhlenberg County, 4)

13. C. Vann Woodward, *Origins of the New South, 1877-1913* (Baton Rouge: Louisiana State University Press, 1951), 154-155, 157.

14. William Turner, interview transcript, in *Freedom on the Border*, ed. Catherine Fosl and Tracy E. K'Meyer, 35.

15. Hugh Sweatt (personal communication, 2021).

16. R[ufus] B. Atwood, "Enactment of Civil Rights Program Now," address delivered by R. B. Atwood, President, Kentucky State College, at the Southern Baptist Theological Seminary, Louisville, Kentucky, February 15, 1951, in *Kentucky Negro Educational Association Journal* 22, no. 3 (April 1951): 17.

17. Derrick Bell, "*Brown v. Board of Education* and the Interest Convergence Dilemma,"93 *Harvard Law Review* 518 (1980), rpt. in *The Derrick Bell Reader*, ed. Richard Delgado and Jean Stefanic (New York and London: New York University Press, 2005), 35.

18. Thanks to Darrel McClellan, Bevier-Cleaton and Rochester, and Hugh Sweatt, Central City, for affirming and adding to my memory of the "Impeach Earl Warren" billboard. Sweatt believes it occupied the footprint of the present Central City Elementary School on U.S. 431. This type of political signage sprouted across the South and beyond after several Warren Court decisions, especially in the two school desegregation cases. The national John Birch Society (formed in 1958) sponsored the signs.

19. Arianna Johnson, "Why the Racial Wealth Gap Hasn't Shrunk Since MLK's Death: A Look at the Numbers," *Forbes* (Jan. 14, 2023).

20. Kriston McIntosh, Emily Moss, Ryan Nunn, and Jay Shambaugh, "Examining the Black-White Wealth Gap" (Brookings Institution, Feb. 27, 2020).
https://www.brookings.edu/blog/upfront/2020/02/27/examining-the-black-white-wealth-gap/; Nora Cahill and William G. Gale, "Narrowing the Racial Wealth Gap Using the EITC and CTC" (Brookings Institution, Feb. 2, 2022). https://www.brookings.edu/blog/how-we-rise/2022/02/02/narrowing-the-racial-wealth-gap-using-the-eitc-and-ctc/; Heather McGhee, *The Sum of Us: What Racism Costs Everyone and How We Can Prosper Together* (New York: One World, 2021), 81.

I do not posit that race is the only or best rubric for examining this problem by listing these racial disparities. In other words, the differentials do not necessarily identify a cause.

21. Rachel Mayer, Alison Dingwall, Juli Simon-Thomas, Abdul Sheikhnureldin, and Kathy Lewis," The United States Maternal Mortality Rate Will Continue to Increase Without Access to Data," *Health Affairs Forefront* (Feb. 4, 2019). https://www.healthaffairs.org/do/10.1377/forefront.20190130.92512/full/

22. Annie E. Casey Foundation, table, "Children in Extreme Poverty (50 Percent Poverty) by Race and Ethnicity" (Kids Count Data Center, n.d.). www.datacenter.kidscount.org

23. Ta-Nehisi Coates, "The Case for Reparations," *The Atlantic* (June 2014). https://www.theatlantic.com/magazine/archive/2014/06/the-case-for-reparations/361631/

24. Jonathan Scott Holloway, *Jim Crow Wisdom: Memory and Identity in Black America since 1940* (Chapel Hill: University of North Carolina Press, 2013), 1

25. Kimberlé Williams Crenshaw, "The Eternal Fantasy of a Racially Virtuous America," *The New Republic* (March 22, 2021). https://newrepublic.com/article/161568/white-supremacy-racism-in-america-kimberle-crenshaw?utm_source=newsletter&utm_medium=email&utm_campaign=tnr_daily

26. Isabel Wilkerson, guest panelist, *The Last Word with Lawrence O'Donnell* (MSNBC Television Network, June 23, 2015) (my transcription).

27. Javier M. Rodriguez, Arline T. Geronimus, John Bound, and Danny Dorling, "Black Lives Matter: Differential Mortality and the Racial Composition of the U.S. Electorate, 1970-2004," *Social Science & Medicine* 136/137 (July 2015): 193-199. National Library of Medicine. https://www.ncbi.nlm.nih.gov/pmc/articles/PMC4465208/#

28. Rodriguez et al., 199.

29. David Cottrell, Michael C. Herron, Javier M. Rodriguez, and David A. Smith, "Mortality, Incarceration, and African American Disenfranchisement in the Contemporary United States," *American Politics Research* 47, no. 2 (March 1, 2019): 195-237. Abstract: https://journals.sagepub.com/doi/pdf/10.1177/1532673X18754555

30. David Cottrell, Michael C. Herron, Javier M. Rodriguez, and David C. Smith, "Nearly 4 Million Black Voters Are Missing. This Is Why," *Washington Post* (April 11, 2018). https://www.washingtonpost.com/news/monkey-cage/wp/2018/04/11/nearly-4-million-black-voters-are-missing-through-early-death-or-over-incarceration-that-distorts-u-s-politics/

31. John Ed Pearce, *Divide and Dissent: Kentucky Politics, 1930-1963* (Lexington: University Press of Kentucky, 1987) 165.

32. Daniel Matlin, review of *Psychology Comes to Harlem: Rethinking the Race Question in Twentieth-Century America* by Jay Garcia, *Journal of American Studies* 48, no. 1 (2014): 340.

33. James A. Jackson, Jr., interview by Maureen Mullinax, transcript 1992OH006ff191, *African-American Farmers Oral History Project* (Louie B. Nunn Center for Oral History, University of Kentucky Libraries, Dec. 30, 1991) (emphasis added). https//oralhistory.uky.edu/oh/render.php?cachefile=1992oh006_ff191_jackson_ohm.xml

34. Jack Glazier, *Been Coming Through Some Hard Times*, 4.

35. Annie L. Bard, Central City (personal communication, handwritten letter, May 1, 2017).

36. George C. Wright, "Race Relations after 1865," in *Our Kentucky: A Study of the Bluegrass State*, 2nd ed., ed. James C. Klotter (Lexington: University Press of Kentucky, 2000), 135.

37. bell hooks, *Feminist Theory: From Margin to Center* (New York and London: Routledge, 2015 [1984]), xvii.

38. Don Mitchell, "Landscape," in *Cultural Geography: A Critical Dictionary of Key Concepts*, ed. David Atkinson, Peter Jackson, David Sibley, and Neil Washbourne (London and New York: I.B. Tauris, 2005), 53; Richard T. Ford, "Urban Space and the Color Line: The Consequences of Demarcation and Disorientation in the Postmodern Metropolis," *Harvard Blackletter Law Journal* 9 (1992): 117.

39. Jeff Taylor, Hopkinsville and Central City (personal communication, Feb. 3, 2023). A few years previous, the Taylors probably could not have eaten in any restaurant's kitchen. However, this anecdote shows that the racial climate rapidly changed beginning ca. 1963 with school integration.

40. Isabel Wilkerson, *Caste: The Origins of Our Discontents* (New York: Random House, 2020), 208-209.

41. Annie L. Bard, Rev. Otis Cunningham, Roger Frazier, and Willie Parker supplied the toponym of "white section" for the area of Central City outside of Colored Town. To be clear, as their interlocutor, I was not sure there was an actual name they used for the white section in the past. In addition, these four claimed they had no name for the segregated Black area of town (interview with the author, April 8, 2017).

42. Stephanie M. H. Camp, *Closer to Freedom: Enslaved Women and Everyday Resistance in the Plantation South* (Chapel Hill: University of North Carolina Press, 2004), 12.

43. James Baldwin, "White Man's Guilt," in *Collected Essays* (New York: Library of America, 1998), 725.

44. Lillian Smith, *Killers of the Dream* (New York and London: W. W. Norton, 1994 [1949]), 39. Smith's childhood town was Jasper, Florida, on the state line with Georgia. Like Central City, she knew the Black section of her town as "Colored Town."

Chapter 11: Jim Crow Education

1. This epigraph comes from James Baldwin, "The Crusade of Indignation," *The Price of the Ticket*, 168.

2. Gary S. Becker, *Human Capital: A Theoretical and Empirical Analysis, with Special Reference to Education*, 3rd ed. (Chicago: University of Chicago Press, 1993). In contrast to cultural capital, social capital refers to extensive social networks.

3. Amy Traub, Laura Sullivan, Tatjana Meschede, and Tom Shapiro, "The Asset Value of Whiteness: Understanding the Racial Wealth Gap," *Demos* (2017), 5 (emphasis added). http://www.demos.org/sites/default/files/publications/Asset%20Value%20of%20Whiteness_0.pdf

4. Nikky Finney, "National Book Award for Poetry Acceptance Speech" (2011). http://nikkyfinney.net/yxLS9.So.79.pdf.

5. William E. Ellis, *A History of Education in Kentucky* (Lexington: University Press of Kentucky, 2011), 88; Leslie Shively Smith, *Around Muhlenberg: A Black History* [suppl. 1980] [Evansville: Infographic, rpt. 2000; and Russellville, KY: A.B. Willhite, rpt. n.d], 26.

6. Interview in Smith, 26-27, 78.

7. W[illiam] D[ecker] Johnson, "W. H. Ross," in *Biographical Sketches of Prominent Negro Men and Women of Kentucky*, 16-17 (Lexington: Standard Print, 1897), 16. In 1886, Ross left teaching in Muhlenberg to start a thriving business as a grocer in Madisonville.

8. Inter-State Publishing, *History of Daviess County* (Chicago: Inter-State Publishing Co., 1883; Rpt. Evansville: Unigraphic, 1966), 363, 367. https://archive.org/details/cu31924028845787

9. Wilbur Greeley Burroughs, *The Geography of the Western Kentucky Coal Field* (Frankfort: Kentucky Geological Survey, 1924), 192, Table 30.

10. Yvonne Honeycutt Baldwin, *Cora Wilson Stewart and Kentucky's Moonlight Schools: Fighting for Literacy* (Lexington: University Press of Kentucky, 2006). Stewart became the first female president of the Kentucky Education Association.

11. Esther Nall, quoted in Leslie Shively Smith, *Around Muhlenberg*, 49.

12. Clyde Earl Vincent, "History of Education in Muhlenberg County," master's thesis (University of Kentucky, 1931), 82, Table 13.

13. William E. Ellis, *A History of Education in Kentucky*, 106.

14. Kentucky Dept. of Education, *Biennial Report of the Superintendent of Public Instruction of Kentucky* (Frankfort: Kentucky State Journal Pub. Co., 1911), Part II, 194, table. Biennial Report of the Superintendent of Public Instruction of Kentucky - Google Books

15. David W. Blight, *Race and Reunion*, 277; James C. Cobb, *Away Down South: A History of Southern Identity* (Oxford and New York: Oxford University Press, 2005), 101. UDC chapters also formed in the North and West, from Boston to Tacoma, Washington.

16. Mildred Lewis Rutherford, *A Measuring Rod to Test Text Books, and Reference Books in Schools, Colleges and Libraries* (n.p. [Atlanta]: United Confederate Veterans, n.d. [1920]), 5. https://archive.org/details/measuringrodtot00ruth/mode/2up. These textbook guidelines are verbatim quotes, except for the inserted ellipsis.

17. Mildred Lewis Rutherford, Miss Rutherford's Scrap Book; Valuable Information about the South (Athens, GA, 1923-1927) (emphasis in the original); quoted in Lester J. Cappon, "The Provincial South," *Journal of Southern History* 16, no. 1 (Feb. 1950): 23.

18. Reinette F. Jones, *Library Service to African Americans in Kentucky*, 38; Appendix A, 149; 138.

19. Jones, 4, 44, 73.

20. Alicestyne Turley-Adams, *Rosenwald Schools in Kentucky, 1917-1932* (Frankfort: Kentucky African American Heritage Commission, 1997).

    The one-room Rhodes School, south of Greenville, was one of 33 schools built in Kentucky between 1917 and 1920 before Rosenwald established the Julius Rosenwald Fund (26). Tuskegee Institute in Selma, Alabama, supervised the construction. Funds came from Julius Rosenwald, the General Education Fund, and Tuskegee. Later, funding always required local contributions. For example, the Rosenwald Fund helped build Greenville School (1921-1922) and Drakesboro School (1930-1931). Other Rosenwald-funded schools in western Kentucky included Beaver Dam School (1925-1926), Sturgis School (1928-1929), and Trenton School in Todd County (1930-1931). In addition, Logan County had a highly active Rosenwald program with nine schools, including Russellville School (1917-1920). Other regional schools included Madisonville School (1930-1931), two in Calloway County, seven in Christian County, two in Henderson County, and four in McCracken County. Finally, Daviess County had two Rosenwald Schools, including Green's Chapel School and Pleasant Ridge School, which Leslie Shively Smith attended. (See Appendix 1 in Turley-Adams, *Rosenwald Schools in Kentucky*.)
    https://heritage.ky.gov/Documents/RosenwaldSchoolsinKY.pdf

21. Reinette F. Jones, *Library Service*, 89.

    Both the Greenville Training School and Drakesboro Community School received a Rosenwald Library. Reinette Jones (of the University of Kentucky Libraries) verifies that in 1932, the Kentucky Library Commission (KLC) sent two officers through the Commonwealth to inspect each of the Rosenwald Libraries. This tour included the Black school libraries in Greenville and Drakesboro. Muhlenberg had two of the sixteen towns visited. The officers reported to the KLC that all the libraries were in good condition (Jones, 96-97).

22. Kristina DuRocher, *Raising Racists: The Socialization of White Children in the Jim Crow South* (Lexington: University Press of Kentucky, 2011), 45.

23. Caroline Randall Williams, Opinion, "You Want a Confederate Monument? My Body Is a Confederate Monument," New York Times (June 26, 2020). https://www.nytimes.com/2020/06/26/opinion/confederate-monuments-racism.html

24. Emily Bingham, *My Old Kentucky Home*, 229.

25. William E. Ellis, *A History of Education in Kentucky*, 279.

26. Information for these two paragraphs comes from the Notable Kentucky African Americans Database, which lists Black high schools in western Kentucky by county. http://nkaa.uky.edu/subject.php?sub_id=189; and the sports history of many of these schools in Louis Stout, *Shadows of the Past: A History of the Kentucky High School Athletic League* (Lexington: Host Communications, 2006). For Alice Dunnigan and Knob City High, see her *Alone at the Top*, 29-30.

27. *Muhlenberg Echo*, untitled news item (Sept. 20, 1888), 3. The state required each county to conduct an annual summer teachers' institute for training and certification. Most likely, there were separate arrangements for Black educators (Manuscripts & Folklife Archives, Library Special Collections, Western Kentucky University TopSCHOLAR. Retired teacher Lexie Mitchell Albach told me that she was impressed by the high quality of the Drakesboro Community staff when she worked with some of these teachers after the school closed (personal communication, May 2023).

28. Kentucky Commission on Human Rights (KCHR), "Comparative Preparation of Negro and White Teachers Employed in Kentucky's Public Schools," table, data adapted from *Teacher Education Circular*, No. 102 [1956], Kentucky Dept. of Education), in *Kentucky's Black Heritage: The Role of the Black People in the History of Kentucky from Pioneer Days to the Present* (Frankfort: Kentucky Commission on Human Rights, Commonwealth of Kentucky, 1971), 109, chart.

29. KCHR, 109, chart.

30. Not until 1966-1967 did Simpson County fully integrate.

31. Adam Fairclough, *A Class of Their Own: Black Teachers in the Segregated South* (Cambridge, MA, and London: Belknap Press of Harvard University Press, 2007), 419-420.

Chapter 12: School Integration, 'As Conditions Warrant'

1. This epigraph comes from Ken Burns, *Remembering the Sand Creek Massacre*, a UNUM Short Video (Nov. 21, 2021). https://www.pbs.org/kenburns/unum/playlist/remembering-the-sand-creek-massacre#remembering-sand-creek-massacre

2. George C. Wright, *A History of Blacks in Kentucky*, 194; Allan M. Trout, "Kentucky Gives the Negro Best Education in the South," *Louisville Courier-Journal* (May 24, 1953), sec. 3: 40.

3. R. Everett Ray and Lyman T. Johnson, letter to the editor, "Kentucky Negro Schools," *Louisville Courier-Journal* (June 6, 1953), 6.

4. George C. Wright, *A History of Blacks in Kentucky*, 195.

5. John A. Hardin, "Education, Kentucky African American Institutions, Movements, and Persons," in *The Kentucky African American Encyclopedia*, 163.

6. Leslie Shively Smith, *Around Muhlenberg*, 76.

7. Daisy James, "Oral History Interview with Daisy James" (transcript), in *Civil Rights Movement in Kentucky*, Oral History Project, Catalog no.20 B 19 (Kentucky Historical Society, 1999). http://www.kyhistory.com/cdm/ref/collection/Ohist/id/2678

8. George T. Taylor, quoted in Harry Bolser, "Easy Integration Likely in Western Kentucky," *Louisville Courier-Journal* (May 18, 1954), Sec. 1: 3 (ellipsis in the original; emphasis added).

   The other cities' "problems" that Supt. Taylor expected Central City would avoid were the issues of classroom space. However, in this same *Courier-Journal* article, Sam Pollack, Madisonville schools superintendent, explained: "Because of the merger of the City and County school systems our physical properties will not be adequate to meet the challenge" [of adequate space]. (Sam Pollack, quoted in Harry Bolser, "Easy Integration Likely in Western Kentucky," 1:3.)

   I presume that Supt. Taylor retained enough authority to speak on behalf of the Central City School Board. For this reason, we could understand this first quote by Taylor as official or semi-official. The case for its being only semi-official (or less) is that it came in an interview, not a written statement from the Board. It could be that the reporter for the *Courier-*

Journal appeared unexpectedly at the superintendent's office and found him unprepared to make an "approved" statement.

9. *Central City Messenger*, "City Education Board Opposes Segregation End" [May 20, 1954, 1]) (emphases added). http://tar.stparchive.com/Archive/TAR/TAR05201954P01.php. In other words, in this local article (published after the *Courier-Journal*'s), the Central City School Board proclaims that it desired to continue segregation. Here is the rest of Supt. Taylor's statement to the *Courier-Journal* :

> We've been thinking about that problem [of school integration] for some time. But we will not encounter the problems that face other cities. Central City has lost much of its Negro population in recent years. We have a five-room Negro school [the 1938 school], but two of those rooms are vacant now. Actually our Negro school census shows only 70 [children] from ages 6 to 18. *I don't anticipate any sentiment against the end of segregation here.*[my emphasis]

It is difficult to understand why seventy school children, distributed from grades 1 to 8, used only three out of five classrooms in the Central City Colored School. Why were two rooms empty? (In 1939, students in grades 9 to 12 went to Drakesboro Community High School.) With only three rooms, the number of students per room calculates as an average of 23.3 students in multi-age groupings, perhaps grades 1-2, 3-5, and 6-8. Unused classroom space was most likely due to the Central City School District's choosing not to hire additional teachers. (See George C. Wright, *A History of Blacks in Kentucky*, 193.)

The brothers Larry L. and Amos E. Stone, originally from Graham, Muhlenberg County, were co-editors from 1947 until the 1970s of the *Central City Messenger* (and the *Times-Argus* after the *Messenger* ceased publishing in Oct. 1968). For full disclosure, I am Larry's son and Amos's nephew.

10. George C. Wright, *A History of Blacks in Kentucky*, 193.
11. Robert Penn Warren, *Segregation: The Inner Conflict in the South* (New York: Random House, 1956), 58.
12. George C. Wright, *A History of Blacks in Kentucky*, 193.
13. Madisonville Supt. Sam Pollack, quoted in Harry Bolser, "Easy Integration Likely in Western Kentucky," 1:3.
14. George C. Wright, *A History of Blacks in Kentucky*, 198.

15. Order no. 121, the directive to send the Greenville superintendent to the desegregation workshop; and Order no. 122 (emphasis added), to formulate an integration plan—in the "General Record Book, July 1948 to June 1956," of the Greenville School District.

    Officials have archived this bound volume (and a few subsequent years) in the Muhlenberg County School Board offices, Powderly. It contains the minutes and directives of Greenville and the county district's school boards (before consolidation). Unfortunately, no volumes exist for the entire past of the Central City school district, according to a district employee when I visited there ca. 2016.

16. "General Record Book, July 1948 to June 1956," Order no. 122 (emphasis added).

17. Allan M. Trout, "School at Clay Is Ruled Able to Bar Negroes," *Louisville Courier-Journal* (Sept. 14, 1956), Sec. 1: 1, 18. At the same time, Attorney General Jo M. Ferguson also served as chairman of the Southern Conference of Attorneys General.

18. Herald-Leader Editorial Board, "The Herald and Leader Got It Wrong. Our Apology to the Woman Who Integrated Lexington Schools" (June 25, 2021).

    The Lexington newspaper had published the family's home address, leaving them vulnerable to attacks.

19. This information about the integration of Wayne County and the Lexington and Fayette County schools comes from the Kentucky Commission on Human Rights (KCHR), *Kentucky's Black Heritage: The Role of the Black People in the History of Kentucky from Pioneer Days to the Present* (Frankfort: Kentucky Commission on Human Rights, Commonwealth of Kentucky, 1971), 104. Logan County integrated Russellville High in the fall of 1956, with the closing of Knob City High.

20. William E. Ellis, *A History of Education in Kentucky* (Lexington: University Press of Kentucky, 2011), 283.

21. George C. Wright, *A History of Blacks in Kentucky*, 198.

22. Wright, 202.

23. The percentage of integrated school districts in 1956 (and the information that western Kentucky lagged) comes from William E. Ellis, *A History of Education in Kentucky*, 283.

24. Kentucky Department of Education, *Racial Integration in the Public Schools of Kentucky* (Frankfort: Kentucky Dept. of Education, 1971), 50-169; David L. Wolfford, "Resistance on the Border: School Desegregation in Western Kentucky, 1954-1964," *Ohio Valley History* 4, no. 2 (2004): 62n56.

25. Murray Kempton, "'If You Got the Guts…,'" in *Reporting Civil Rights; Part One: American Journalism, 1941-1963* (New York: Library of America, 2003), 332; previously published in Murray Kempton, *America Comes of Middle Age: Columns 1950-1962* (Boston: Little, Brown, 1963).

26. Stephen Pickering, "Howard, James Leonard," in *The Kentucky African American Encyclopedia*, 256.

27. Jo M. Ferguson, interview by George G. Humphreys, "Interview with Jo McCown Ferguson, June 7, 2011," interview accession 2011oh182_wkp012 (Louie B. Nunn Center for Oral History, University of Kentucky Libraries, 2011).

28. Jo M. Ferguson, quoted in Allan M. Trout, "School at Clay Is Ruled Able to Bar Negroes," 1.

29. Ferguson, in Trout, 18.

30. Jo M. Ferguson believed Black leaders rushed integration. ("Interview with Jo McCown Ferguson")

31. David L. Wolfford, "Resistance on the Border."

32. Allan M. Trout, "Progress Forecast in Integration," *Louisville Courier-Journal* (Aug. 21, 1957), 16.

33. Herbert Wey and John Corey, *Action Patterns in School Desegregation* (Bloomington, IN: Phi Delta Kappa Commission Project, 1959).

34. Ibram X. Kendi, *Stamped from the Beginning*, 4.

35. Tom Wallace, *Golden Glory: The History of Central City Basketball* (Morley, MO: Acclaim Press, 2015), 200.

The naming of the Drakesboro Community High School (DCHS) sports teams as the Buffaloes relates closer to local history and geography than the name of the landlocked Central City High School sports teams—the Golden Tide (with no ocean tides within 600 miles). First, American buffaloes (the woods bison) flourished in pre-settlement Muhlenberg and western Kentucky. Their well-worn trails ("traces") were still visible even in the 1930s when Agnes Harralson visited an old track. (See Harralson, *Steamboats on the Green*, 11; Otto A. Rothert, *A History of Muhlenberg County*, 12-13.) Two buffalo traces crossed at the Muhlenberg County Courthouse. Second, the Green River was named the Buffalo River once (Harralson, 12).

Moreover, the name is also reminiscent of the Black Buffalo Soldiers Division (the segregated 92nd Infantry Division), which, in WW I, participated in the Meuse-Argonne Offensive. In WW II, the 92nd saw action in the Italian Campaign. (See Chapter 6 about a Black Muhlenberger's death in this campaign.) The name "Buffalo Soldier" originated with the U.S. Army's Black regulars, who served in the western United States for three decades post-Civil War. From an article in the *Smithsonian*:

> Despite a recent wave of interest in the professional African-American soldiers of the 19th century, many writers have treated them as a footnote to the history of the frontier. In fact, Black regulars took center stage in the Army's high Western drama, shouldering combat responsibilities far out of proportion to their numbers (which averaged 10 percent of the military's total strength). Over the course of three decades on the frontier, the buffalo soldiers emerged as the most professional, experienced and effective troops in the service. (T. J. Stiles and Arthur Shilstone, "Buffalo Soldiers," *Smithsonian* 29, no. 9 [1998])

For these reasons, the sports team name for DCHS—the Buffaloes—was historically apropos for a school in Muhlenberg. However, the mascot name—the Bisons—of Howard University, a historically Black institution in Washington D.C., may have influenced DCHS school officials. Note: In her text (*Around Muhlenberg*), Leslie Shively Smith uses this alternate spelling of the mascot.

36. See lists of Drakesboro Community graduates in Lesley Shively Smith, *Around Muhlenberg*, 268-277, Appendix C.

37. Drakesboro Community built its gymnasium in 1937 (with federal Works Progress Administration labor and materials). Besides the sports teams of DCHS, the Central City Colored School sponsored girls' and boys' basketball teams, playing Black teams from Princeton, Hopkinsville, Owensboro, and others. Unfortunately, Smith does not provide the exact years. (Smith, 77; see 272, photo).

38. *Central City Messenger*, "Greenville Draws Bye into Semis; Graham to Play Negroes in District" (January 2, 1958), 6.

    Former Central Citian Bill Hicks comments: "[L]eading up to the game," Wayne T. Ewing (1933-2005)—the coach of the Graham Nighthawks boys' basketball team—"went to great lengths to get the Drakesboro Community star, Leroy Willis, disqualified [from playing in the 1958 district tournament]. Coach Ewing based his claim on the grounds [that] he was too old. He failed, and Leroy, aka Kilroy, played." [And] "Willis did not have a birth certificate. He was born at home. If I remember correctly, the family came up with a family Bible with his birth recorded in it. The court or KHSAA [most certainly, the latter], whoever was conducting the inquiry accepted the Bible record, and he was declared eligible." Hicks offers this opinion: "I don't think Ewing's motive was necessarily racial, as much as it was [about] winning. [But] It was one more obstacle DCHS had to face in playing on equal terms with the white schools" (personal communication, 2017). DCHS won the game, 48 to 39. In the next contest, CCHS defeated DCHS 83 to 62.

39. *Central City Messenger* (January 2, 1958), 3. Laura Robinson crowned Mae Helen Rice as homecoming queen. Her escort was William Mitchell.

40. *Central City Messenger*, "Central City to Integrate Grades 7-12 on Aug. 26" (Aug. 8, 1963), 1.

41. At least one local person, retired teacher Lexie Mitchell Albach, thinks that the Central City School Board (and possibly the other two) had been making some plans for integration beginning in the spring of 1963. So perhaps, they foresaw that the KDOE would issue an ultimatum that summer. Interestingly, she also says Joanne Taylor told her that parents, ministers, and teachers at Drakesboro Community were preparing the Black students for integration that spring (personal communication May 2023).

42. Larry Elliott (personal communication, 2015).

43. George C. Wright, *A History of Blacks in Kentucky*, 204.

44. Central City had thirty-eight students of color in the top seven grades (6-12). This number comes from the photos I counted in the 1963 school yearbook.

45. Leslie Shively Smith, *Around Muhlenberg*, 79.

46. KCHR, *Kentucky's Black Heritage*, 103.

47. Jo M. Ferguson, "Interview with Jo McCown Ferguson."

    The former Kentucky attorney general may have illogically reasoned that Mittie K. Render wanted to delay school integration due to the students' hypothetical behavior. How would Black and white youths have more time to "get along better" when they lived segregated in nearly all aspects of life? Only by integration would there be substantial intermingling. However, my informants revealed significant interracial comradery among adolescents in Drakesboro.

48. See Mitte K. Render's biography in Roger Grady Givens, *African-American Life in Butler County*, 67-69.

49. Dorothy Martin, former Muhlenberg teacher (personal communications by telephone interviews [December 20, 2018, and July 31, 2021]). Martin remembers that Black teachers were concerned they would lose their jobs. But, as it turned out, she thinks that none lost their jobs due to integration, except for a few who decided to retire. One of these retirees was a long-time teacher who did not have a teaching degree.

    Martin had a lengthy career teaching in Muhlenberg, beginning in 1953 at Drakesboro Community. She is the last person alive (in 2018 and 2021) with firsthand knowledge of these matters.

50. Leslie Shively Smith, *Around Muhlenberg*, 80.

51. KCHR, *Kentucky's Black Heritage*, 107; William E. Ellis, *A History of Education in Kentucky*, 288.

52. KCHR, *Kentucky's Black Heritage*, 107 (my calculations).

53. Jo M. Ferguson, "Interview with Jo McCown Ferguson."

54. *Greenville Leader*, editorial (Sept. 5, 1963), quoted in Leslie Shively Smith, *Around Muhlenberg*, 79.

55. KCHR, *Kentucky's Black Heritage*, 108.

56. Nikki Brown, "Lillian Horace and the Respectable Black Woman: Black Women's Activism in Combating Jim Crow," 246.

57. KCHR, 108.

58. Rev. Otis Cunningham, Central City; interview with the author, April 8, 2017. I have since learned that a Black English teacher taught at Muhlenberg County High School in the 2020-2021 school year.

Rev. Cunningham, the Ebenezer Baptist Church pastor and city council member, and three others from Muhlenberg met with George Humphreys and me at the church for an interview session. The other interviewees were Annie L. Bard, long-time head of the Muhlenberg branch of the NAACP; Roger Frazier, Drakesboro city council member; and Willie Parker, a county constable. (See "Bard, Annie, interview by Lee Durham Stone, April 8, 2017," *West Kentucky Politics Oral History Project* [Louie B. Nunn Center for Oral History, University of Kentucky Libraries]. Interview with Annie Bard, Roger Frazier, Otis Cunningham, and Willie Parker, April 8, 2017 · SPOKEdb (kentuckyoralhistory.org).)

59. Greg Toppo, and Mark Nichols, "Decades After Civil Rights Gains, Black Teachers a Rarity in Public Schools," *USA Today* (Feb. 1, 2017). www.usatoday.com/story/news/nation-now/2017/02/01/decades-after-civil-rights-gains-black-teachers-rarity-public-schools/96721684/

60. John Marshall Harlan (1833-1911) was born into a slaveholding family five miles west of Danville and grew up on his family's slave-worked estate near Frankfort. He graduated from Centre College and the Transylvania Law School. Harlan was an antagonist of postwar Black rights but changed his thinking after the atrocities by the Klan and other white supremacist groups. As was common in families with enslaved people, Harlan had a mixed-race sibling, an older brother, whom his father raised in the household as a family member, except he was enslaved legally, thus without rights as a person. Harlan's relationship with his older half-brother may have influenced him to argue for equal rights under the law in *Plessy v. Ferguson* (1896), the dissent for which he is most known. Harlan became known as the "Great Dissenter" due to his many dissents in cases that restricted civil liberties. In 2022, newly installed Supreme Court Justice Katanji Brown Jackson swore her oath on two Bibles. One was the Harlan Bible of Justice Harlan.

61. Doris Y. Wilkinson, "Integration Dilemmas in a Racist Culture," *Society* (Mar./April 1996): 27.

62. Kristan McCullum, "(Re)Locating Sites of Memory in Appalachia through Black Spaces and Stories," *Black Perspectives* (Dec. 10, 2021). https://www.aaihs.org/relocating-sites-of-memory-in-appalachia-through-black-spaces-and-stories/

63. Annie L. Bard, Central City (personal communication, 2018).

64. KCHR, *Kentucky's Black Heritage*, 107, chart.

65. Gloria Ladson-Billings, "Culturally Relevant Pedagogy," *American Educational Research Journal* 32, no. 3 (1995): 465-491.

Django Paris and others have developed a newer concept, "culturally sustaining pedagogy." See Django Paris, "Culturally Sustaining Pedagogy: A Needed Change in Stance, Terminology, and Practice," *Educational Researcher* 41, no. 3 (2012): 93-97.

66. Drakesboro Community continued to 1963-1964, its final school year, so some Black teachers kept their jobs for that year. With Drakesboro Community closing the following year, Dorothy Martin taught English at Muhlenberg Central High, and Dorothy Hightower Bibbs taught at Graham Elementary. William Traylor, who became principal at Drakesboro Community in 1957, stayed through its last year, then went to Drakesboro Consolidated as a teacher. Mittie K. Render and Mabel Render were among the teachers remaining at the Central City Colored School. Central City High hired Mittie K. as a reading instructor. Later, she worked as a substitute teacher in the Central City School District for many more years.

67. Barack Obama, *Dreams from My Father: Race and Inheritance* (New York: Three Rivers Press, 1995), 99-100.

68. Sherrilyn Ifill, "What's Left Out of *Brown*," in *Race, Rights, and Redemption: The Derrick Bell Lectures on Law and Critical Race Theory*, ed. Janet Dewart Bell and Vincent M. Southerland (New York and London: The New Press, 2020), 294.

69. Ifill, 295.

70. Ifill, 297.

71. Ifill, 297.

Chapter 13: Resistance and Change

1. This epigraph comes from James W. Loewen and Edward H. Sebesta, *The Confederate and Neo-Confederate Reader: The 'Great Truth' About the 'Lost Cause'* (Jackson: University Press of Mississippi, 2010), 392.

2. Gov. George Wallace, quoted in Dan T. Carter, *The Politics of Rage: George Wallace, the Origins of the New Conservatism, and the Transformation of American Politics*, 2nd ed. (Baton Rouge: Louisiana State University Press, 2000), 174.

3. Two former Black students at CCHS revealed they were targets of racial taunts and epithets during the first year of school integration. Additionally, Larry Elliott, a former Black student at GHS, informed me that in the fall of 1963, the school held an assembly at the start of the first day. When Elliott walked into the auditorium, he saw only one vacant seat near the front. The white girl beside him promptly stood and walked away as he sat down. This microaggression was unmistakable (personal communication, 2015). On the other hand, a former white student at Muhlenberg Central observed she was "[t]hankful and proud that there were no protesting or ugly remarks [by whites] that I am aware [of]"—when she was a freshman in 1963 (personal communication, name withheld, 2020).

4. Rev. Cecil Phillips, quoted in Angela Oliver, "Boycott that Sparked a Civil Rights Movement Remembered by Locals," *Owensboro Messenger-Inquirer* (Dec. 5, 2015).

5. In a retrospective of the 1960s, the Owensboro newspaper printed this record (small photo and caption) about the 1964 Owensboro delegation to Frankfort. (*Owensboro Messenger-Inquirer*, "It Happened in Owensboro in the Sixties" [Jan. 4, 1970], D1).

6. Roger Grady Givens, *African-American Life in Butler*, 127.

7. Dorothy Mae Alexander Woods (1890-1988), her biography and quote in Turner Publishing Co., *Muhlenberg County, Kentucky: History and Families* (Paducah, KY: Turner Publishing, 1996), 294-295.

8. Jon Meacham, *The Soul of America: The Battle for Our Better Angels* (New York: Random House, 2018), 224-225.

9. Jack Glazier, *Been Coming Through Some Hard Times*, 29.

10. Frye Gaillard, *Cradle of Freedom: Alabama and the Movement that Changed America* (Tuscaloosa: University of Alabama Press, 2004), 341.

11. *Central City Messenger*, "Greenville Negro Dances with Greenville White Girls at Dance Saturday" (Sept. 5, 1963), A1 (emphasis added).

12. *New York Times*, editorial, Mar. 7, 1930, in Lerone Bennett, Jr., "What's in a Name?" *Ebony* (Nov. 1967), 50.

13. *Central City Messenger*, "Greenville White Girls Sat Down When Negro Joined Circle, G'ville Boys Say" (Sept. 12, 1963), A3.

14. *Central City Messenger*, A3.

15. *Central City Messenger*, A3.

16. *Central City Messenger*, A3.

17. *Greenville Leader*, editorial (Sept. 5, 1963), quoted in Leslie Shively Smith, *Around Muhlenberg*, 79.

18. Muhlenberg Republican Campaign Committee, advertisement in the *Central City Messenger* (Sept. 12, 1963), 3 (capitalization in the original).

19. James C. Klotter, in James C. Klotter and Craig Thompson Friend, *A New History of Kentucky*, 2nd ed. (Lexington: University Press of Kentucky, 2018), 397.

20. Klotter, 397.

21. Those local Republican politicians who won in 1963 were J. C. Noffsinger for sheriff, Reid Summers, circuit court clerk, and Fred Wallace, Jr., state representative.

22. Otto A. Rothert, *A History of Muhlenberg County*, 357.

23. Rothert, 356.

24. Richard T. Martin, quoted in Rothert, 358.

25. *Central City Messenger*, "Greenville Negro Dances with Greenville White Girls," A1.

26. Avidit Acharya, Matthew Blackwell, and Maya Sen, *Deep Roots: How Slavery Still Shapes Southern Politics* (Princeton, NJ, and Oxford: Princeton University Press, 2018).

27. Assuredly, some Black intellectuals interpret the American past in other ways. For example, concerning the meaning of the enslavery era for later times, John McWhorter posits it differently, as indicated by the title of his essay: "Slavery Does Not Define the Black Experience," in *Red, White, and Black: Rescuing American History from Revisionists and Race Hustlers*, ed. Robert L. Woodson, Sr. (New York and Nashville: Emancipation Books, 2021).

28. Larry L. Stone, "Mulebergers" (column), *Central City Messenger* (Oct. 17, 1963), 3.

29. George G. Humphreys, *The Fall of Kentucky's Rock: Western Kentucky Democratic Politics since the New Deal* (Lexington: University Press of Kentucky, 2022), 262.

30. Eric Schickler, *Racial Realignment: The Transformation of American Liberalism, 1932-1965* (Princeton, NJ, and Oxford: Princeton University Press, 2016).

31. James C. Klotter, in *A New History of Kentucky*, 2nd ed., 376.

32. I found a copy of this fourteen-point Muhlenberg GOP pamphlet at the *Central City Times-Argus* office in July 2018.

33. Leslie Shively Smith, *Around Muhlenberg*, 165.

34. Smith, 167, 176.

35. Rev. Dan Washington, interviewed by Edward Owens, "Interview with Dare [sic] Washington, January 12, 1979," Black Church in Kentucky Oral History Project, 1979Oh096 027 (Louie B. Nunn Center for Oral History, University of Kentucky Libraries, 1979). https://kentuckyoralhistory.org/catalog/xt7pg44hqc4p

36. Mervin Aubespin, "Kentucky Has Fewer Blacks in Elective Jobs," *Louisville Courier-Journal* (Nov. 2, 1982), 8.

37. James T. Wooten, "Out Where Majority Is…Quiet," *New York Times* (Nov. 17, 1969), 43.

38. Wooten, 43.

39. Hugh Sweatt, "Black History Month," Hugo's Hometown Blog. http://hughdogg6.blogspot.com/2010/11/black-history-month.html?showComment=1447268977999#c1966101504435138539

40. Reinette Jones, *Library Service to African Americans in Kentucky, from the Reconstruction Era to the 1960s* (Jefferson, NC, and London: McFarland Pub., 2002), 161, Appendix I; 159, Appendix H.

    Drakesboro Community designated Ada Holloway as either a librarian or a teacher-librarian. In 1950, Carrie D. Smith filled this position.

41. Thanks to Bill Hicks for drawing attention to this publication about the Black Indianapolis Clowns baseball team and the anecdote about their appearance in Central City.

42. Alan J. Pollock, *Barnstorming to Heaven: Syd Pollock and His Great Black Teams*, ed. James A. Riley (Tuscaloosa: University of Alabama Press, 2006), 349.

43. This Black/white handshake mirrors the image emblazoned on the Kentucky State Flag. It also suggests the desideratum (or imperative, or even warning) of the State Motto: "United We Stand; Divided We Fall." In addition, this Central City handshake is reminiscent of the encounter between journalist Ray Jenkins and E. D. Nixon during the Montgomery Bus Boycott in 1955-1956. Nixon was crucial for organizing this eventful struggle in the civil rights movement. He explained that his handshake with Jenkins was the first in his 60-year life that a white man publicly shook his hand. (Frye Gaillard, *Cradle of Freedom*, 8-9). Gaillard points out that obtaining respect lay at the heart of the movement.

44. Ralph Ellison, "Perspective of Literature," in *The Collective Essays of Ralph Ellison*, ed. John F. Callahan (New York: Modern Library, 2003), 783; quoted and discussed in Tom Fielder, "Psychoanalysis and Anti-Racism," 204.

Epilogue

1. Shahzad Bashir and David Gary Shaw, "Race, History, and Understanding," *History and Theory* Virtual Issue 3 (Feb. 2021): 2 (emphasis in the original).

2. W. E. B. Du Bois, *The Souls of Black Folk*, 253. Du Bois published this four years after his infant son Burghardt died of diphtheria in 1899 at age two. Du Bois and his wife, Nina Gomer Du Bois, believed the segregated hospital system in Atlanta, where they could not obtain proper care, was partly responsible for their son's death. Du Bois suggested in his wife's obituary five decades later that she never fully recovered from the resulting depression. (Paul Ryan Schneider, "Du Bois, Nina Gomer," in *W. E. B. Du Bois: An Encyclopedia*, ed. Gerald Horne and Mary Young (Westport, CT, and London: Greenwood Press, 2001), 57.

3. Diana L. Gustafson, "White on Whiteness: Becoming Radicalized about Race," *Nursing Inquiry* 14, no. 2 (2007): 153-161.

4. According to the ornately termed but under-theorized "doctrine of first effective settlement" (credited to geographer Wilbur Zelinsky), the initial group to effectively settle an area "will be of singular importance in shaping the [subsequent] cultural landscape of that area" (Richard L. Nostrand, "The Spanish Borderlands," in *North America: The Historical Geography of a Changing Continent*, ed. Robert D. Mitchell and Paul A. Groves [Savage, MD: Rowman & Littlefield, 1990], 62). The first group

not only leaves material-cultural imprints on the land—the "landscape impress"—it also helps shape the cultural lifeways that influence later arrivals. That is, if the first group can "effect a viable, self-perpetuating society." (Wilbur Zelinsky, *The Cultural Geography of the United States* [Upper Saddle River, NJ: Prentice-Hall, 1973], 13). The cultural landscape is not an inert or accidental object. Local actors purposefully created, defended, and maintained the human imprints.

5. Otto A. Rothert, in his *A History of Muhlenberg County*, narrates the so-called Negro Equality Panic (356-360), the 1870 lynching of Bob Gray (361-365), and merely notes the 1874 lynching of Dudley White (365).

6. Abraham Lincoln, "Annual Message to Congress—Concluding Remarks" (Dec. 1, 1862).
http://www.abrahamlincolnonline.org/lincoln/speeches/congress.htm

7. Michelle L. Norris, "Students Need to Learn about the Haters and Helpers of Our History," Opinion, *Washington Post* (July 23, 2021).
https://www.washingtonpost.com/opinions/2021/07/23/students-need-learn-about-haters-helpers-our-history/?fbclid=IwAR0jMixYAUfsV0B0XDLxmEhuVy8kKO0_DZAPbuFmTMJBgllVSls7AHXrGSg

8. Robert Penn Warren, "Why Have I Wandered the Asphalt of Midnight?" in *The Collected Poems of Robert Penn Warren*, ed. John Burt (Baton Rouge: Louisiana State University Press, 1998), 395.

9. Beverly Southgate, *History: What and Why: Ancient, Modern, and Postmodern Perspectives* (London and New York: Routledge, 1996), 106.

10. Southgate, 106 (emphasis added).

11. Jelani Cobb, "The Republican Party, Racial Hypocrisy, and the 1619 Project," *The New Yorker* (May 29, 2021).
https://www.newyorker.com/news/daily-comment/the-republican-party-racial-hypocrisy-and-the-1619-project

12. Nikole Hannah-Jones, "Our Democracy's Founding Ideals," para. 10.

13. Matthew Karp, "History As End: 1619, 1776, and the Politics of the Past," *Harper's* (July 2021): 29-30.

ABOUT THE AUTHOR

Lee Durham Stone retired after 26 years of teaching high school social studies in three states (including 15 years of A.P. Human Geography) and at community colleges.

The author grew up in Muhlenberg County, graduated from the University of Kentucky (1970), and was a Peace Corps Volunteer in Jamaica (1979-82). He earned four master's degrees from state universities (Ohio University, University of Southern Mississippi, and California Polytechnic State University) and a Ph.D. from Texas State University (2013). In addition, Dr. Stone recently completed an M.A. in American history from Gettysburg College (2023) in the program associated with the Gilder Lehrman Institute of American History. His thesis explores how, when, and why Kentucky became Southern. Dr. Stone plans to turn this into a book.

So why this book on the western Kentucky Black experience? After moving back to the Bluegrass State in 2011, Dr. Stone discovered these words of the Nobel Laureate and Pulitzer Prize winner Toni Morrison: "If there's a book you really want to read, but it hasn't been written yet, then you must write it." He thought he might be the singular person to extract the has-not-yet-been-written from the silent archives.

    Author's webpage:
    https://kentuckyhistorybooks.wixsite.com/stone

INDEX

A

abortion, 134-137, 266n10
activity space, 162 (def.)
Adair County, 187, 190
Adairville, Logan County, 188
Alabama, 8, 40, 44, 138, 159, 174, 204, 238n13, 276n20
Alexander, Harrison, 39-40, 73-89, 107, 138, 205, 252n7
Allen, Henry, 122-130
Allensville, Todd County, 84
Allison, Harry Thomas, 144
American Expeditionary Force, WW I, 141
American hierarchical psychosis, 220
American imagination, 132
American Tobacco Company, 98
Anderson, Marian, concert singer, 154
Angelou, Maya, writer, 9, 10
anti-Black riots, race riots, 24, 140, 269n22
anti-Blackness, 12, 23, 24, 34, 95, 107, 120, 140, 160, 184, 214, 230n11
apartheid, 25, 34 (def.), 97, 140, 143, 196, 219, 235, 220
archaic romanticism, 154
archival cultures, 14
"as conditions warrant," 185, 186
Atwood, Rufus B., college president, 142, 155
Auburn, Logan County, 188

B

Bailey, Ora Lee, educator, 134, 135, 265n7
Bailey, Robert Thomas, M.D., 58, 133-139, 180, 265n7, 265n9
Baker, Charles E., 144
Baldwin, James, writer, 17, 19, 132, 166
Ballard County, 116, 153
Banks, Annie Simms, educator, 149
Banks, Ernie, baseball player, 193
Bard, Annie Louise, v, 161, 274n41, 285n58,
Bard, Houston, 170
Barkley, Alben, politician, 87
"Beaumont to Detroit: 1943," poem, 146, 269n22
Beckham, J. C. W., governor, 45, 74, 78, 80, 83, 86, 87, 251n2
Beech Creek, 151
behavioral path dependence, 212
Bell, Derrick, legal theorist, 155
Beaver Dam Bruce High, 175
Bevier-Cleaton, 42, 57, 59, 60, 78, 80, 126, 127,
Bibbs, Bernes L., 216
Bibbs, Dorothy (Hightower), 286n66
Bingham, Emily, historian, 15, 47, 175
Birth of a Nation, The, movie, 31, 32, 140
Black agency, 18, 19, 170

293

"black beast" ("menace"), 31, 32, 33, 78, 86, 87
Black-owned businesses, 20, 26, 40, 41, 61-68, 264n31
Black churches, 25, 38, 169, 180, 195, 204, 206, 266n9
Black criminality, 157
Black Diamond Mine, 66
black lung disease, 67, 71, 250n49
Black middle class, 26, 156
Black migration, 26, 64, 152
Black miners, 24, 68, 69, 70, 72; 70, Table 1
Black missingness, 158, 159
Black Patch, region, 98, 99, 117, 118
Black physicians, 62, 64, 146
Black schools, 168, 169, 173, 179, 180, 199, 200
Black teachers, 176, 177, 196, 197, 198, 199, 201
Black testimony, 80, 253n15
Black trauma narrative, 19
Black Wall Street, Tulsa, 63
Black women, 62
Black workers, 64, 67, 68, 107, 114
Black writers, 19
blackface minstrelsy, 39, 40, 44, 46, 47, 54, 55, 154, 223
Black-owned businesses, 24, 37, 38, 57-60, 63, 64, 167, 247n31
Blasengane, Paul, 145
Blight, David, historian, 19, 52, 98
bloodlust, 20, 91, 92
blues, music genre, 228n9
Border South, 153
Bowling Green, 61, 175, 180

Bowling Green Academy, 175
Bowling Green High Street High, 175
Bowling Green State Street Junior and Senior High, 175
Boyer, Robert, 101
Bratcher, W. D., Republican County Chairman, 213
Breathitt, Ned, governor, 155, 211, 215
Browder Mine, 65, 68
Browder, Rufus, 100, 102
Brown v. Board of Education, Supreme Court decisions, 155, 161, 179, 181, 184, 185, 187, 188, 194, 199, 203
Buckner, Ellis, 111
Buckner, Simon Bolivar, CSA general, 154
Buffalo Soldiers, 145, 282n35
bushwhackers, 131
Butler County, vi, 104, 106, 107, 113, 116, 175, 180, 195, 205, 211, 229n3, 244n6
Byrd, Sr., Harry F., politician, 194
C
cabin maids, 54, 55
Caise, Helen Carey, 187
Calloway County, 116, 188
Campbell, Sallie L. (Waddleton), educator, 42
Campbell, William Joseph, labor leader, 40, 41, 42
Camplin, Paul, local historian, vi, 86, 104
Carbondale, Hopkins County, 109
Carnegie Corporation, 172

Cash, W. J., journalist, 27
Caudill, Harry, journalist, 67
caverns of night, 72
Cayton, Jr., Horace, journalist, 147
Central City, downtown, 58
Central City Board of Education, 182, 183, 186, 194, 278n8, 279n9, 283n41
Central City Colored School, 9, 42, 135, 184, 260n34, 261n34, 279n9, 282n37, 286n66
Central City Colored Town, 50, 57, 134, 162-166, 180, 218, 219, 242n39, 259n15, 274n41
Central City High, 46, 191, 241n30, 281n35, 286n66
Central City Law and Order League, 134
Central City Lions Club, 46, 47, 241n30
Central City Messenger, 134, 182, 192, 194, 203, 209, 210, 232n25, 265n9, 266n9, 268n14, 279n9
Central City School District, 180
Central City Times-Argus, 122, 126, 203, 232n25, 268n14, 279n9
Central City Youth Center, 207, 208, 209, 210
Central Coal & Iron Co., 76, 249n49
Central Mine (Dupont), 65, 71
Chandler, Happy, governor, 127, 189
Chicago, 84, 116, 135, 152, 193
Christian, Edmund, 110, 111

Christian socialist camp meeting, 116
Christian County, 13, 84, 90, 99, 116, 119, 155, 160, 161, 172, 229n3, 276n20
Christmas Scare (1856), 85
church discipline, 118
civil rights movement, 8, 147, 159, 192, 204, 205, 290n43
Civil War, 9, 27, 29, 31, 46, 49, 50, 51, 52, 64, 89, 92, 93, 94, 96, 97, 98, 104, 113, 117, 118, 131, 140, 141, 143, 145, 151, 153, 170, 178
Civil War veterans, Black, 31, 52, 142, 216, 233n5
Civil War veterans, Confederate, 10, 24, 28, 29, 30, 52, 89, 110, 240n26
Civil War veterans, trauma, 93, 233n5
Clay, Webster County, 189, 190, 196, 203
coal miners' blues, music genre, 65, 71, 72, 250n60
coal mining, 14, 60, 64, 66, 68, 69, 72, 119, 167
Coates, Ta-Nehisi, writer, 157
Cobb, Jelani, journalist, 94, 224
Cobb, W. E., 59
code language, 81, 183
collective amnesia, 14
collective trauma, 89
color line, 10, 11, 13, 14, 166, 175, 223, 235, 236, 238, 244n7
Columbia School District, 201

Combs Civil Rights Executive Order (1963), 210, 211
Combs, Bert T., governor, 210, 211
community of suffering, 43
Confederacy (Confederate States of America), 23, 31, 35, 94, 95, 172
Confederate monuments, 30, 35
Confederate reenactment, 223, 270n12
Confederates, 24, 28, 29
contributionist narrative, 88
convict lease, 28
Co-operative Coal Co., 114
Corbin, Whitley, Knox, and Laurel counties, 131
Cornelius, Amos, 59
Cornette, Elmer, 121-128, 262n51
Cox, J. P., 126
Crabtree, Mari N., trauma scholar, 73
Crawford Cemetery, Central City, 51, 242n40
Crenshaw, Kimberlé Williams, legal theorist, 157
Crescent Mines, 66
criminal coverup, 126
Crittenden County, 99, 211
Crofton, Christian County, 84
cross-racial dancing (event) (1963), 206-209, 217
cultural impress, landscape impress, 222-223, 291n4
cultural landscape, 12, 13, 14 (def.), 21, 27, 50, 52, 72, 131, 154, 162, 163, 164, 208, 219, 220, 225, 240n22, 255n1, 290n4, 291n4
cultural unconscious, 47

culturally relevant pedagogy, 201
culture of violence, 117, 119, 131
Cunningham, E., 68
Cunningham, James S., 100
Cunningham, Rev. Otis, v, 273n41, 285n58
Curse of Ham, 24
Curwood, Anastasia, historian, 20

D

"danger was double," 72
Danville, Boyle County, 95, 285n60
"dark forebodings of a fearful future," 212
Daviess County, 125, 185, 186, 194, 202, 276n20
Davis, Jefferson, CSA president, 89, 141, 171
Debs, Eugene V., politician, 116, 117
Declaration of Independence, 205
"deficiency view" (of Black schools), 199
Democratic Party, 27, 28, 29, 161
disfranchisement, 23, 146, 158, 159
Divine, Jay, vi
Dixon, Webster County, 31, 203
dominator culture (bell hooks's term), 14, 27, 47, 111, 120, 137, 213, 230n11
double consciousness, 43, 72
Double V Campaign, WW II, 145, 146, 147
Douglass, Frederick, 51, 228n7
Dove, Rita, poet, 44, 48
Drakesboro, v, 9, 42, 57, 59, 60, 66, 68, 109, 141, 145, 173, 175, 180,

191, 192, 193, 194, 195, 199, 200, 201, 215, 216, 217

Drakesboro Community School, 173, 175, 180, 191, 192, 193, 194, 195, 199, 200, 201, 217
Dred Scott Supreme Court decision (1857), 31
Du Bois, W. E. B., scholar, 12, 19, 25, 41, 42-43, 52, 72, 116, 163, 221, 228n7, 228n9, 242n39, 290n2
du Pont, T. Coleman, industrialist, 40
dueling consciousness, 43
Dulin, Joe, 76
Dulin, Maggie, 9
Duncan, Pete, 141
Dunnigan, Alice Allison, journalist, 176

E
Earlington, Hopkins County, 81
Earlington Bee, 129, 130
East St. Louis race riot, 140
Ebenezer Baptist Church, 180, 266n12, 385n58
Elkton, Todd County, 81
Elliott, Larry, v, 287n3
Ellison, Ralph, writer, 139, 219
emancipation, 19, 31, 49, 50, 92, 94, 96, 177
Emancipation Day, 84
endemic lawlessness, 92
ethnic cleansing, 109, 131
Evansville, 24, 55
Everly, Ike, musician, 72
extreme poverty, 156

F
Faubus, Orval, Arkansas governor193
Faulkner, William, novelist, 137
Faust, Drew Gilpin, historian, 9, 93, 227n4
Feland, John, attorney, 77, 78, 79, 82, 83
Ferguson, Jo M., attorney general, 186, 189, 190, 196, 197, 280n17, 281n30, 284n47
Finch, Blake, 57
Finney, Nikky, poet, 168
Forrest, Nathan Bedford, CSA general, Historical Marker, 218, 222
Fortson, Bettiola Heloise, poet, activist, 149
Foster, Stephen Collins, songwriter, 45, 47, 175
Frankl, Viktor, philosopher, 221
Franklin Lincoln School, 191
Franklin, Simpson County, 100, 177, 229n3
Frazier, Earl, 215
Frazier, Roger, v, 266n12, 273n41, 285n58
Freedmen's Bureau, 95
Fulton County, 142

G
Gaines, Ernest, novelist, 89
Galilee, Central City neighborhood, 76, 107, 259n15
Gates, Jr., Henry Louis, historian, 32
geography of containment, 164, 165
Gettysburg, Pennsylvania, 52, 205

Gibraltar Coal Co., 105
Gilded Age, 113
Givens, Roger, local historian, vi
Glazier, Jack, anthropologist, 13
global color line, 143
Goldwater, Barry, politician, 214
Gone with the Wind, movie, 48
Gordon, Louise, 189
Graham, 192
Grant, Donald, 143
Graves County, 116
Gray, Bob, 39, 85, 89, 138
Gray, W. H., 122, 126
Great Depression, 135, 214
Great Migration, 64
Green River, 12, 54, 55, 56, 102, 108, 225
Green River Country, 14, 55, 225, 243n5
Greenville Board of Education, 185, 186, 194
Greenville gallows, 76, 80, 89
Greenville High School (GHS), 194-195, 207, 261n34, 287n3
Greenville Leader, 198, 203
Greenville Record, 39, 44, 99, 122
Greenville Tobacco Works, 114
Greenville Training School, 173, 218, 276n21
Griffith, D. W., movie director, 31, 32, 33, 140
Guelzo, Allen, historian, 95
Guthrie, Todd County, 98

H

Hall, Robert, 39
Hamilton, Nattie, 176
Harding, Vincent, historian, 97
Harding, Warren G., president, 149
Harlan, John Marshall, Supreme Court justice, 200
Harlem Hellfighters, WW I, 142
Harralson, Agnes S., local historian, 54-55, 56, 121-22, 123, 128, 243n2, 262n51, 268n14, 282n35
Hazel Creek Missionary Baptist Church, 118
Heltsley, Charlie, 127
Henderson, Henderson County, 38, 84, 91, 111, 116, 117, 172, 173, 175, 188
Henderson Frederick Douglass High School, 175
Hickman, Fulton County, 142, 175
Hickman Riverview School, 175
Hicks, Bill, vi, 227n3, 283n38, 289n41
Hillside, 107, 121, 122, 125, 127
Hillside Coal Co., 121
historical revisionism, 17, 18, 29, 35, 93, 224
historiography, 17, 29, 88
Hollywood films, 10, 48
Home Guard, 117
hooks, bell, writer, theorist, 14, 19, 161, 162, 164, 165, 175, 230n11
Hopkins County, 64, 112, 169
Hopkinsville, vi, 9, 63, 77, 78, 79, 81, 83, 84, 149, 154, 161, 164, 175, 204, 205, 211
Hopkinsville Attucks High School, 161, 175
Hopkinsville Kiwanis Club, 154
Horse Branch, Ohio County, 111

Index

Hughes, Langston, poet, 19, 62, 146, 154
human capital, 167
Humphrey, Hubert, politician, 214
Humphreys, George G., historian, v, 213, 229n3, 285n58
Hurston, Zora Neale, writer, anthropologist, 10, 11, 228n6

I
idea of Kentucky, 20, 225
Ifill, Sherrilyn, legal theorist, 201
Iler, Arthur Triplett, county judge, 126-127, 128, 263n63, 264n70
Illinois, 24, 138, 153
Illinois Central Railroad (ICRR), 57, 62
Indiana, 23, 131
Indianapolis Clowns, 218
Industrial Workers of the World (IWW, or Wobblies), 113
infant mortality rate, 159
interest convergence principle, 155
interracial unionism, 40
intersectionality, 62
invisibly present, 40

J
Jackson, James A., 160
Jackson, Lannie, mayor, labor leader, 131
Jackson, Mahalia, concert singer, 205
James, Daisy, 181
James, Jesse, outlaw, 56, 57, 244n8
Jefferson, Thomas, 107, 205
Jim Crow in uniform, 147
Jim Crow(ism), 9, 23, 24, 25, 26, 27, 32, 34, 49, 51, 52, 56, 62, 64, 65, 94, 96, 97, 100, 102, 119, 132, 140, 143, 147, 148, 152, 157, 161, 162, 174, 177, 178, 196, 213, 214
Johnson, Lyman, 179
Johnson, Lyndon, U.S. president, 214, 215
Johnson, Pauline, 134
Jones, John, 101
Jones, Kennedy, musician, 72
Jones, Virgil, 101

K
Kendi, Ibram X., historian, 43, 191
Kennedy, P. H., clergyman, 38
Kentucky civil rights, 215
Kentucky Board of Education (KBOE), 174
Kentucky Commission on Human Rights (KCHR), 197
Kentucky Court of Appeals, 83, 87, 100
Kentucky Department of Education (KDOE), 183, 185, 194
Kentucky General Assembly, 24
Kentucky High School Athletics Association (KHSAA), 192
Kentucky Lake, 152
Kentucky Moonlight Schools, 170
Kentucky Socialist Party, 117
Kentucky State University, 142, 155
Killgrew, George, 68
Kimley, W. S., 38
Kincheloe, Mrs. D. H., blackface entertainer, 44
King, Jr., Rev. Martin Luther, 8, 10, 155, 204, 205, 206, 213

Kirkpatrick, Lewis, 99
Klotter, James C., Kentucky historian, vi
Knights of Labor, 114, 115
Knob City School, Logan County, 176
Ku Klux Klan, 23, 31, 32, 110, 131, 204, 222

L

La Meade Opera House, 39, 44, 54, 81
labor, mining, unions, 26, 40, 41, 42, 64, 106, 112, 113, 114, 115, 116, 117, 120, 132, 238n13 (see UMWA)
Ladson-Billings, Gloria, pedagogical theorist, 201
Langley, J. D., police chief, 127, 130
Lawrence, Henry, state adjutant-general, 84
Lears, Jackson, historian, 113
Lee, Robert E., CSA general, 30
Legal Defense and Educational Fund (LDF), 201
legal lynching, 82
Lepore, Jill, historian, 19
Lester, Eugene G., 60
Letcher County, 200
Lewisburg, Logan County, 188
Lewisburg High, 188
Lexington, vi, 33, 45, 63, 187, 200
Lexington Frederick Douglass High, 187
Lincoln Memorial, 150, 205, 213-214

Lincoln, Abraham, 95, 150, 171, 205, 215, 223
Lincoln, Mary Todd, 150
Lincoln, Robert Todd, 150
Lindley, Ves, 38
literacy, illiteracy, 129, 130, 168, 170
Littlepage, "Aunt" Rowena E. (Smith), 151
Littlepage, "Uncle" Rufus, 151
Livermore, McLean County, 102, 117
localism, 118
Logan County, 59, 99, 100, 101, 116, 172, 188
Lost Cause, 29, 30, 31, 34, 35, 140
Louisville, v, 26, 30, 32, 34, 50, 52, 58, 63, 84, 99, 112, 130, 171, 173, 179, 185, 190, 195, 206
Louisville & Nashville Railroad (L&N), 57, 62, 164
Louisville Courier-Journal, 26, 52, 80, 101, 102, 103, 129, 130, 179, 181, 182
Love, Smoloff Pallas, county judge, 212
loyal slave trope, 44
Lumpkin, Katherine Du Pre, writer, 10, 11
LuRay Hotel, 57, 62
lynching, 19, 23, 24, 28, 34, 39, 49, 50, 73, 81, 82, 84, 85, 89, 92, 94, 95, 96, 101, 103, 111, 138, 139, 223

M

Maddox, Harrison, 108, 109

Index

Madisonville, Hopkins County, 30, 34, 45, 60, 89, 106, 175, 184, 187, 240n26, 275n7, 276n20, 278n8
Madisonville Rosenwald School, 175
mammyism, mammies, 44, 47, 48, 241n34
March on Frankfort (1964), 204
March on Washington (1963), 205
Marion, Crittenden County, 188
Marshall County, 152, 270n7
Marshall, Anne E., historian, 33
Marshall, Suzanne, historian, 96, 117
Martin, Dorothy, educator, vi, 284n49, 286n66
Martin, Hugh N., 99
massive resistance, 294
Mathis, "Uncle" Noah, 56
Mathis, B., 59
Mathis, Jack, 59
May, James S., M.D., 58
Mayfield, Graves County, 140, 175, 188
Mayfield Dunbar School, 175
McClellan, Darrell, 271n18
McCoy, Bobby, 216
McCracken County, 116, 172, 190
McCreary, James B., governor, 110, 121
McDaniel, Hattie, actor, 48
McElhinny, William D., mayor, 76
McGhee, Heather, author and policy advocate, 156
McLean County, 102, 103, 104, 116, 188, 229n3, 244n6, 258n38
McNary Corners, 170
McPherson, James, historian, 17
Meade County, 30
memory (mnemonic) justice, 48
Memphis, 84, 173, 206
Meredith, Hubert, commonwealth attorney, 127, 128, 130, 263n63
microaggression, 204, 287n3
mining fatalities, 66-68, 248n46, 249n49 (table)
Mississippian Empire, 55
Mitchell, Frank, 102, 103
Montell, William Lynnwood, folklorist, 92
monuments, 14, 29, 30, 33, 141, 171, 172
Moore, Mike, local historian, vi, 251n2
morality police, 120
Morgan, John Hunt, CSA general, 46, 80, 110
Morganfield Dunbar School, 175
Morgantown, Butler County, 106
Morrison, Toni, novelist, scholar, 19, 292
Morton, Ernest, 141
Moton, Robert Russa, college president, 150
Muhlenberg County Courthouse, 133, 137, 138
Muhlenberg County Republican Campaign Committee, 210, 211
Muhlenberg Republican Party, 213, 215
Murray, Calloway County, 30, 140, 175, 188
Murray Douglass School, 175

"My Old Kentucky Home," song, 45, 47, 100, 175

N

N-word, discussion of its non-use, 239n22
Nall, Esther, 170
National Association for the Advancement of Colored People (NAACP), 25, 73, 103, 149, 179, 180, 187, 190, 201, 207
Negro American League, 218
Negro Equality Panic (1870), 92, 212, 223
Negro impersonator, 45
"Negro problem" ("question"), 51, 96, 97, 172
Negro Spirituals (aka Sorrow Songs), 10
Negro Village (at Kentucky Lake Dam), 152
Nelson Creek Coal Co. mine, 66, 68
neo-Confederate, 29, 30, 45, 94
New South, 26
Niagara Movement, 25
Night Riders, 98, 104, 110, 111, 117, 119, 120
Nineteenth Amendment, 148
Nixon, Richard, 214
93rd Infantry Division, WW I, 141
Norris, Michelle, journalist, 223
Nortonville, Hopkins County, 117
Nunn, Louie B., governor, 211, 215

O

O'Malley, John, 71
O'Neal, King E., 58
Oakland Mine, 122
Oates, "Uncle" John, 33
Obama, Barack, 201
Obama, Michelle, 222
Ohio, 56
Ohio County, 104, 108, 109, 111, 116, 129, 211, 229n3, 246n6
Old South, 27, 32, 45, 51, 93, 119, 154, 168, 174, 216
Olmstead, Logan County, 100, 188
othering in space, 165
otherness, 11
Owensboro, 30, 37, 38, 60, 62, 108, 114, 117, 169, 173, 175, 181, 188, 194, 195, 204
Owensboro Dunbar Elementary, 181
Owensboro High, 181, 194
Owensboro Western High, 173, 176, 181

P

Pace, Richard O., 106
Paducah, 30, 84, 91, 116, 176, 187, 188
Paducah Lincoln High, 176
Painter, Nell Irvin, historian, 18
Parker, Willie, Jr., deputy sheriff, v, 216
Party of Lincoln, 161
Pembroke, Christian County, 160
Penrod, 99, 100
people without history, 224
Perry, Imani, scholar, 62
Peter, Paul and Mary, folksingers, 204
Petition of Seventy-Six, 74, 75, 76, 77, 82, 90, 251n4, 252-253n9
petty apartheid, 62
physicians, 58, 59, 60, 79, 136

Pioneer Infantry, WW I, 141
Pittsburgh Courier, 145, 147
place-world, 13, 17, 160, 245-229n5 (def.)
Planters' Protective Association (PPA), 98
Plessy v. Ferguson, Supreme Court decision (1896), 177
police state, 120
polygenesis, theory of, 23
Porter, Ulysses Simpson, M.D., 60
Possum Hunters, 9, 98, 104–15, 117–18, 120-128, 130, 214, 223
post-Reconstruction, 23, 24, 25, 27, 33, 34, 49, 50, 54, 73, 92, 132
post-traumatic psychopathology, 93
Post-Traumatic Stress Disorder (PTSD), 108
Poston, Ted, journalist, 9, 10
Potter, Will, 102, 103
Powderly, 114, 115, 121, 133, 135, 264n72
Powderly, Terrence Vincent, labor leader, 114, 115
Powers, Georgia Davis, politician, 204
Prestonsburg, Floyd County, 188
Princeton, Caldwell County, 30, 32, 62, 100, 176
Princeton Dotson School, 176
Prohibition, 134
Promised Land, 10, 11, 225
proto-apartheid, 164
protocols of race, 20
psychic costs, 160

psychological distancing, external/internal, 178
psychological triumph, 206
psychosexual fear, 32, 50, 212
push-pull (migration) factors, 65

R

racial protocol, 20
racial uplift agenda, 26
racial wealth gap, 156
racialization, 230n10 (def.),
racialization of space, 14 (def.), of place, landscape, 50, 163, 222
racialized humor, 47
racism, quiet, 160
racism, scientific, 23
racism, systemic, 62, 160
Rager, Mose, musician, 72
"rape-colored skin," 174
Ray, Everette, 179
Ray, Jim, 107
Reconstruction, 13, 26, 27, 28, 31, 32, 33, 34, 41, 44, 49, 50, 92, 93, 95, 96, 98, 132, 153, 168, 196, 214, 223
Red Scare (1917-1920), 113
Redemption (white), 23, 27, 28, 29, 31, 49, 50, 73, 92, 96, 234n14
Reed, Adolph, Jr., scholar, 9, 230n11
Regulators, 92, 104, 111, 117, 120, 255n7
Render, Mittie Keown, educator, 42, 175, 176, 196, 199, 200, 384n47, 286n66
Render, Willie, 66
Republican Party, 28, 38, 40, 41, 101, 116, 132, 138, 149, 158,

210, 211, 212, 213, 214, 215, 238n13, 288n21
re-right history, 18, 225
Reynolds, Edgar T., 216
Reynolds, Will M., 141
Rhodes School, 135
Riley, Joseph, 101
River Queen Mine, 66, 248n43 (1968 fatalities)
Robeson, Paul, concert singer, 193
Robinson, A. J., 61
Robinson, Jackie, activist, baseball player, 204
Robinson, "Uncle" Winton, and Carolyn (Newton), 48-51
Rochester, Butler County, 107, 180
Rockport, Ohio County, 55, 108, 109
Roll, T. L., sheriff, 39
Roller Skating Rink, Greenville, 58
Roosevelt, Theodore, 38, 116
"rope, halter, and strap" (Possum Hunters), 115
Rosenwald Fund, 174
Rosenwald, Julius, philanthropist, 173
Rosie the Riveters, 144
Ross, William Henry, 169
Rosson, Ben, 39
Rothert, Otto A., local historian, vi, 32, 33, 66, 68, 87, 88, 232n25, 236n30, 238n11, 244n8, 252n2, 252n8, 255n1
rousters (roustabouts), 54, 55, 56, 61
Russellville, Logan County, vi, 36, 60, 84, 86, 91, 101, 176, 188

Rutherford, Mildred Lewis, white supremacist educator, 171

S

Sankofa egg, 21, 22
Saulsberry, David and Shelby, 141, 142
school integration, 176, 181, 183, 184, 186, 187, 190, 193, 194, 196, 198, 199, 201, 203, 204, 205, 206, 210, 215
"schooling in prejudice," 95
Scott County, 190
Scottsboro Boys case, 138
self-abortions, 135
sentimental Confederacy, 31, 171
"separate but equal," 138
Separate Coach Law (1892), 62
separate drinking fountains, 138
Shaver, J. A., sheriff, 75
Shelbyville, Shelby County, 58, 187
Short, Frank, 108
Shultz, Arnold, musician, 56, 72, 244n6
Shultz-Travis Region (guitar playing style), 261n6
silent archives, archives of silence, 15, 22, 31, 36, 51, 81, 88, 269n2, 292
Simons, O'Hara, 141
Simpson County, 100
16th Street Baptist Church, Birmingham, 204
slave patrollers, 119, 120
slavery, 31, 44, 47, 50, 51, 52, 92, 95, 96, 159, 164, 274, 236n30, 288n27

Smith, Leslie Shively, educator, local historian, vi, 209, 211, 283n7, 285n5, 286n14, 295n20, 301n35
Smith, Lillian, writer, 166
Smith Burial Ground (aka Smith Cemetery), 46
social infrastructure, 97
social violence, 91
socialistic doctrine, 112, 113, 114, 116
Solid South, 214
Sommerville, Diann Miller, historian, 93
South Carrollton, 37, 42, 56, 57, 60, 61, 65, 66, 68, 165, 181
Southern identity, 35
Southgate, Beverly, historian, 224
St. Joseph Catholic Church, 71
St. Louis, 84
State Guard, 74
State Theater, Central City, v, 8, 10, 217, 227n3
states' rights, 139, 214
steamboat sublime, 55, 56, 243n5
Stephens, Alexander, CSA vice president, 95
Stringer, William, dentist, 134
Stuart, "Uncle" Green, 56
Sturgis, Union County, 189, 190, 196
Sturgis High, 189
sundown county, 152
Supreme Court, U.S., 25, 150, 155, 156, 177, 179, 181, 185, 186, 189, 199, 201, 209

Sweatt, Hugh, mayor, vi, 217, 271n18

T

Taylor, George T., school superintendent, 181, 182, 183, 278n8, 279n9
Taylor, Jeff, vi, 163, 273n39
Ten Commandments, The, movie, v, 8
Tennessee, 49, 92, 96, 98, 117, 148, 150, 152, 159
Tennessee Valley Authority (TVA), 152
Thomas, Jr., Robert Young, commonwealth attorney, 82-87, 141, 254n27
thought monument, 171
369th Infantry Regiment, WW I, 141
Till, Emmett, 16, 184
tobacco, 56, 61, 96, 98, 99, 100, 104, 111, 114, 117, 118, 170
Tobacco Wars, 98, 99, 104, 112, 214
Tocqueville, Alexis de, 95, 96
Todd County, 84, 91, 98, 99, 110, 116, 172, 176, 229n3, 276n20
Todd County Training School, 176
tragic optimism, 221
trauma, traumatic events, 10, 19, 33, 73, 89, 93, 105, 107, 108, 131, 231n16
Travis, Merle, musician, songwriter, 56, 65, 71, 72, 151-152, 244n6, 250n61
Trenton, Todd County, 110
Trenton School, 276n20

Trigg County, 116, 118, 172
Truman, Harry S., 153
Turner, William, local historian, 155
Tuskegee Normal and Industrial Institute (University), 38, 150, 173, 276n20

U

Uncle Tom's Cabin Law (1906), 45, 80
Union Army, 49, 140
Union County, 116, 189
unionization, 114, 121, 128
United Daughters of the Confederacy (UDC), 29, 30, 46, 80, 89, 171 (textbook guide), 241n34
United Mine Workers of America (UMWA), 41, 112
UMWA District 23, 41, 42, 131
Unity Baptist Church, 97

V

Vanlandingham, Peter, 61
Veterans of Foreign Wars (VFW), 216
Vietnam War, 140, 145, 216
vigilantes, violence, (ism), 49, 81, 83, 84, 91, 92, 98, 99, 100, 104, 106, 107, 111, 112, 118, 119, 120, 124, 125, 126, 127, 130, 204, 254n1
violence-prone region, 91

W

Waldrep, Christopher, 118
Wallace, George C., politician, 204
Warren, Earl, Supreme Court justice, 168, 289n18

Warren County, 64, 125, 245n3
Warren Court, 156, 201, 202, 271n18
Warren, Robert Penn, writer, 94, 184, 223
Washington, Booker T., college president, 38, 95, 150, 173
Washington, Dan, mayor, 216
Washington, Harold, mayor, 152
Watterson, Henry, editor, 26
Wayne County, 187
Webster County, 67, 186, 189, 190
Wesley Chapel AME Zion Church, 169
West Kentucky Industrial College, Paducah, 176
West Virginia, 70
Western Coalfield, 64, 65, 104, 112, 113, 116, 117
Western Kentucky University, 188
Western Lunatic Asylum, Hopkinsville, 39, 77
Whitehouse, Florence, 76-79
White House, 32, 38, 140, 222
White Man's Ticket (1870), 212
white Southerners, 28, 93
White, Dudley, 138
whiteness, 10, 44, 151, 157 (def.), 165, 166, 222, 227n2 (why "white" is not capitalized), 230n10
Wickliffe, Robert, 122, 126
Wilde, Oscar, writer, 17, 224
Wilkerson, Isabel, journalist, 163
Wilkins, Roy, NAACP leader, 187
Wilkinson, Doris, sociologist, 200

Williams, Carolyn Randall, poet, 174
Willson, Augustus E., governor, 101
Wilson, Charles Reagan, historian, 29
Wilson, Woodrow, 32, 52, 116, 140
Wing, Charles Fox, county clerk, 154
women's suffrage, 116, 148
Woods, Dorothy Mae (Alexander), 205
Woodson, Carter G., historian, 152
Woodson Mine, 124, 127, 128
Woodward, C. Vann, historian, 153, 154
Workers Alliance of America, 113
Works Progress Administration (WPA), 9, 42
World War I, 26, 44, 60, 64, 68, 108, 140, 141, 142, 149, 152, 171, 214

WW I veterans, Black, 153,154
World War II, 9, 10, 13, 56, 63, 143, 145, 152, 154, 155, 192, 214, 217
Wright, George C., historian, vi, 50, 161, 179
Wright, Richard, writer, 19, 26, 139

Y

Young, George, coroner, 122, 123, 126

Made in the USA
Columbia, SC
26 October 2024

824aa02d-03b0-4be6-a895-7aa2ad0659bfR01